BOYLE CO. PUBLIC LIBRARY
3 6402 4004 5213 8

D0204500

E Q U I

P O S E

CHRISTOPHER MAKOS

EQUIPOSE

PREFACE BY DOTSON RADER

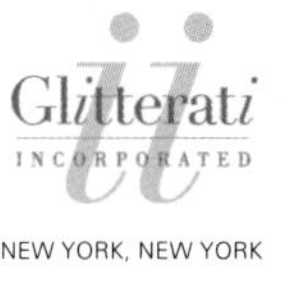

NEW YORK, NEW YORK

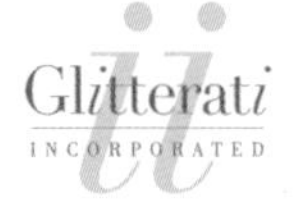

First published in the United States of America in 2005 by
Glitterati Incorporated
225 Central Park West
New York, New York 10024
www.GlitteratiIncorporated.com

First edition, 2005

Photography and Art Direction **CHRISTOPHER MAKOS**
Editor and Title Concept **PETER WISE**
Creative Director **PABLO GARCIA PEREZ**

Library of Congress Control Number 2005926280
Hardcover ISBN 0-9765851-2-X

Printed and bound in China by Hong Kong Graphics and Printing Ltd
10 9 8 7 6 5 4 3 2 1

DEDICATED TO
FREDERIC REMINGTON

SPECIAL THANKS Paul Solberg, Dalia Simmons, Agatha Ruiz de la Prada, Miren, Luis, Christophe, Andrea Kafer, Kelly Klein, Micky Jorda, Jose Luis Talban, Dotson Rader, Natasha Carleton, Jane Holzer, Ralph Pucci, George Krol, Bruce Weber, John Esposito, Jonay N. Cogollos van der Linden, Pablo Garcia Perez, Edmond Franco, Mattias and Gabi Kampl, Dorothy Blau, David Fahey, Paul Washington, Sam Bolton, Patrick McMullan, Paul Bierne, Calvin Klein, Jean Gabrielle Mitterand, Inmaculata Lladro, Francisco Reyes Medina, Patrick Scarlet, Giuseppe Liverani, Pilar Vico, Richard Mishaan, Carmen Calvo, Hunt Slonem, James Moore, Dean Mellon, Sean Strub, Christophe Heinrich, Emilio Saliquet, Alaska, Mario, Jan Des Bourvrie, Michael Ralke, John, Paul, George and Ringo, ManRay, Francisco Costa, Dale Rozmiarek, Alan Laskow, Patrick Mundt, Ingrid Sischy, Sandy Brandt, Brian Clamp, John Batchelor, Robert Lococo, John Demsey, Jason Weinberg, Bruce Brendon, Joseph Batchelor, Steven Bocks, Lisa Silhanek, Robert Jess Roth, Tom Conley, Steven Klein, James Maharg, Kevin Calica, Gregg Ventra, Alexander Galan, Brian Sawyer, Stuart Haber, John Woods, Claire Occonner, Victoria George, Michelle Loud, Steven C. Rosso, Zorione Riezu and the HP family of friends, Marta Hallett, Roseanne Barr, Johnny, Robert Soros, Harald Johnson, Glenn Albin, Christian Deseglise, Anne Cohen, Genevieve Maquinay, Andy Merhi, Isabelle del Grange, Philip del Grange, Robert de Grenier, Frank Andolino, Vinnie, Sam Shahid, Mark Sink, The Tourist Office of Spain, Mina, Boras Bas, Rosemary Feitelberg.

CONTENTS

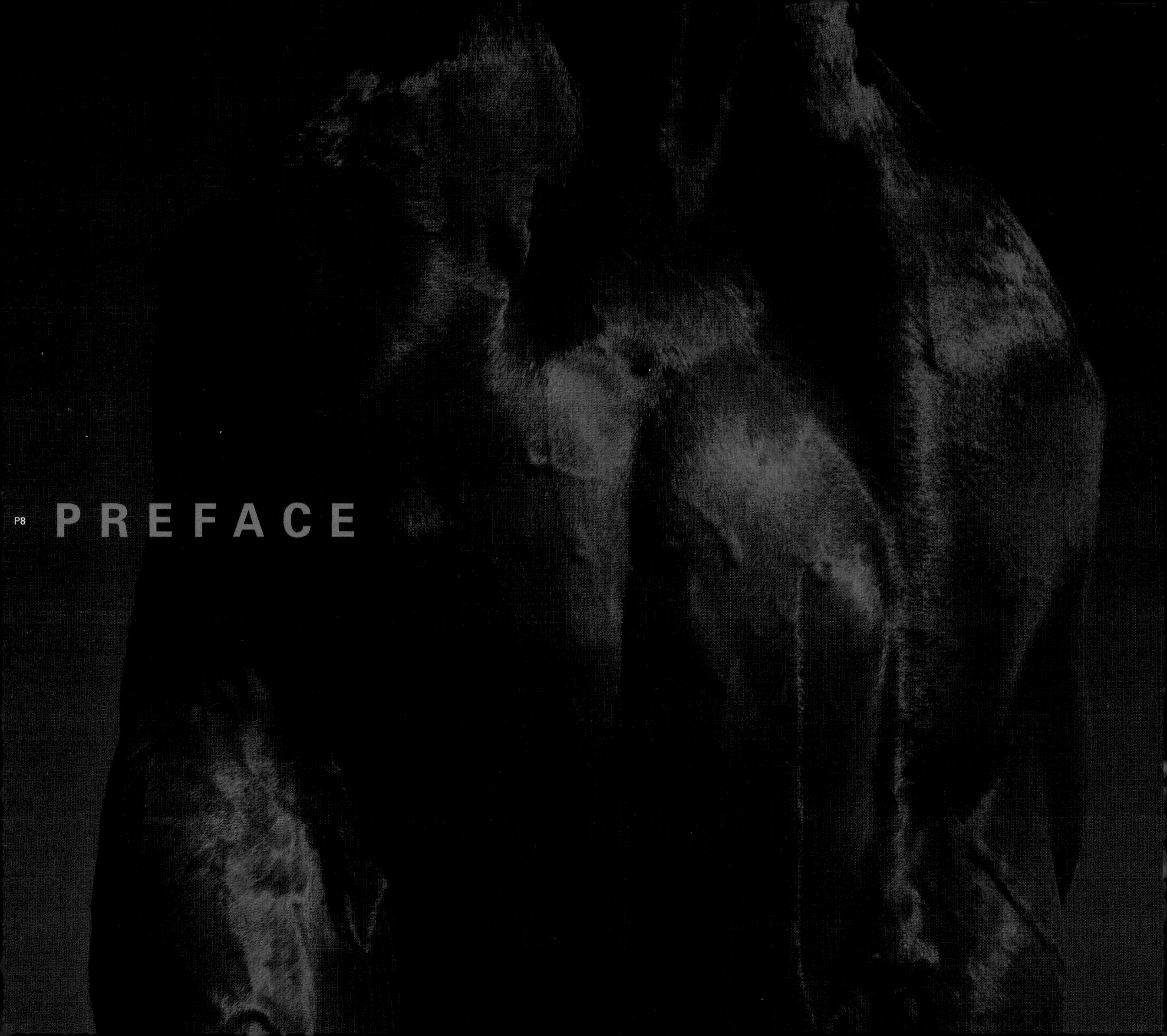

P8

PREFACE

EQUIPOSE is an astonishingly beautiful excursion into pastoral worlds made wondrously new again. It is a stunning achievement. The fact that the photographer is Christopher Makos and the subject is horses makes this collection a unique artistic event.

Makos is widely considered the most important and gifted American photographer of his generation. Since the publication of his first collection, *White Trash* in 1977, Makos' cool, sophisticated, and radically accepting view of urban life, particularly downtown New York, has had a transforming influence on the visual arts.

Until now, Makos' work has been obsessed with the seductive, louche, often dangerous margins of city life–the precincts of the celebrated and debauched, the hustlers and vacant rich, the demi-monde and beau monde, the pretty boys, artists, poets, the crazed, the lost, the glamorous. He captured those lives in photographs of sublime elegance and restraint.

But the subject and setting of **EQUIPOSE** are vastly different from the social and cultural arenas where Makos initially made his reputation. In **EQUIPOSE** Makos leaves the world he knows best in order to visit–unexpectedly, amazingly–"a separate nation," as he calls horses. In that "nation" he paradoxically finds what he thought he had left behind: beauty enlivened by authentic feeling. It is a surprising departure for Makos, and a hugely successful one. Exquisitely photographed and selected, these pictures display the very qualities of disturbing intimacy, irony, exhausted romanticism, playfulness and movement, classical allusion, eroticism, danger, freedom-within-captivity that have long made Makos' art singular and unforgettable. **EQUIPOSE** celebrates nobility in the physical and a beauty breathless in its pressing reality.

Makos, the uneasy outsider, always sees what we do not notice–and sees it often years before the rest of the culture catches up with him. Here, in **EQUIPOSE**, what he sees is another world entirely–more honest, more real, purer than our own. Horses–playful, skittish, sensual, powerful, threatening and desired–brought to life in a way we have never seen before.

Dotson Rader, New York City

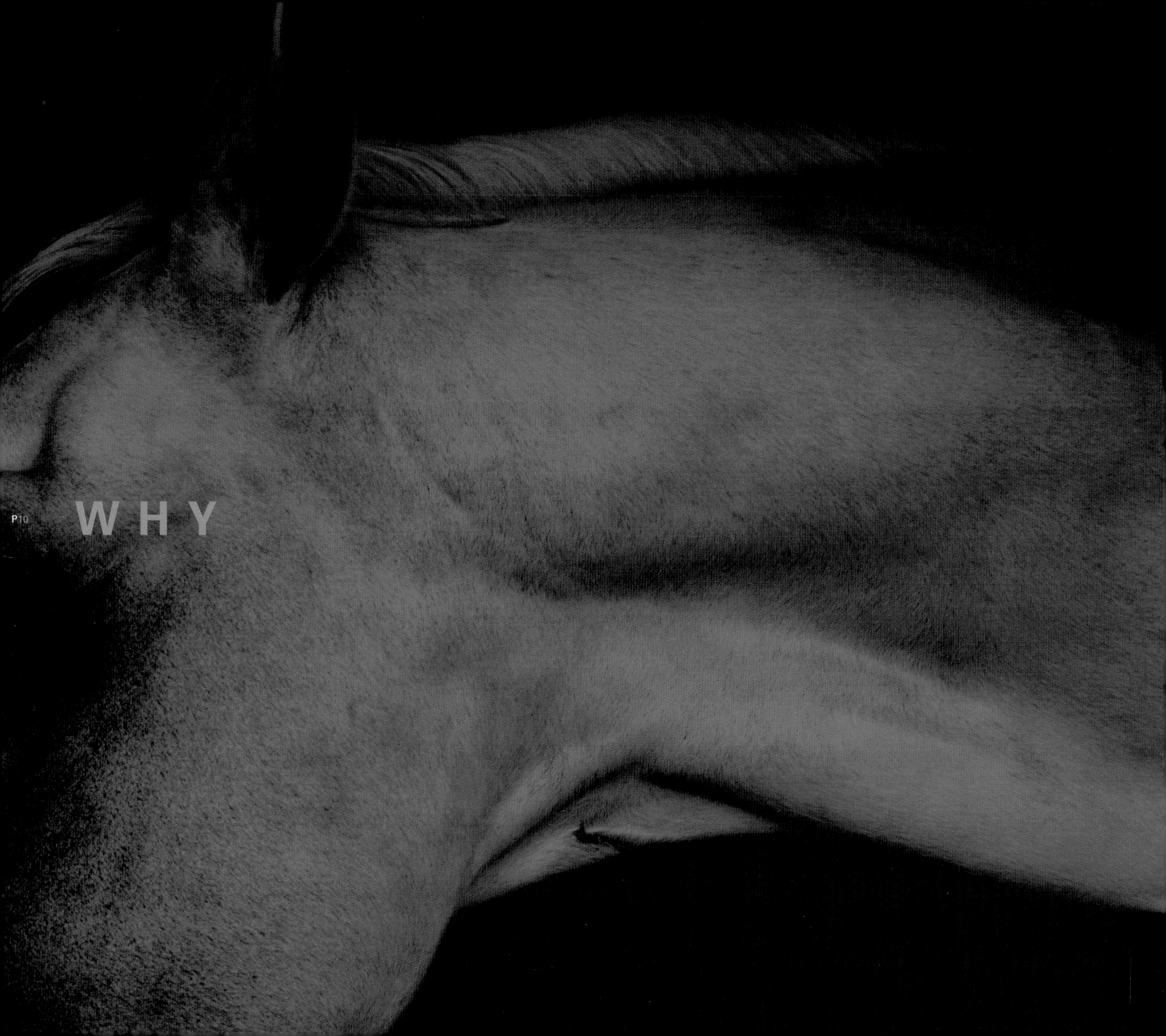

WHY

If this is the first time you're looking at Christopher Makos' photographs, you probably aren't asking the question, "Why," but for those of you who know my work, taking pictures of horses is a departure from my usual shots of buffed boys, exotic locations, sleek machines, and Andy Warhol–to say the least.

This book came about because I have recently been making one-of-a-kind surfboards that incorporate original photographs that are particular to each buyer, and made one for Kelly Klein, an avid horse person and equestrienne. I went to Southampton, New York, to meet her at her horse farm. I was very much impressed photographing these amazing animals, but thought no more of it than creating a component to a unique surfboard. As I usually do when I undertake a new subject, I sent out a few jpegs to some of my "regular" photo recipients, one of whom is the publisher of my last book, **EXHIBITIONISM**. She said, "I've never seen photographs of horses like this, Chris; lets make this your next book!" At first I was very excited, but then the idea of trying to find horses to shoot became a bit of a nag–no pun intended–after all this was a total departure from my usual subject categories; and then I realized I could tap into my amazing resource of friends to find my "subjects" and create a personal work that was totally new for me. What has emerged has been an extraordinary personal and professional journey into the "world" of horses.

I want to alert the viewer of this book that this is not a comprehensive work that defines what horses are, but instead my experience as an artist of what horses are, to me. Like all my projects, when I am allowed to have first impressions, usually I come away with a totally different perspective from that which is usually seen by others. I like to think that I see the "unseen;" those moments that other people have viewed so regularly that it is impossible for them to experience them in a new light. An example of this is the photograph of the horses "kissing" in Valencia, Spain. I turned the corner of the stable, and there they were, those two amazing creatures, bending their necks around the partition of their stable so they could, quite literally nuzzle, kiss, and enjoy what we humans call, "making out." From that very first encounter in the Hamptons when I first started to really look at horses, I have now come to realize that each and every one of these animals has special and unique personalities. They are totally aware–just look at the kissing horses looking at me while I stole some photos of them.

Most of the horses in this book were photographed during a six-month time frame, including two trips to Spain, where some of the most amazing horses in the world reside. When I asked around, I found that friends of mine either owned horses, or had just acquired them–much to my surprise. The horses of Spain shown here were photographed in the royal city of Aranjuez, just outside of Madrid; in Valencia; and, in the south, in Jerez.

I never really understood horses; I think I do now.

This book is for people who love horses. I have become one of you.

Christopher Makos, New York City

IMAGES

P14

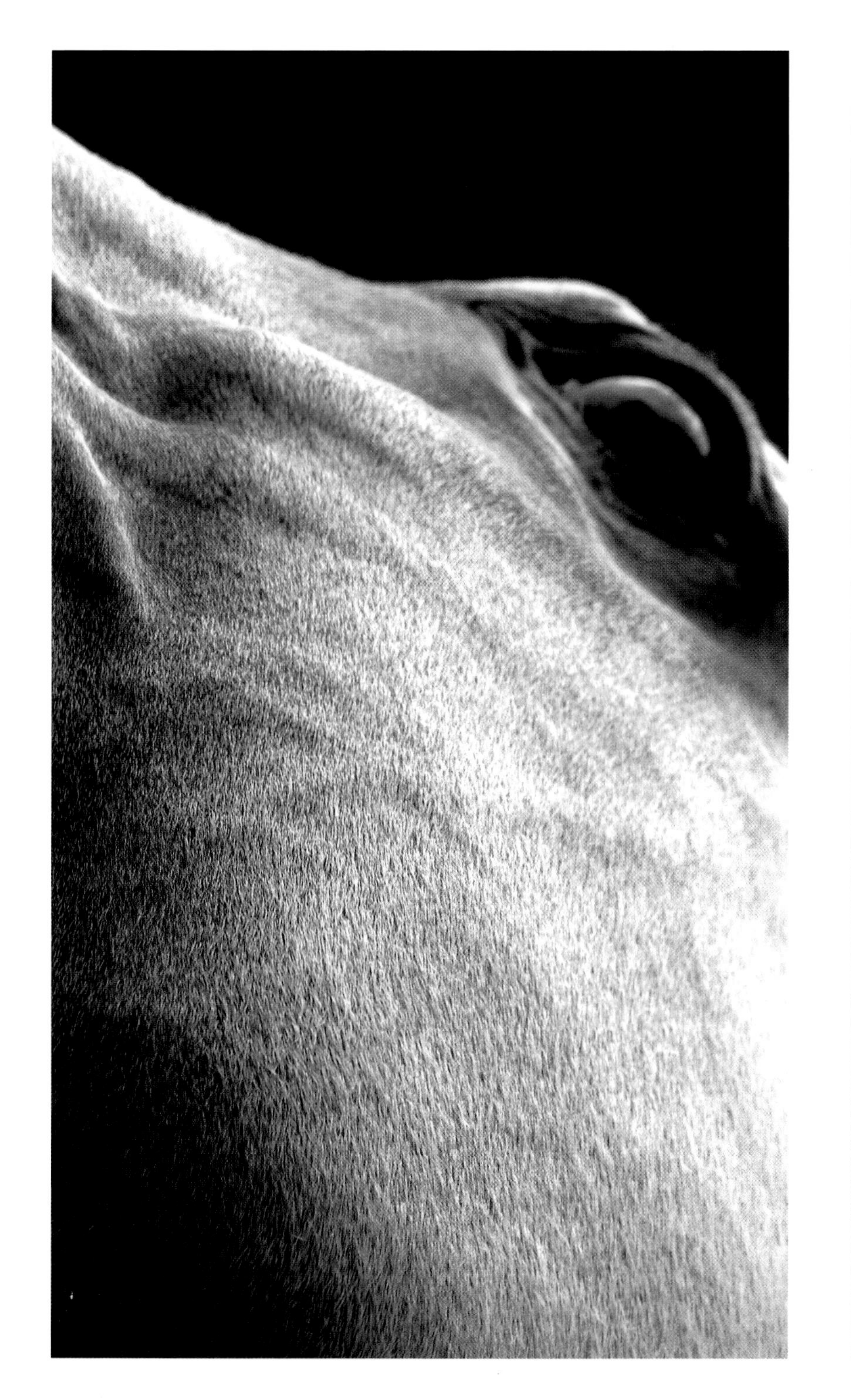

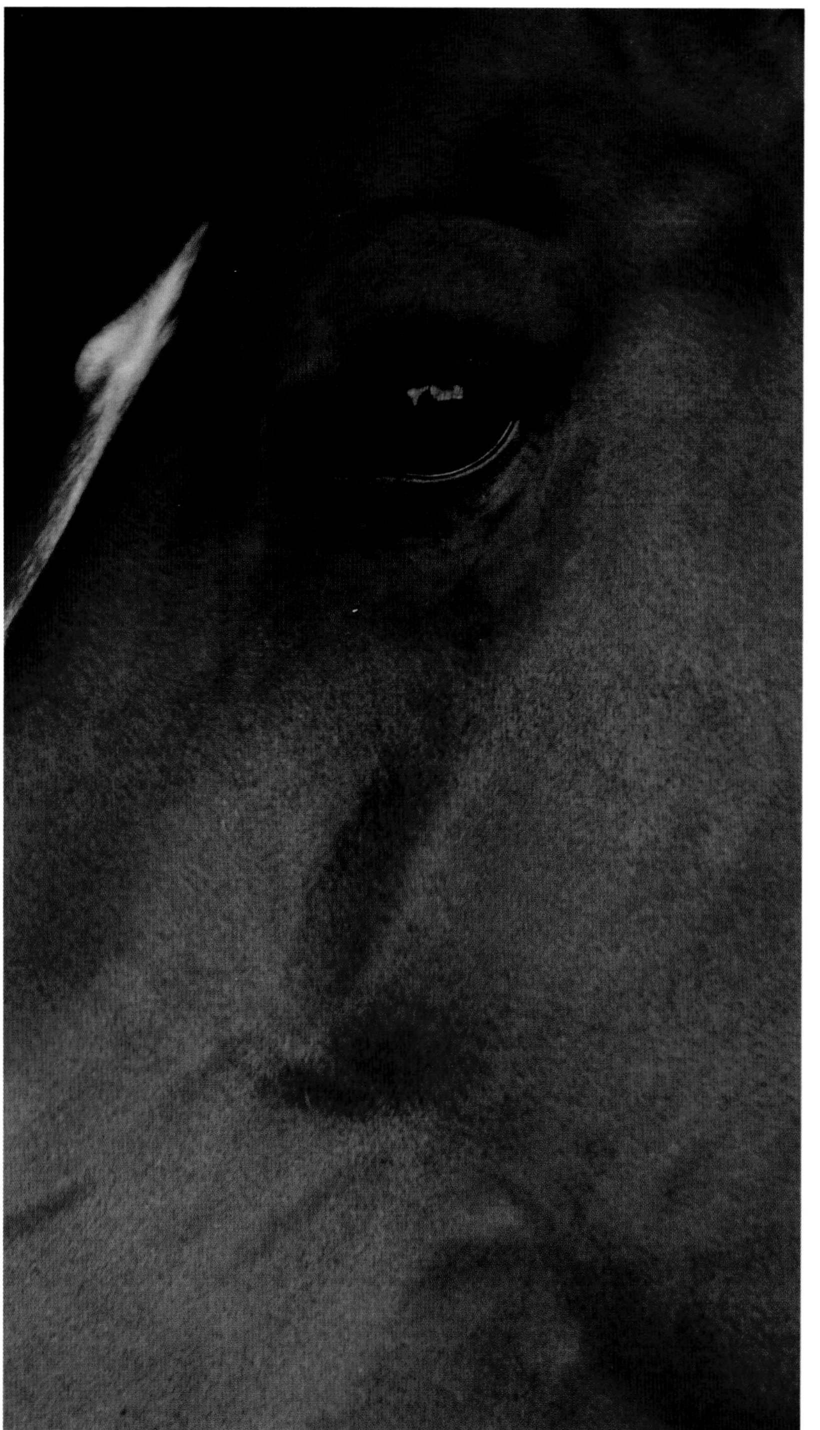

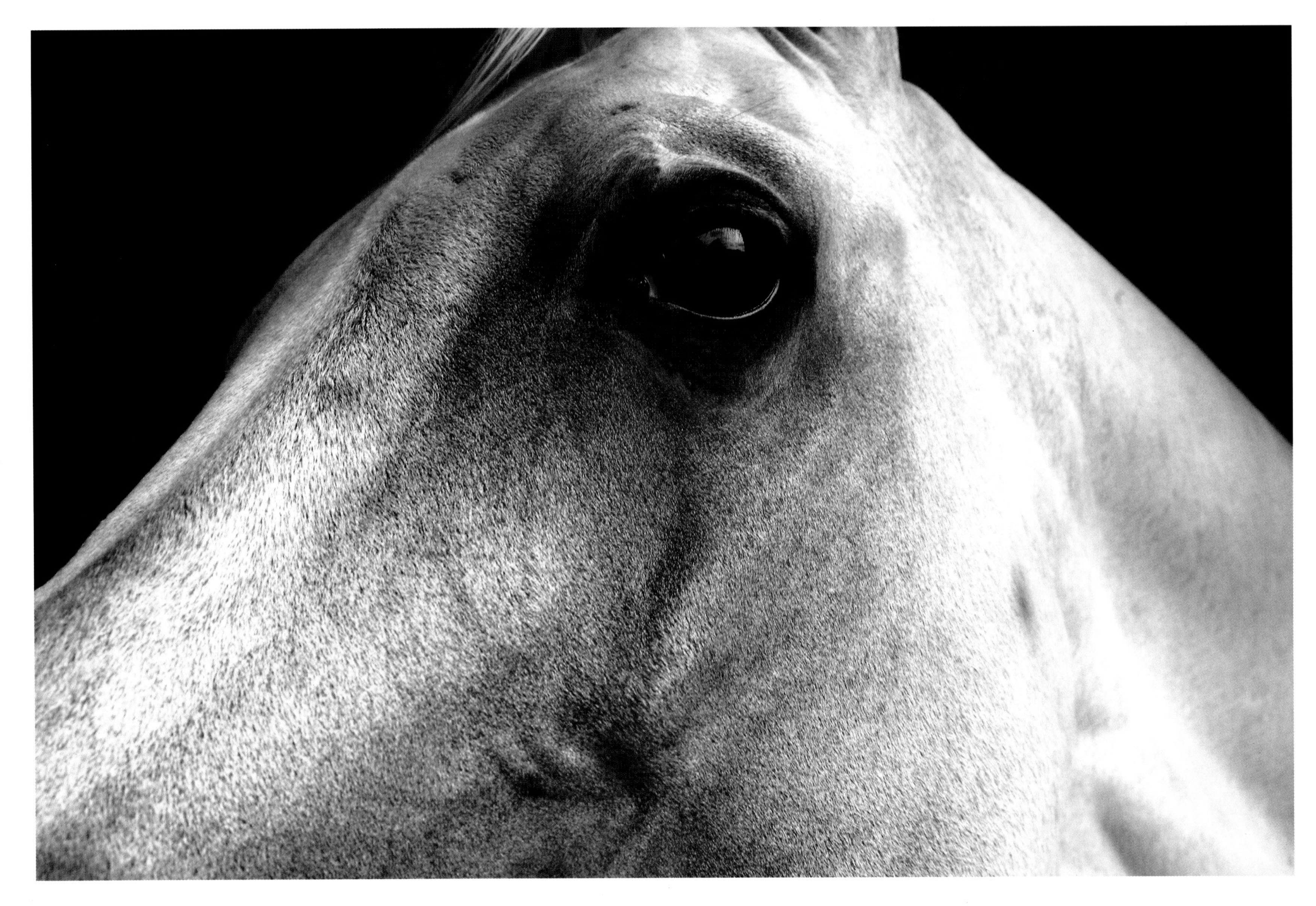

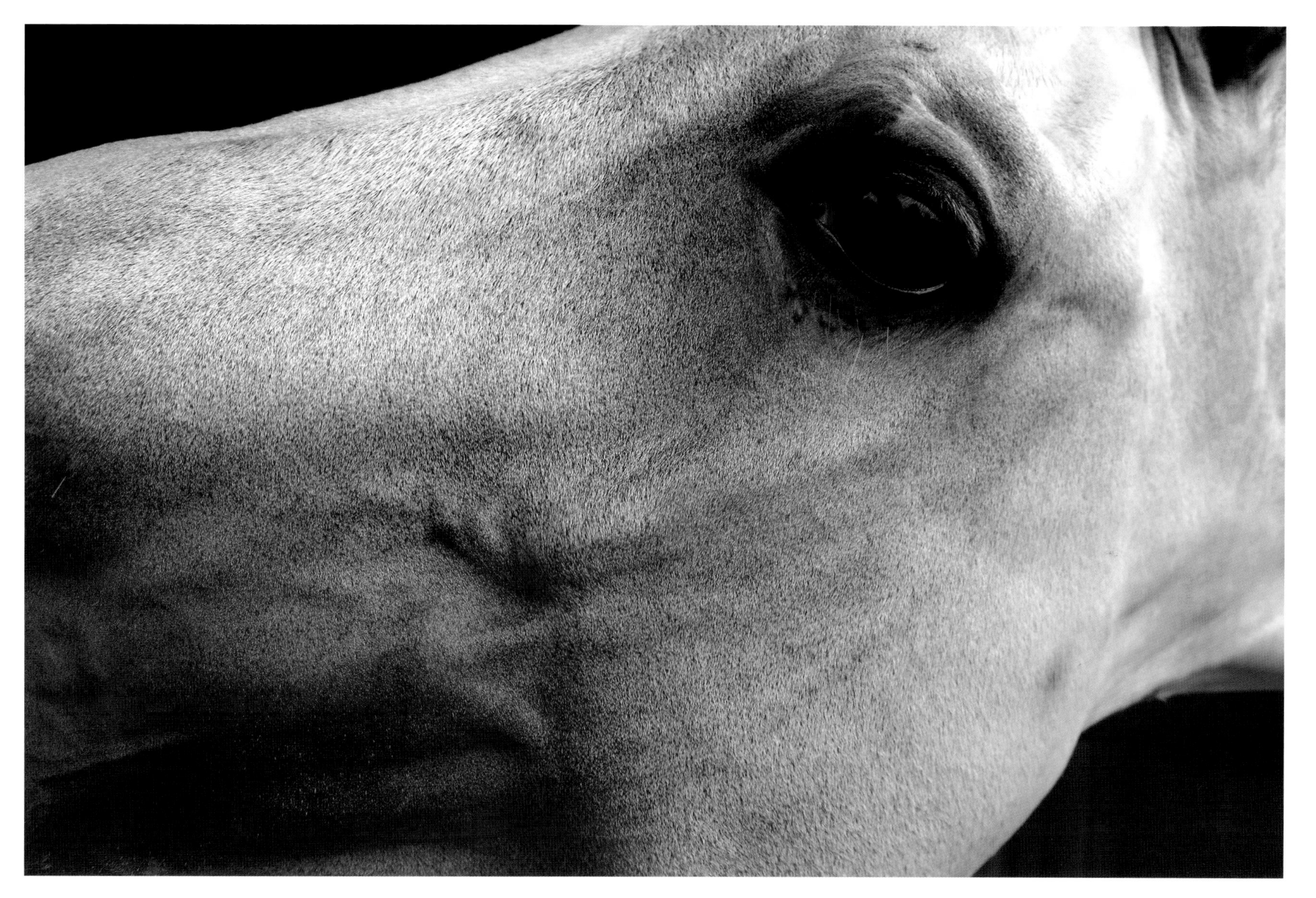

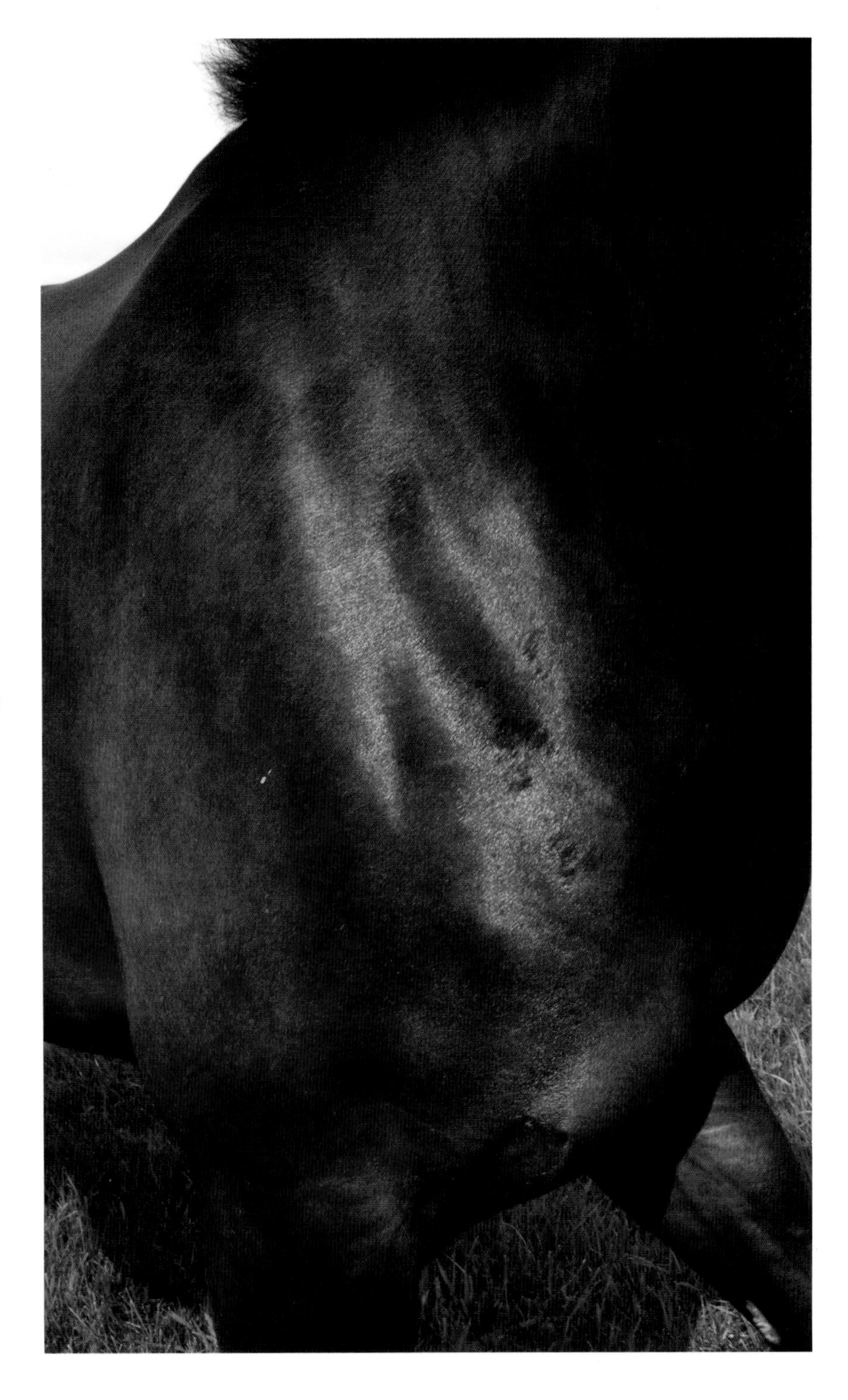

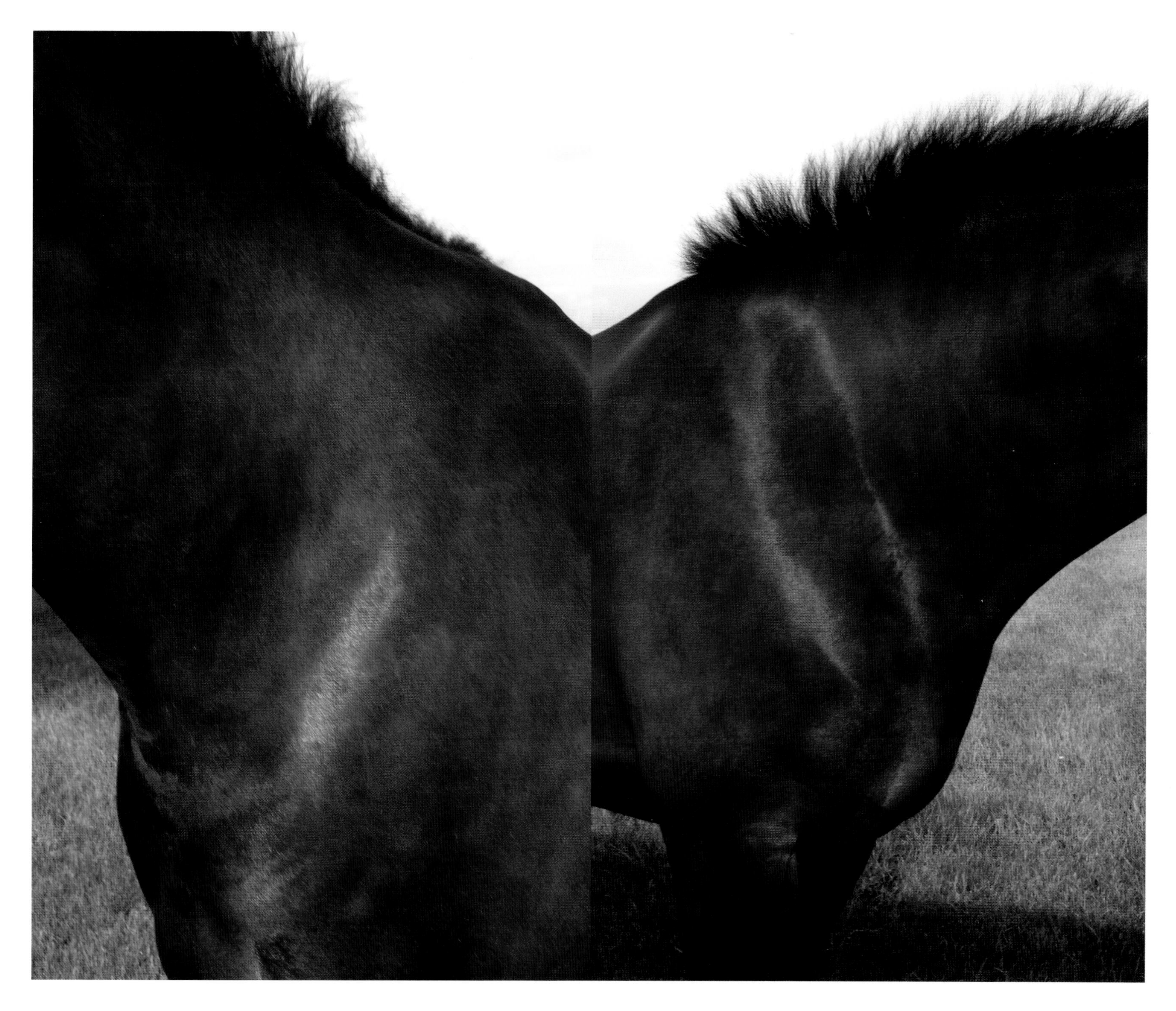

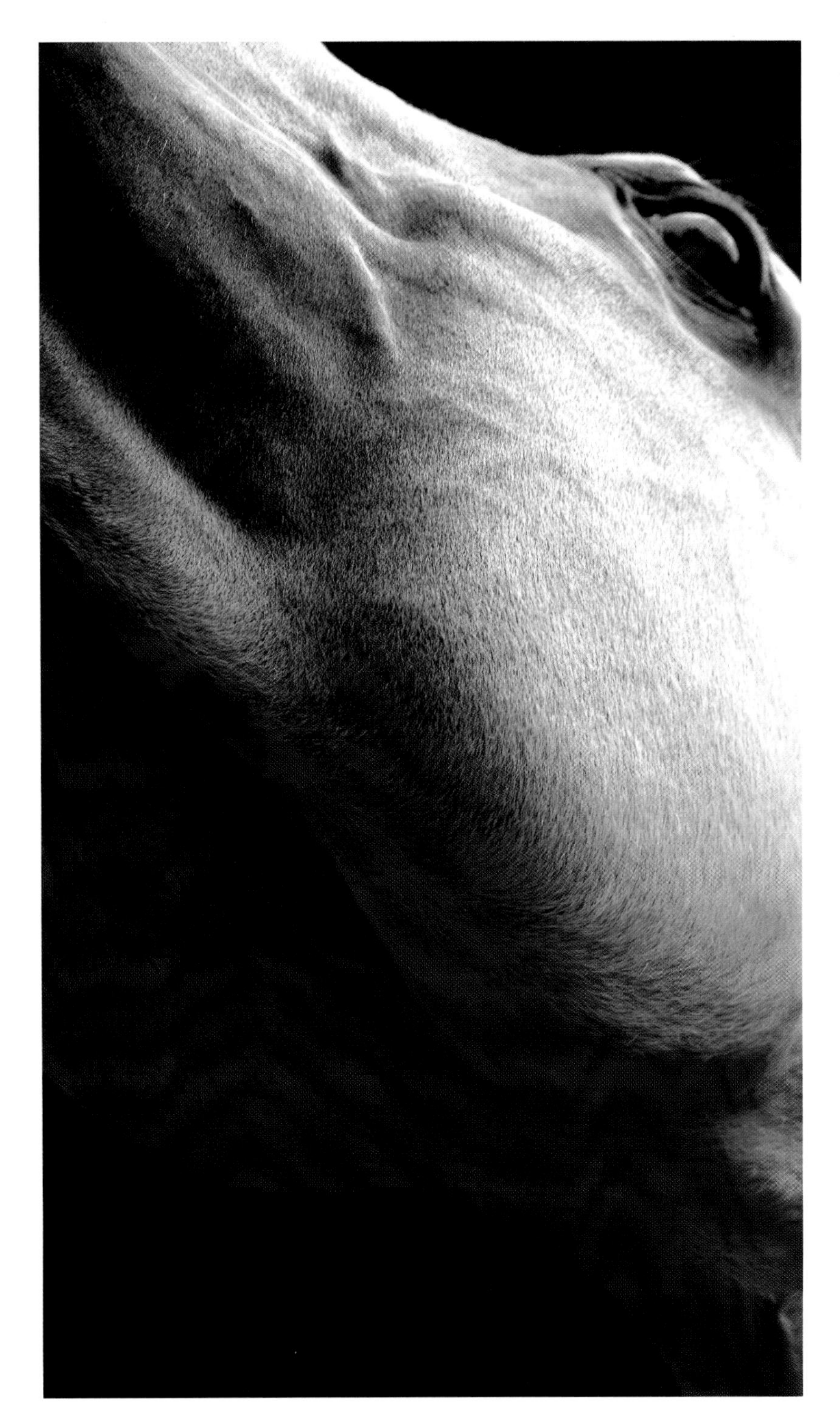

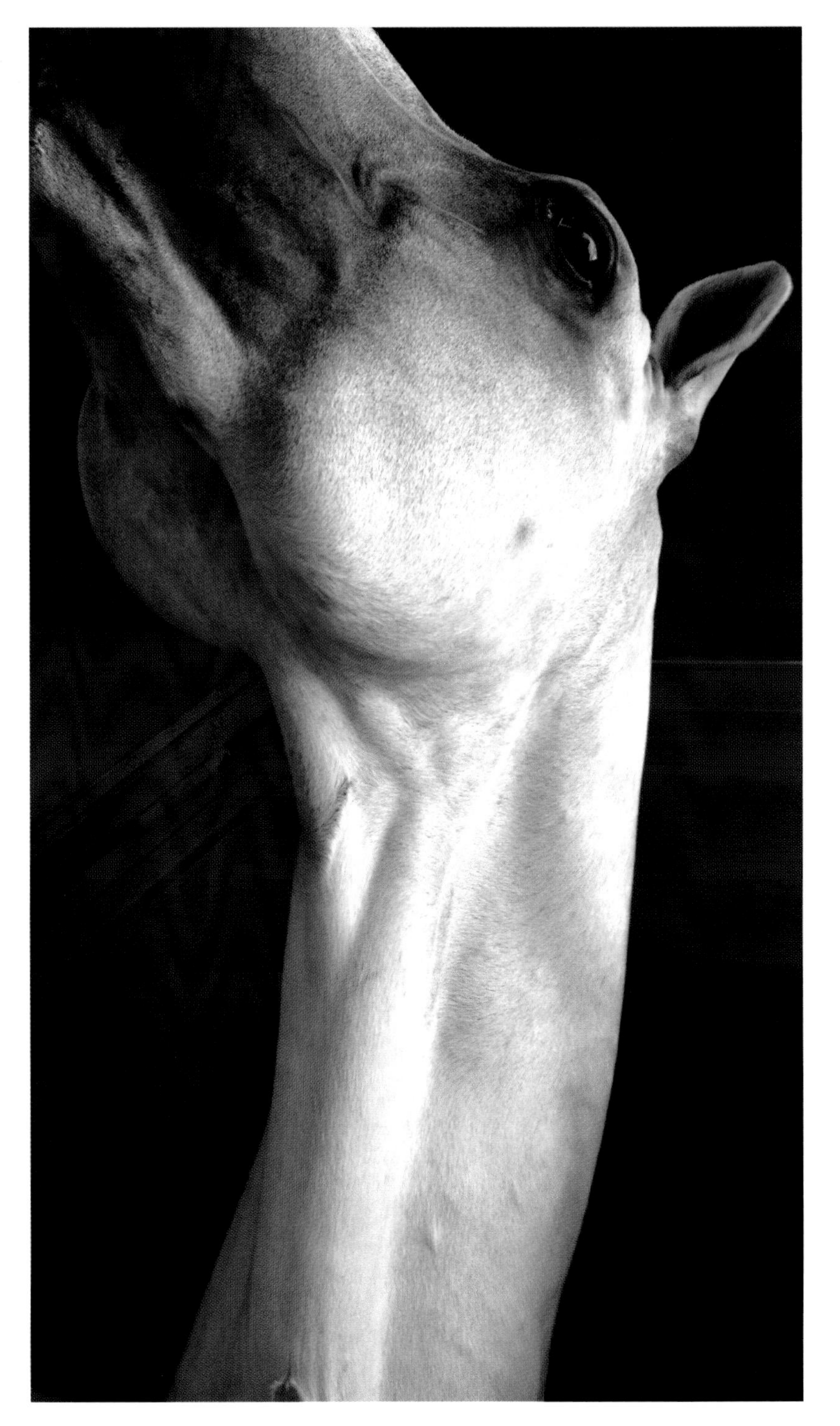

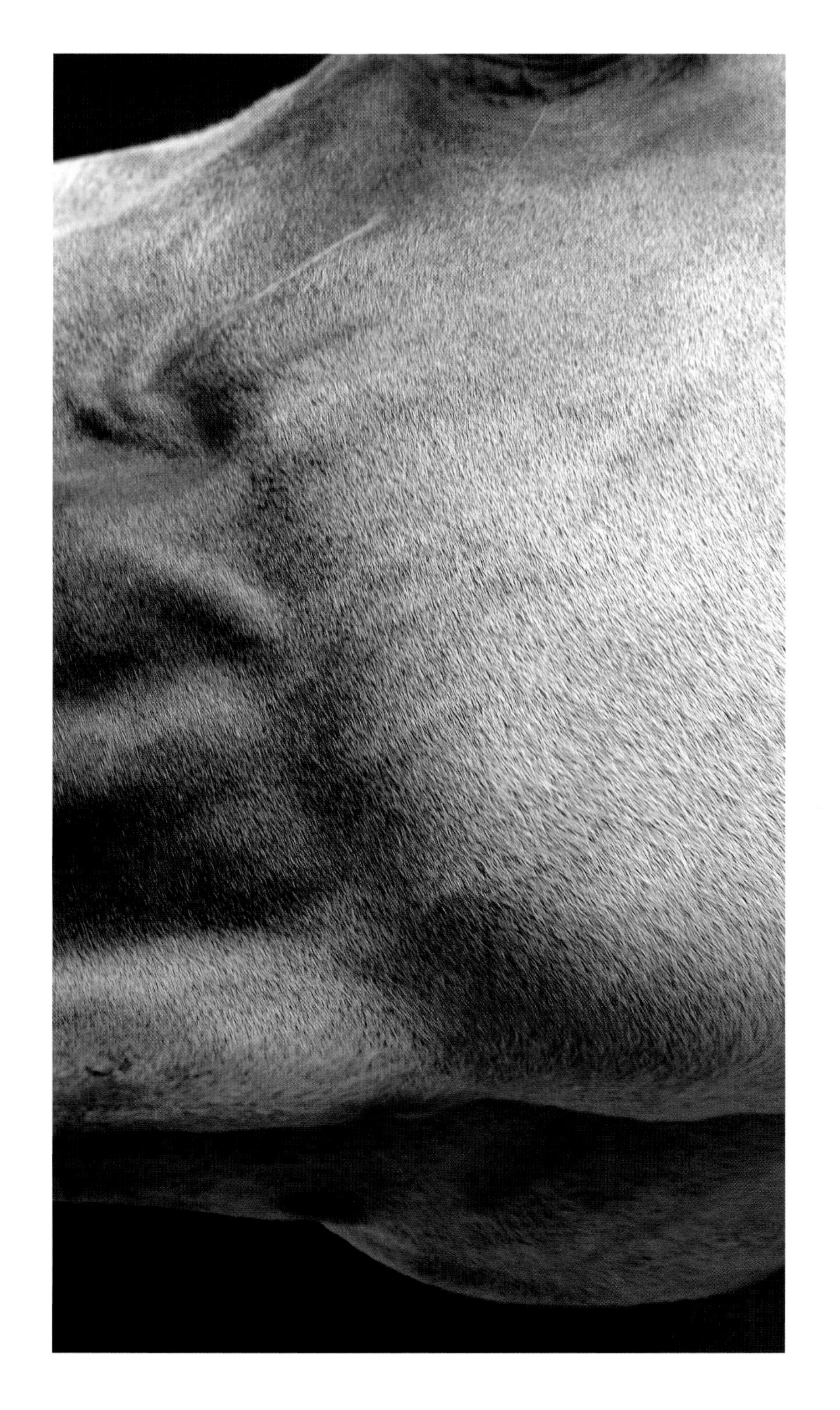

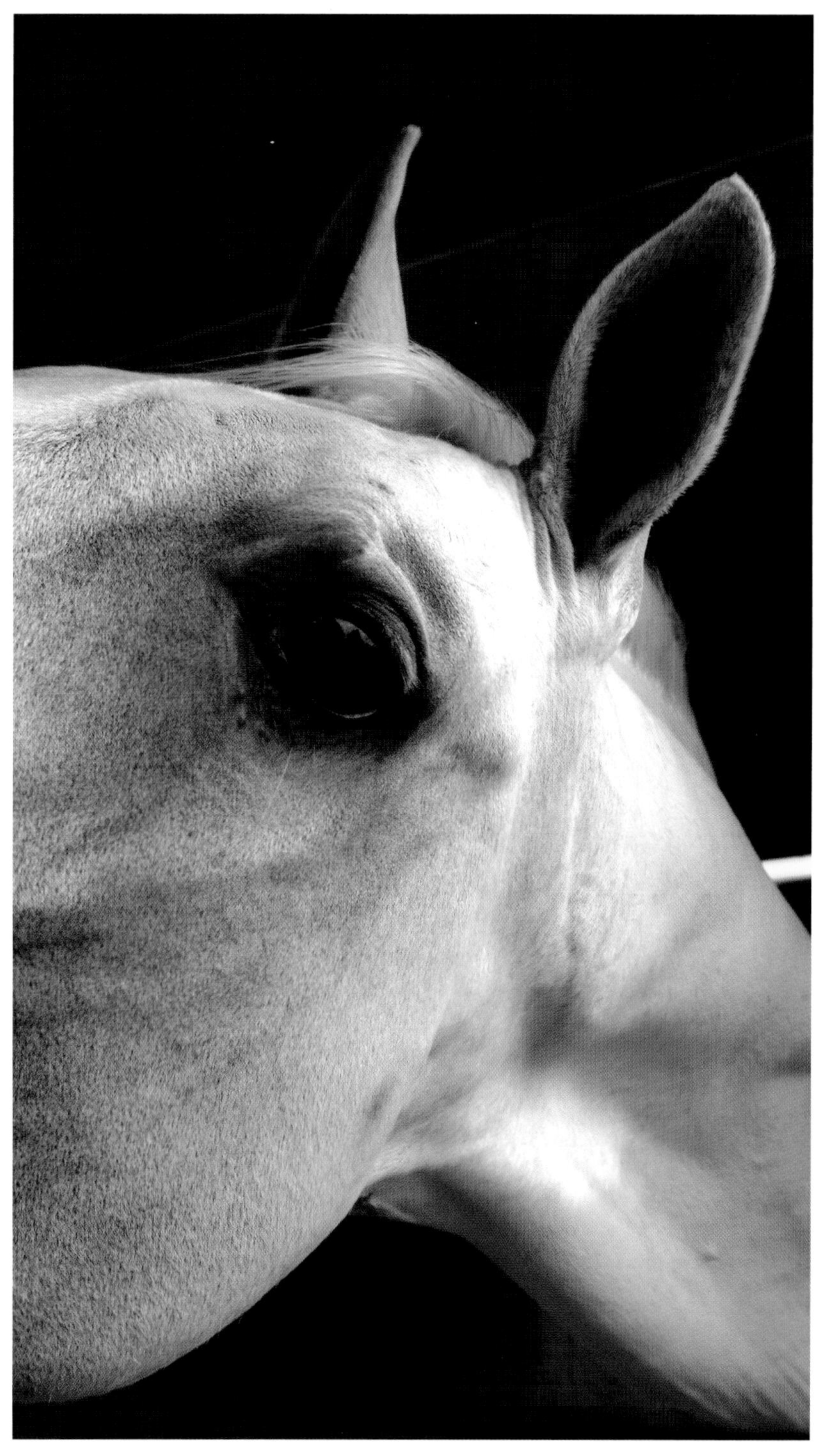

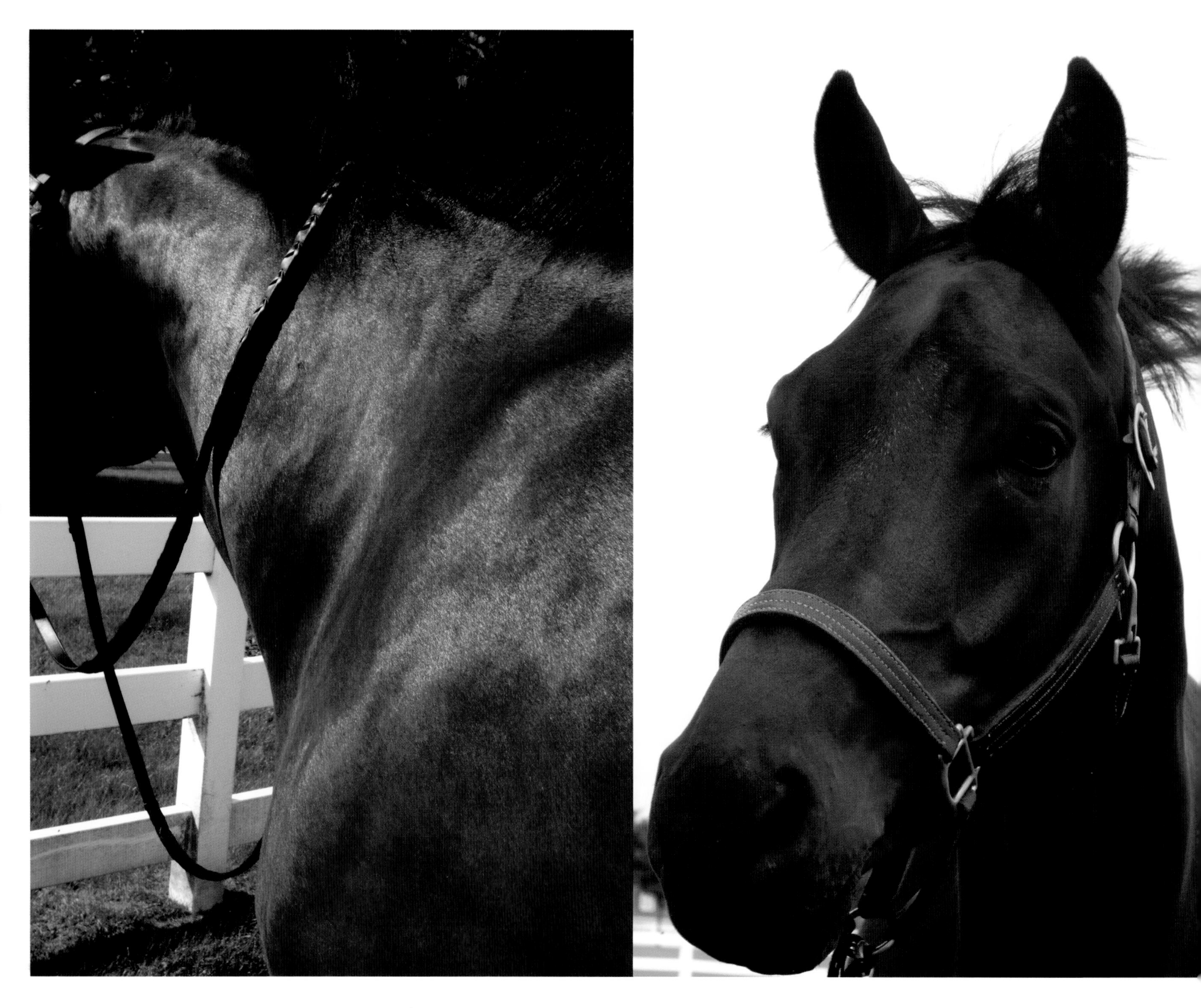

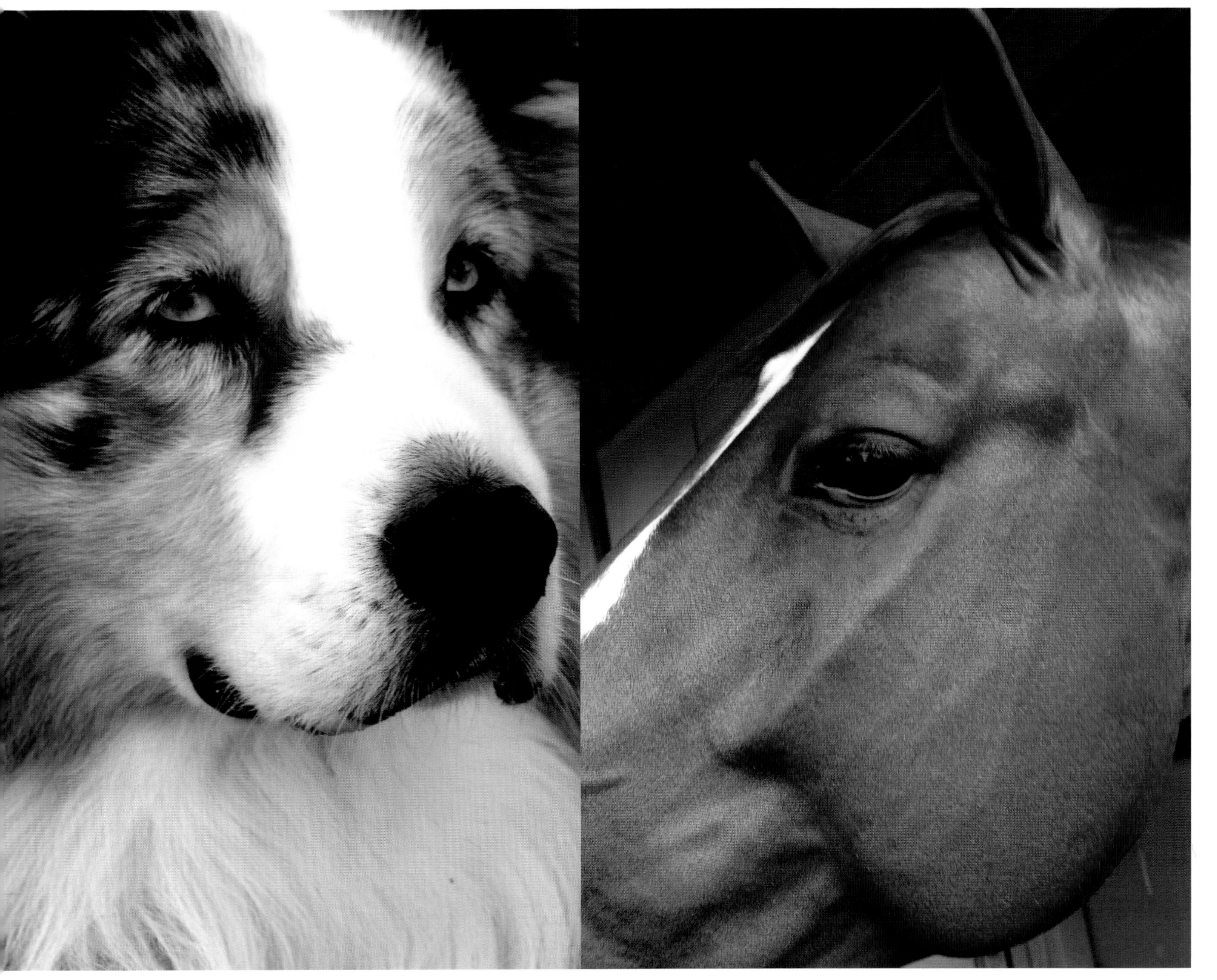

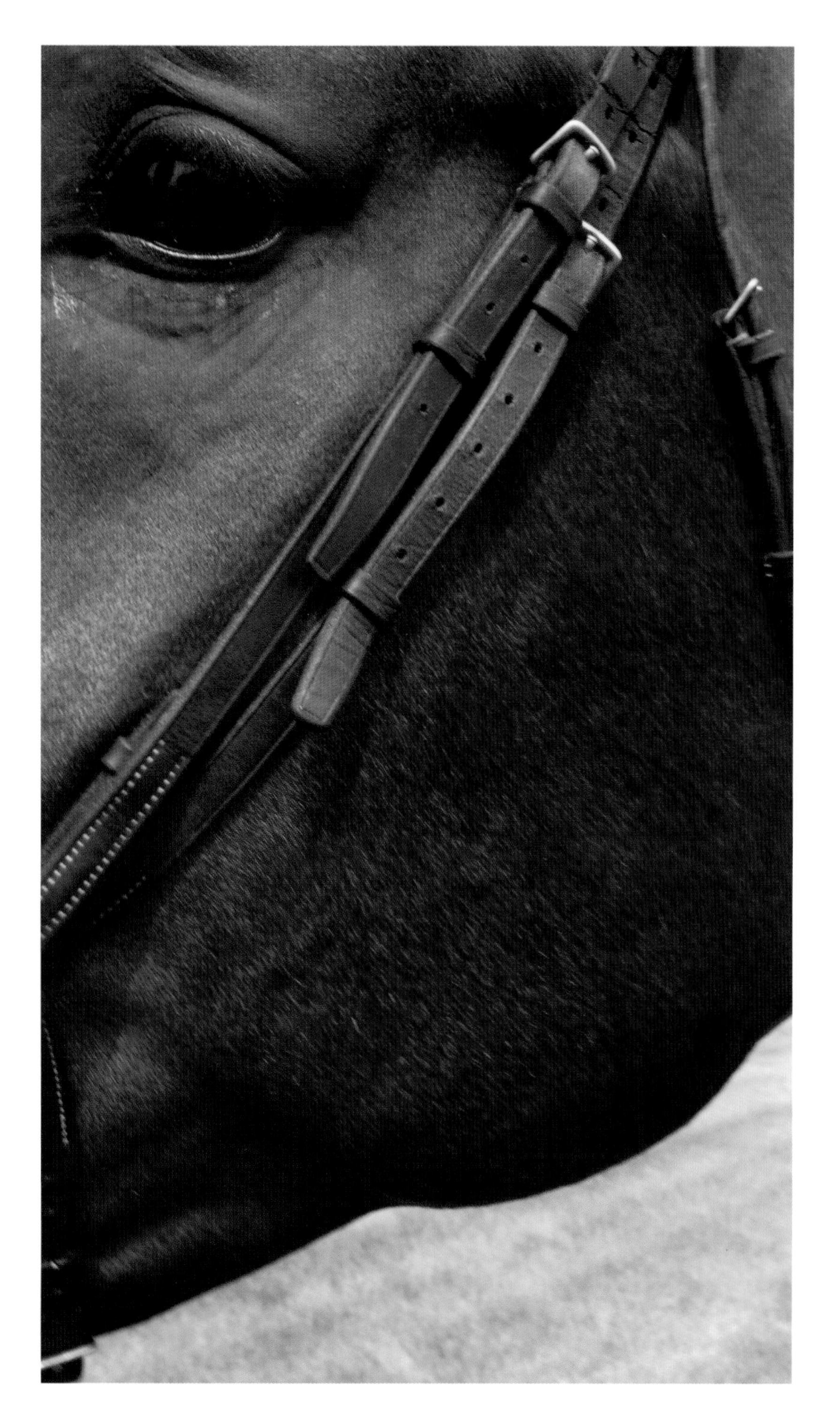

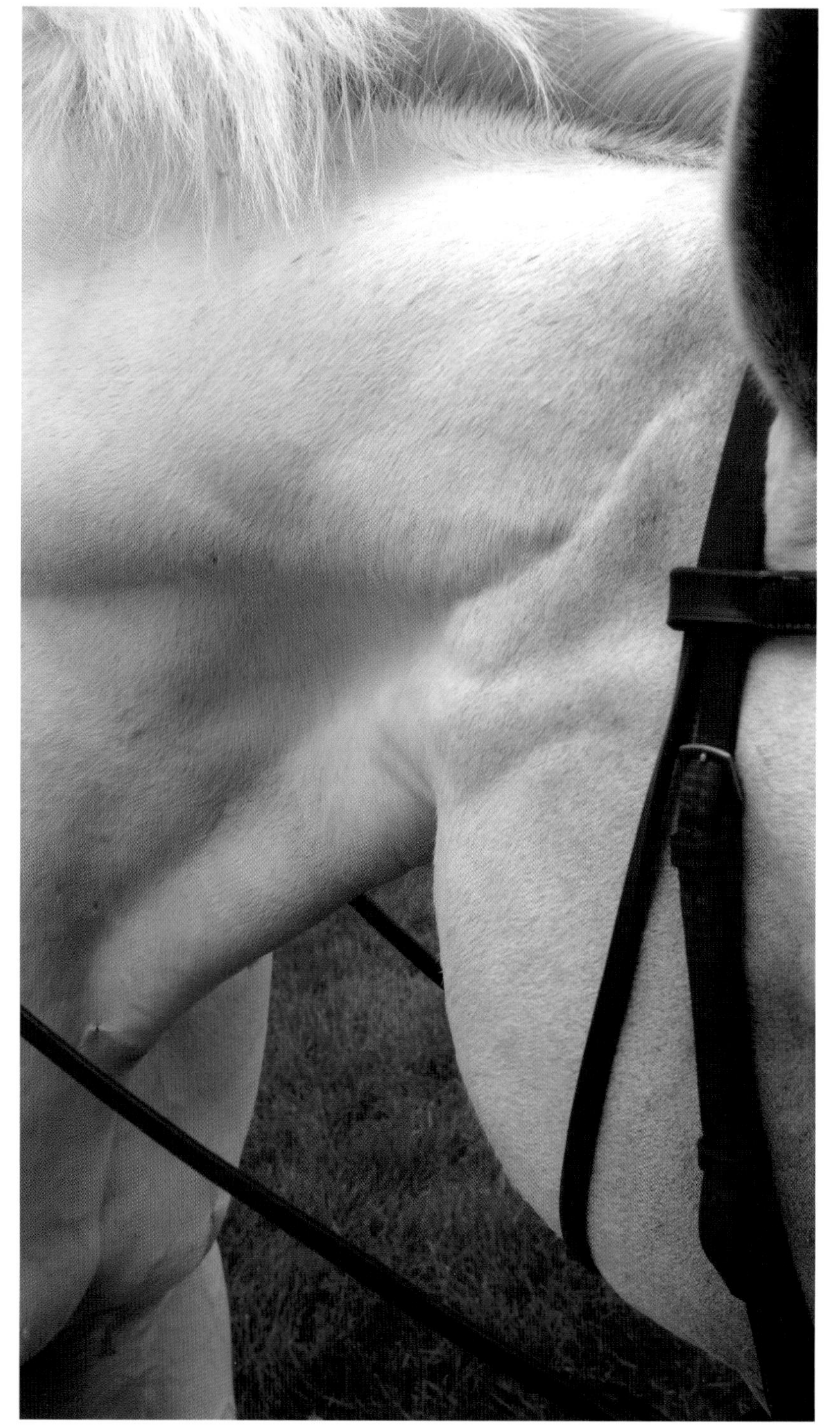

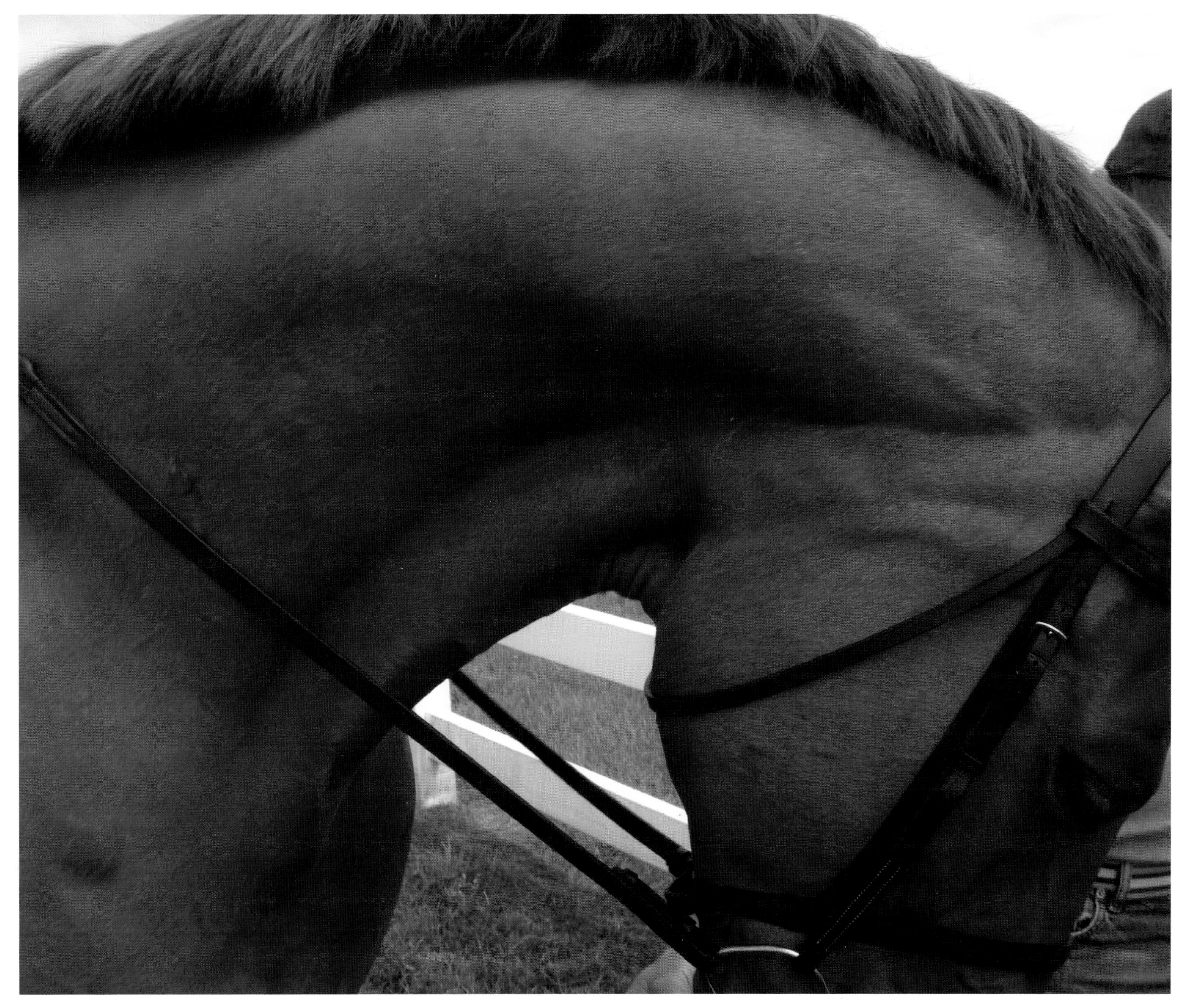

Boyle County Public Library

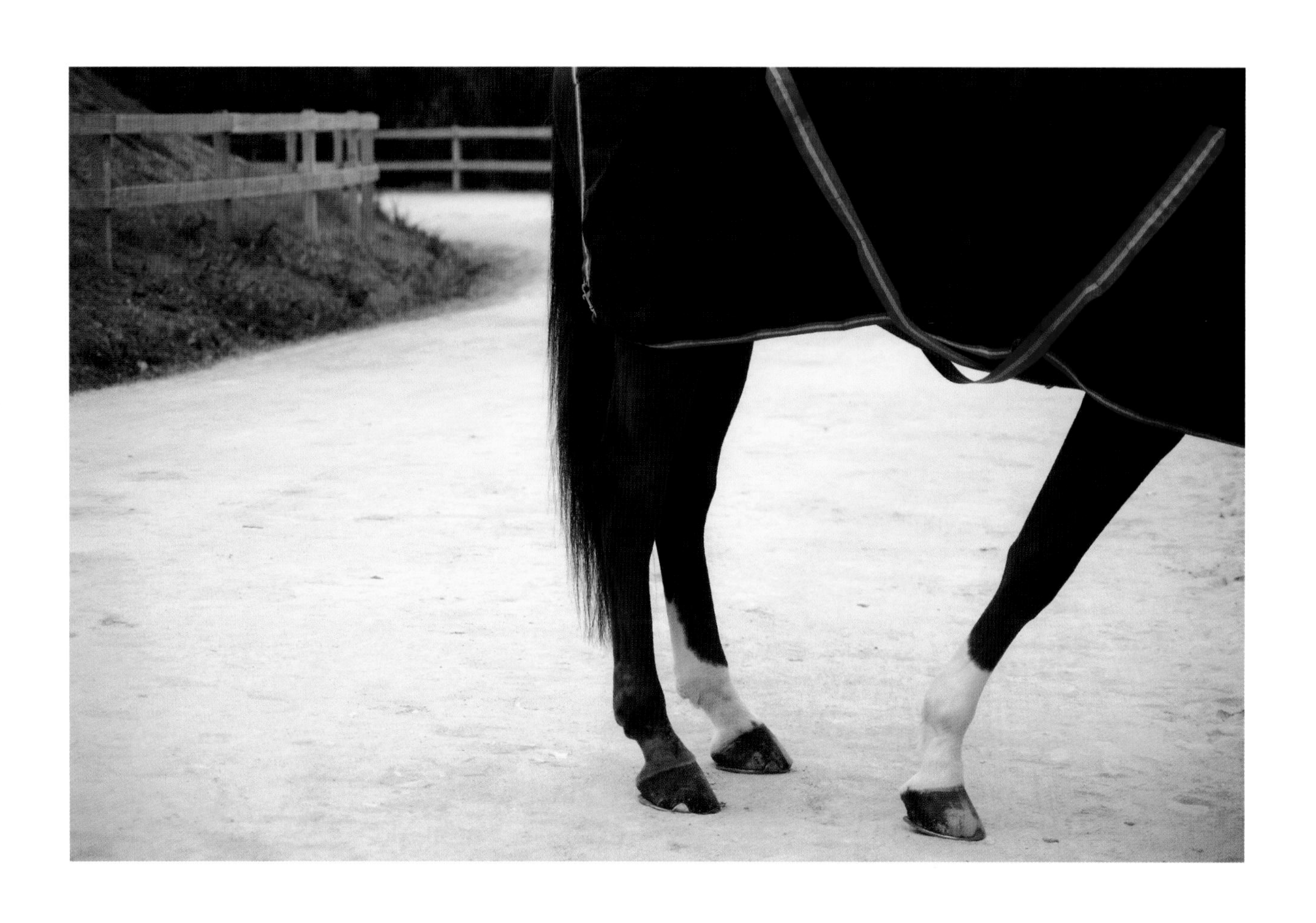

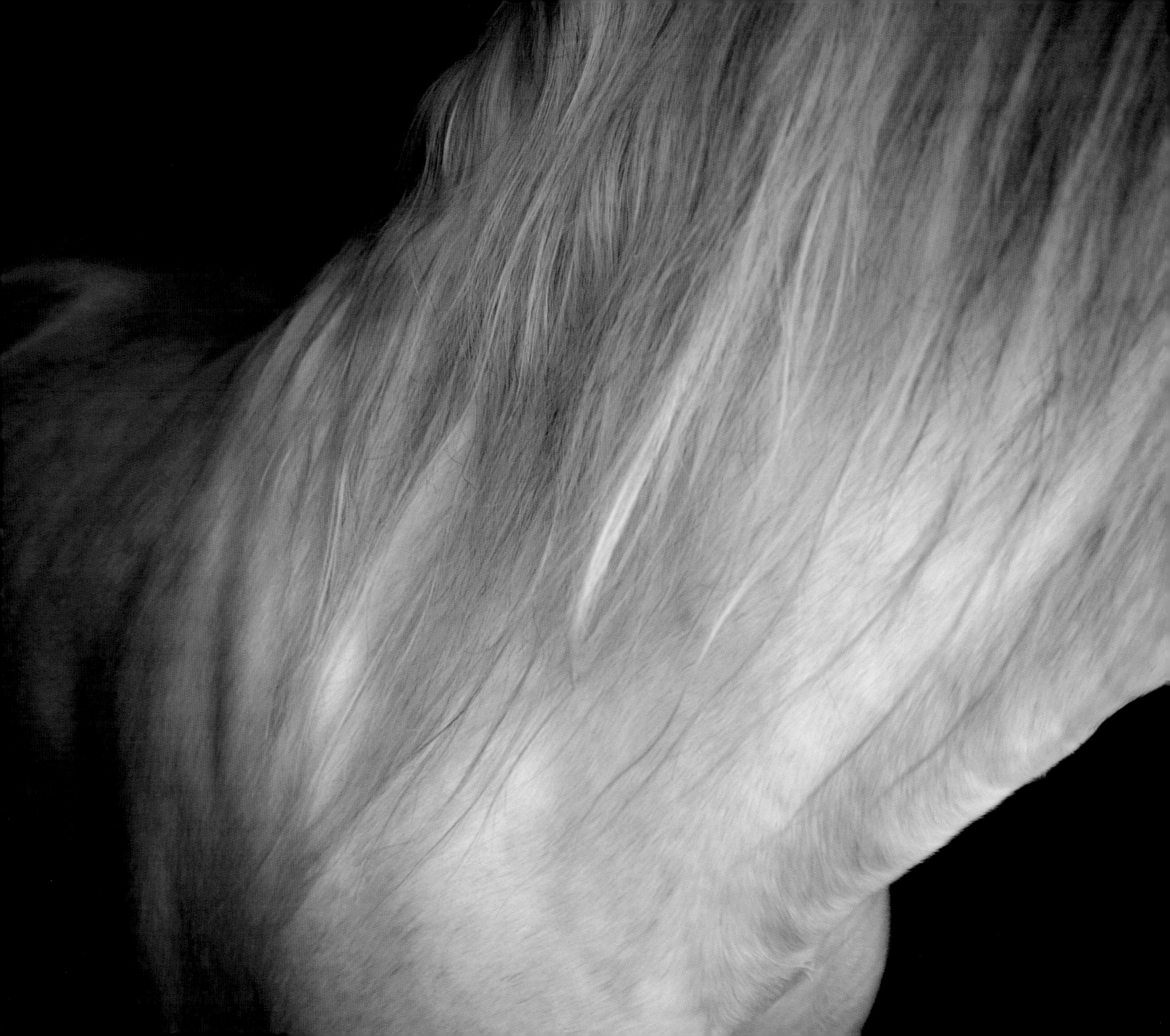

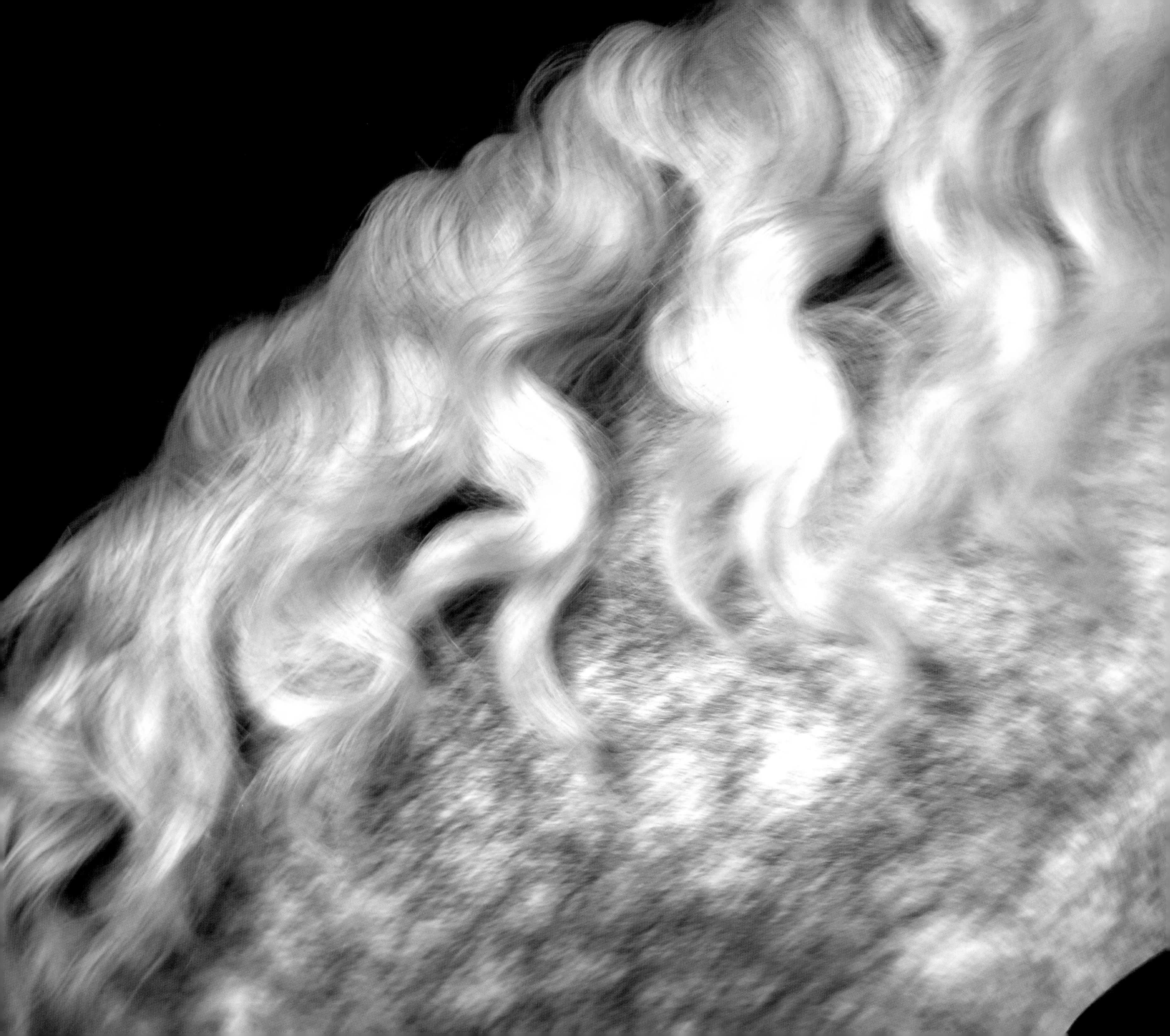

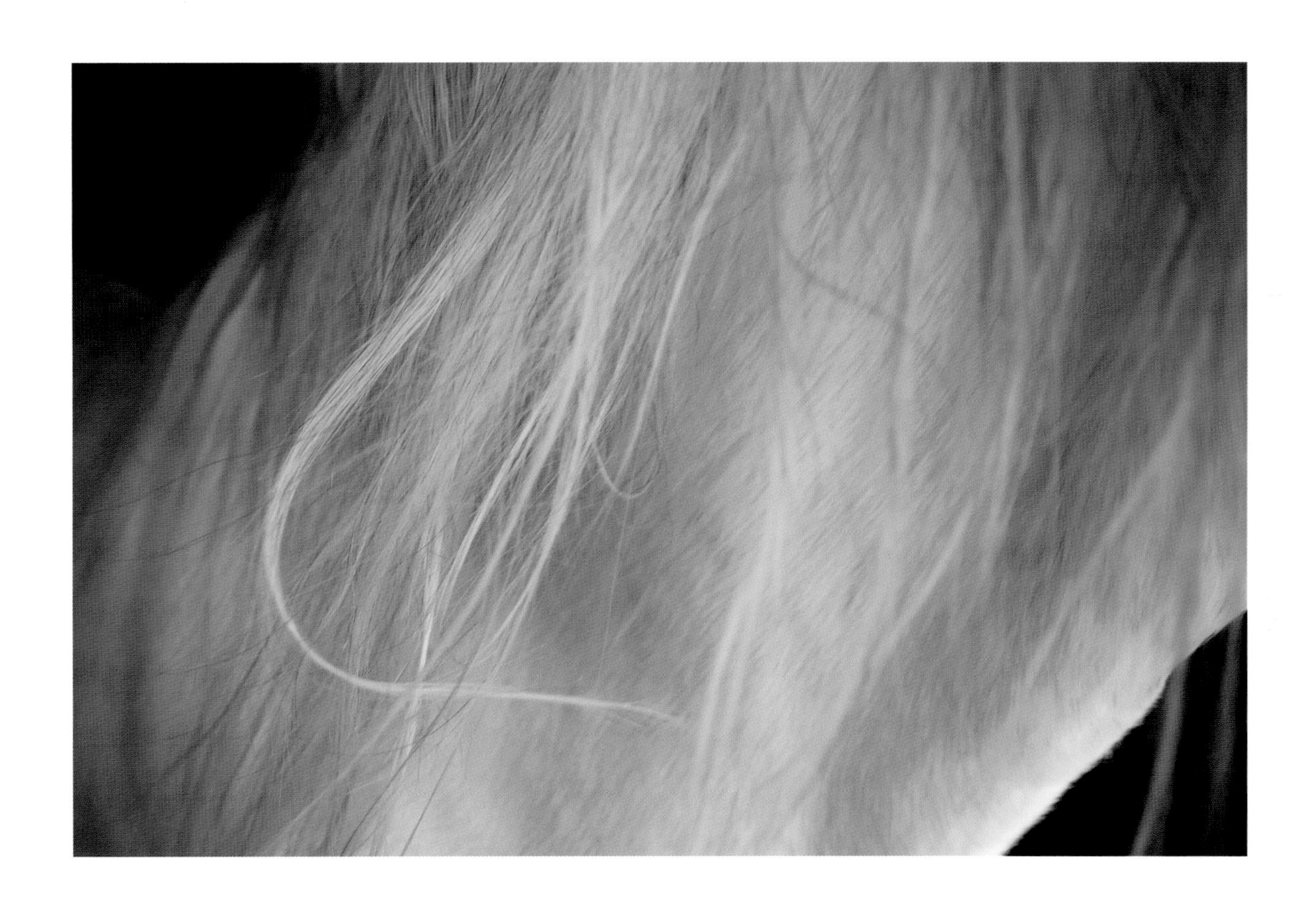

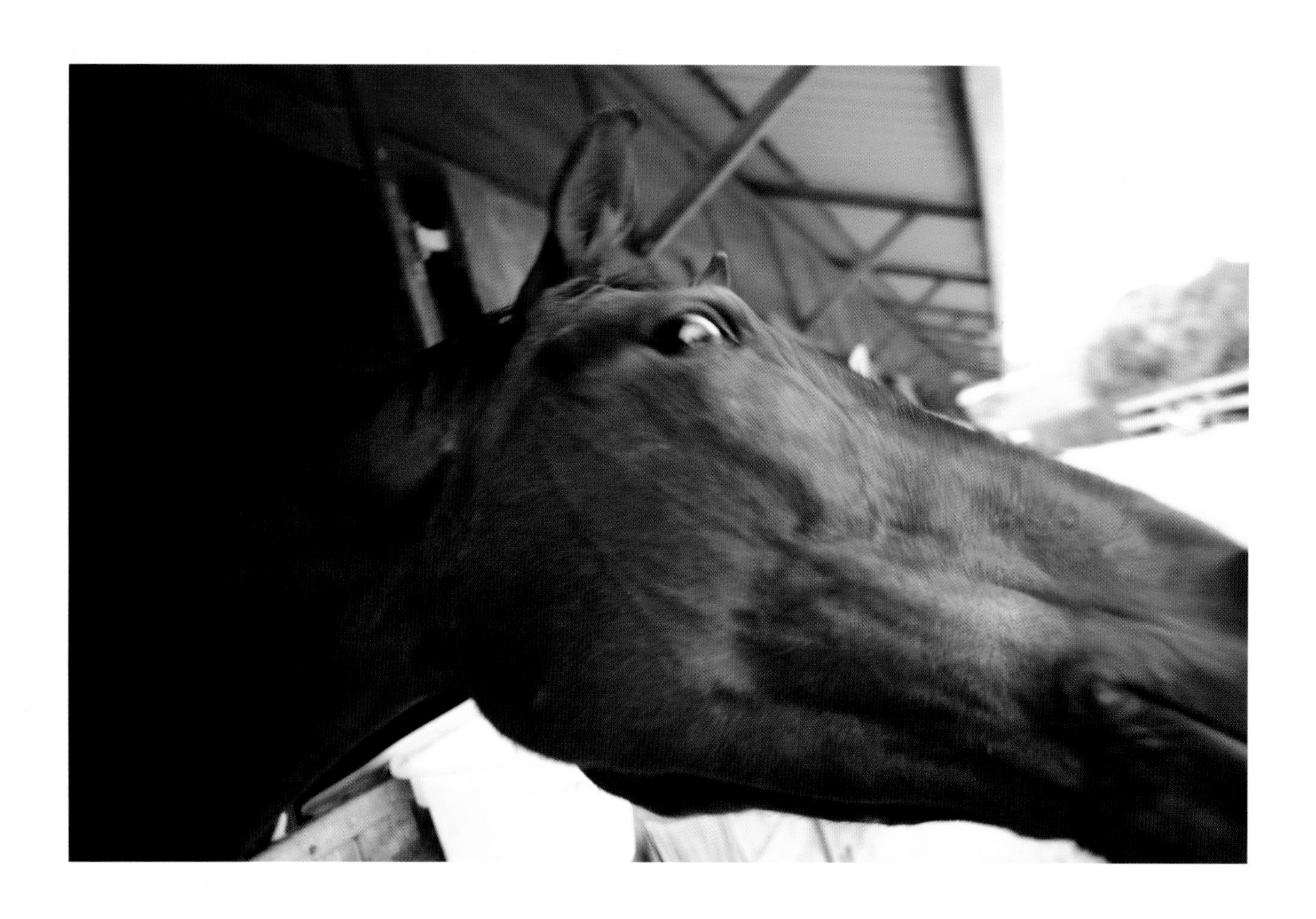

P30

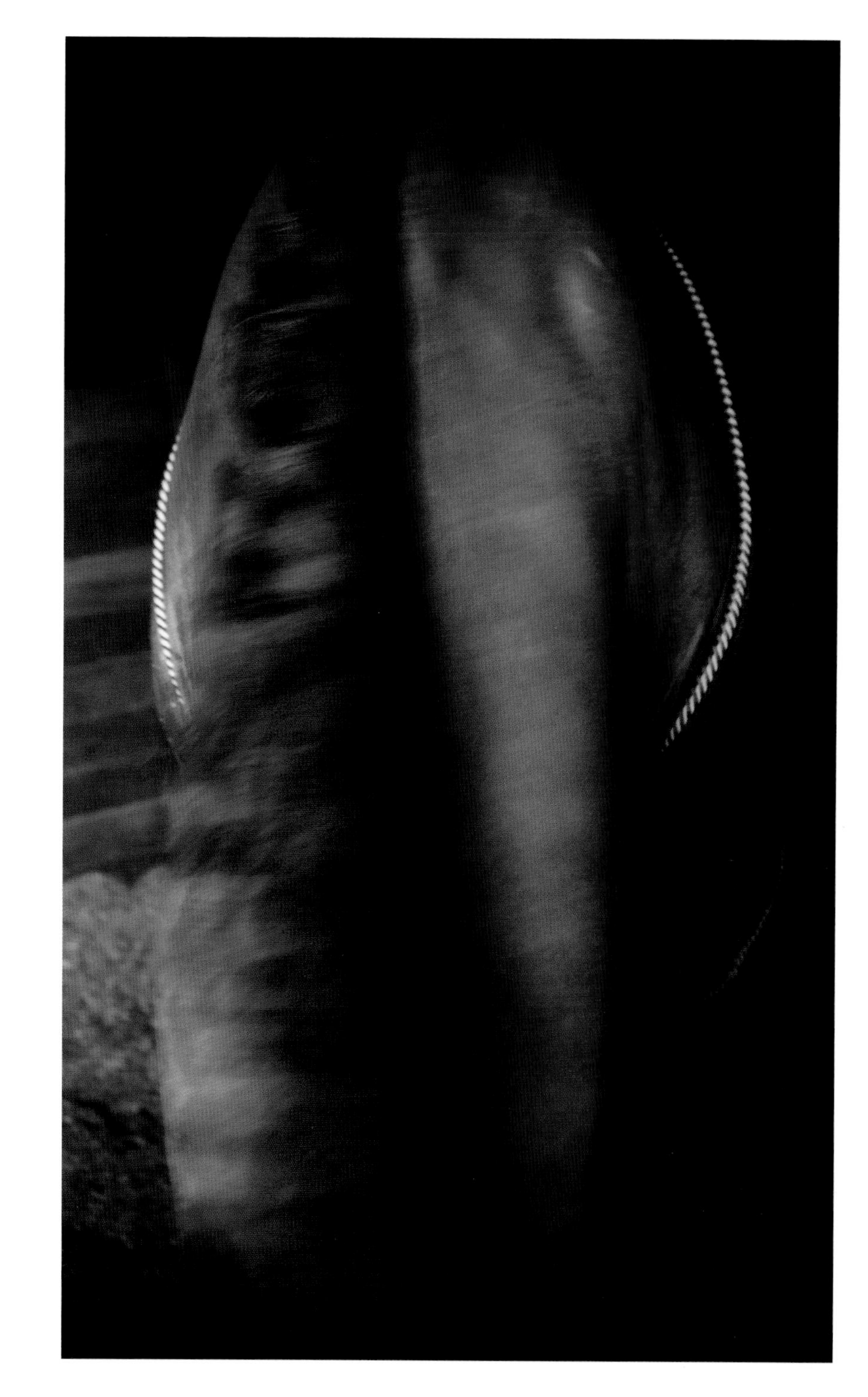

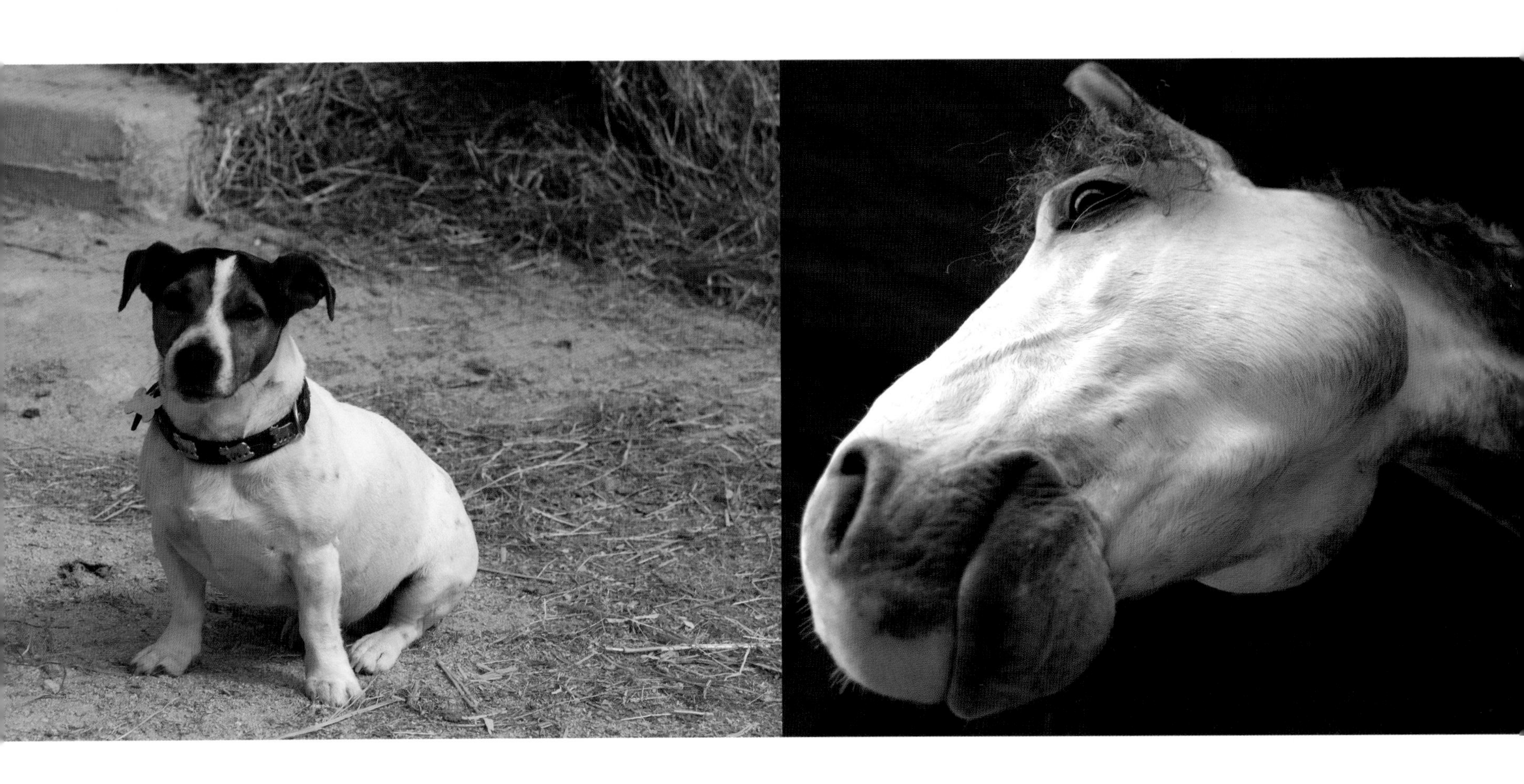

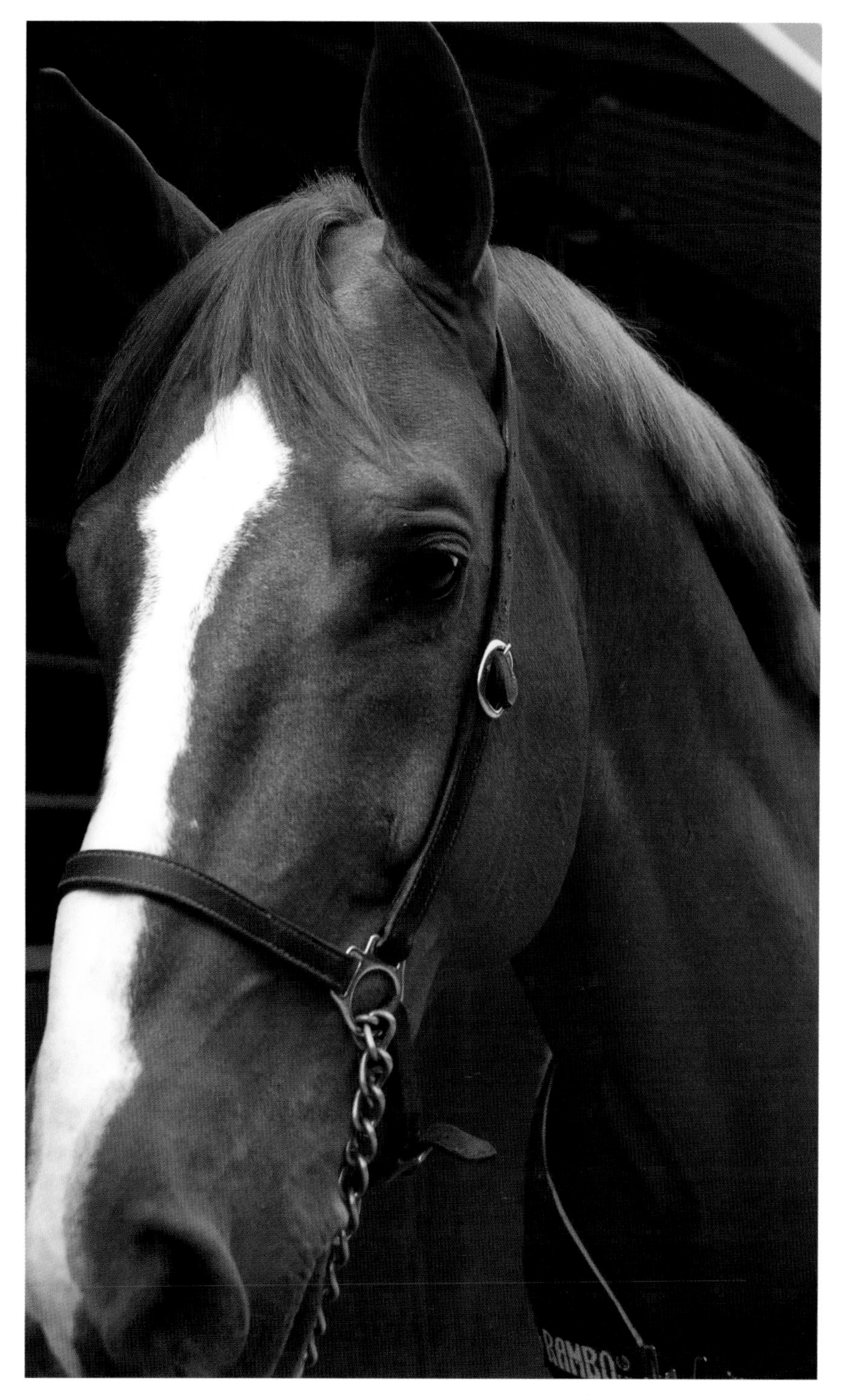
RAMBO

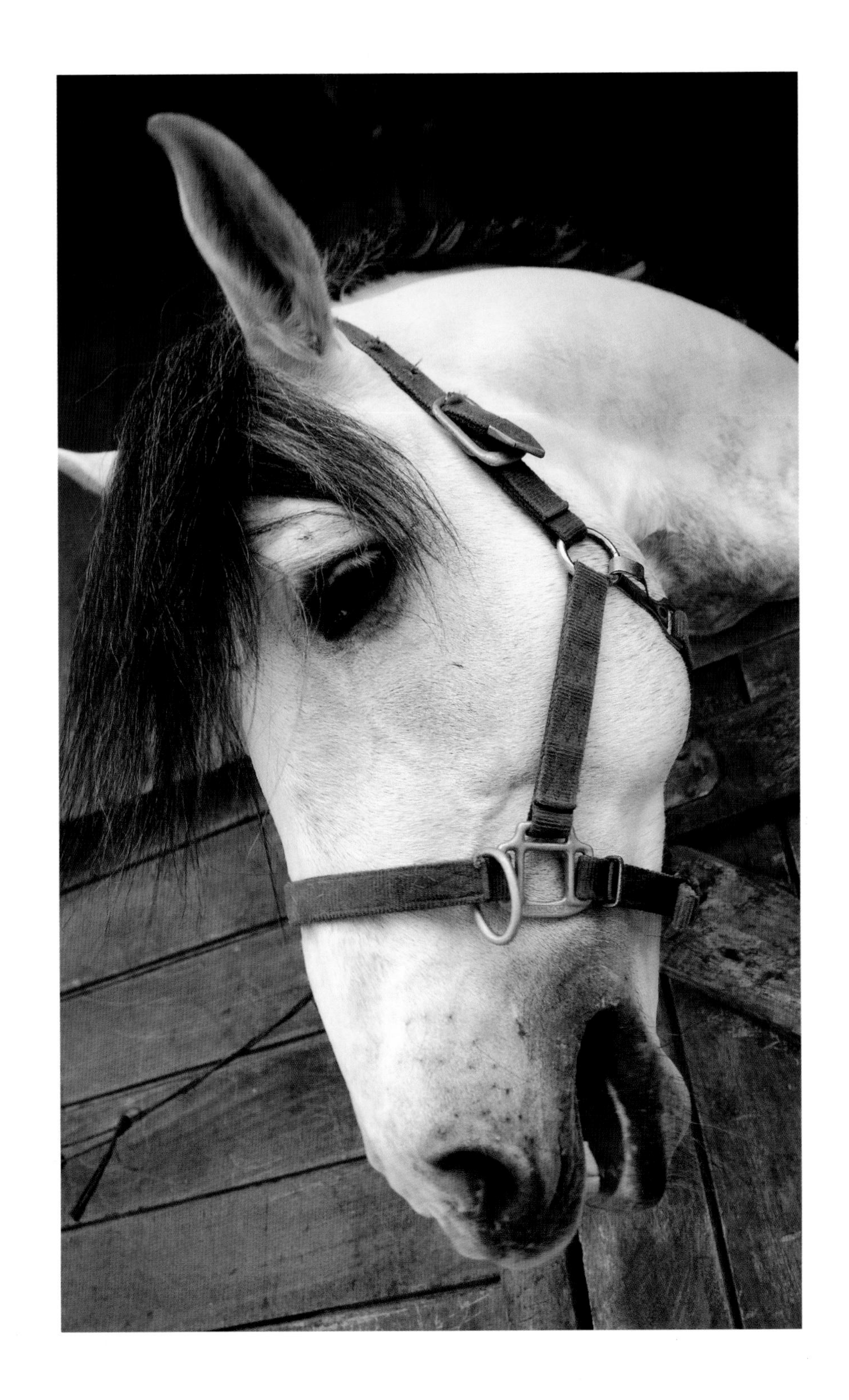

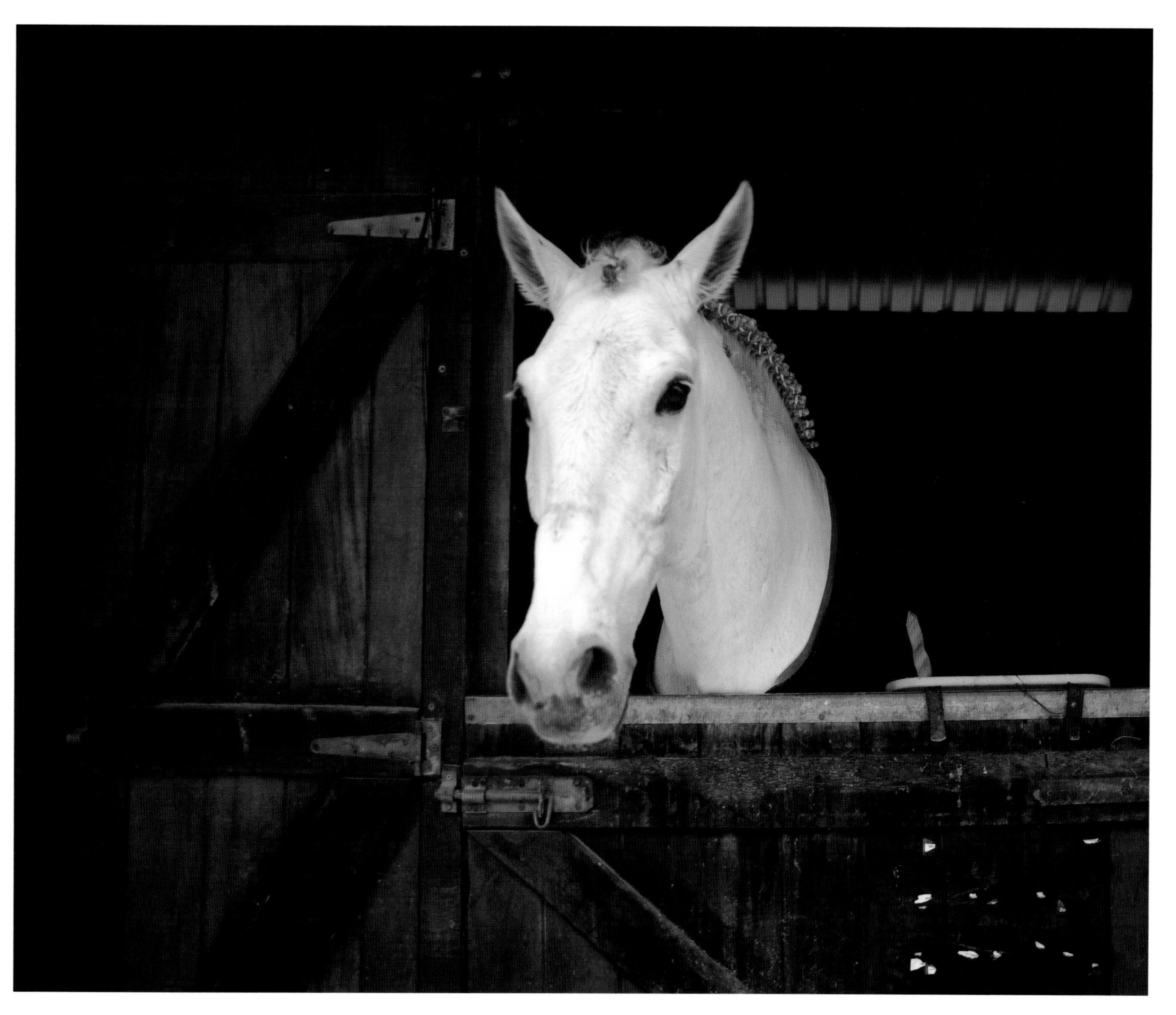

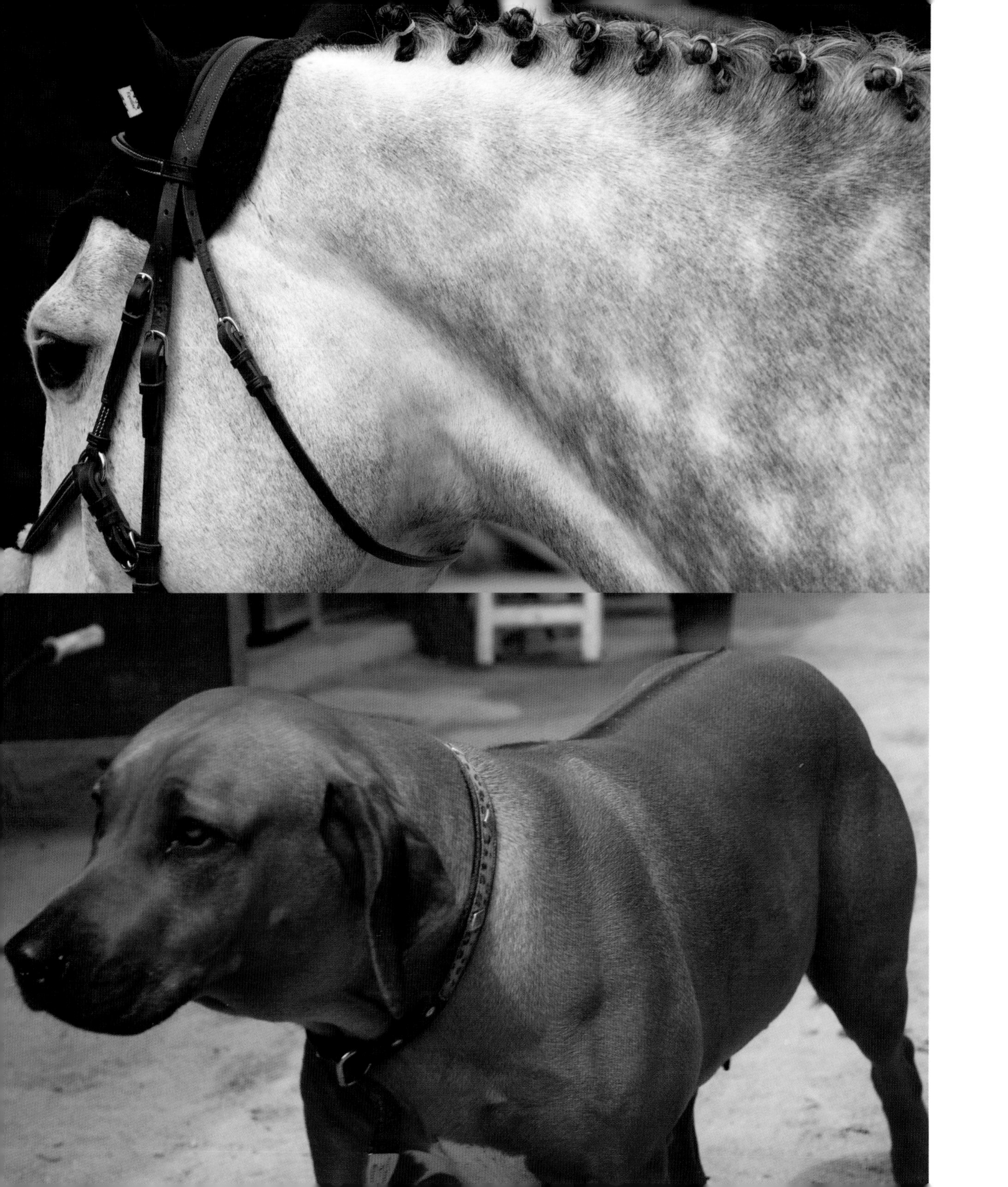

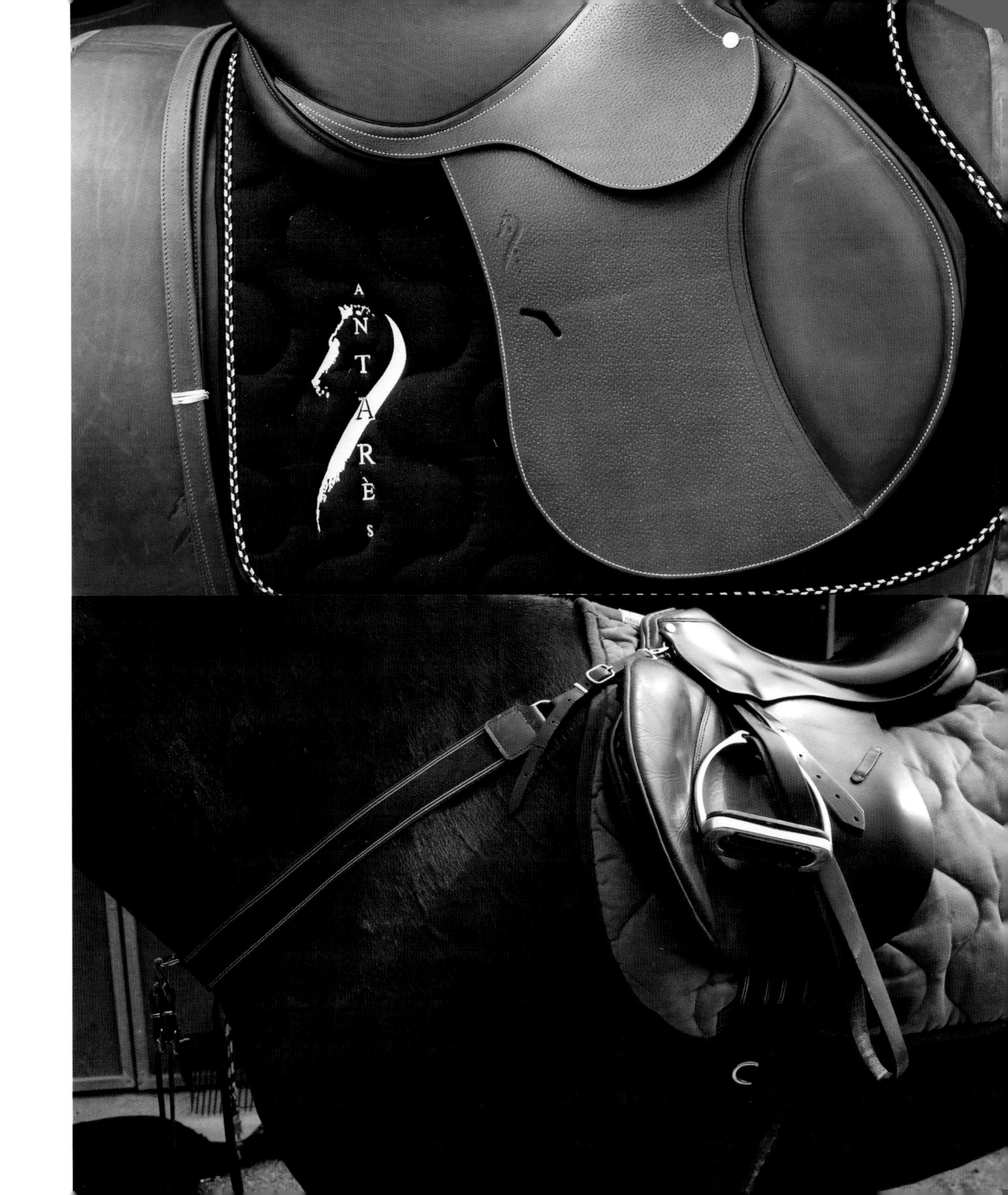
ANTARÈS

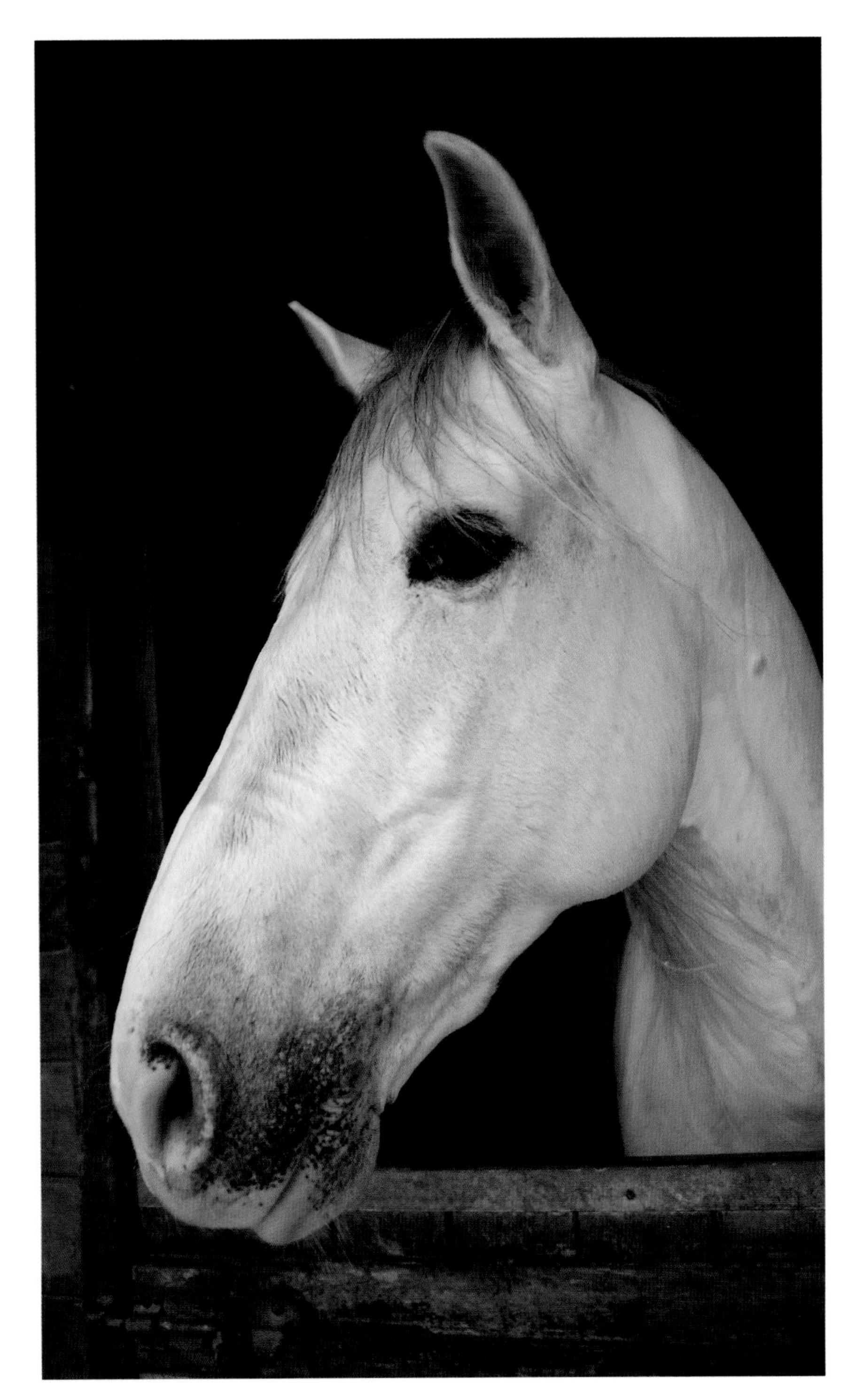

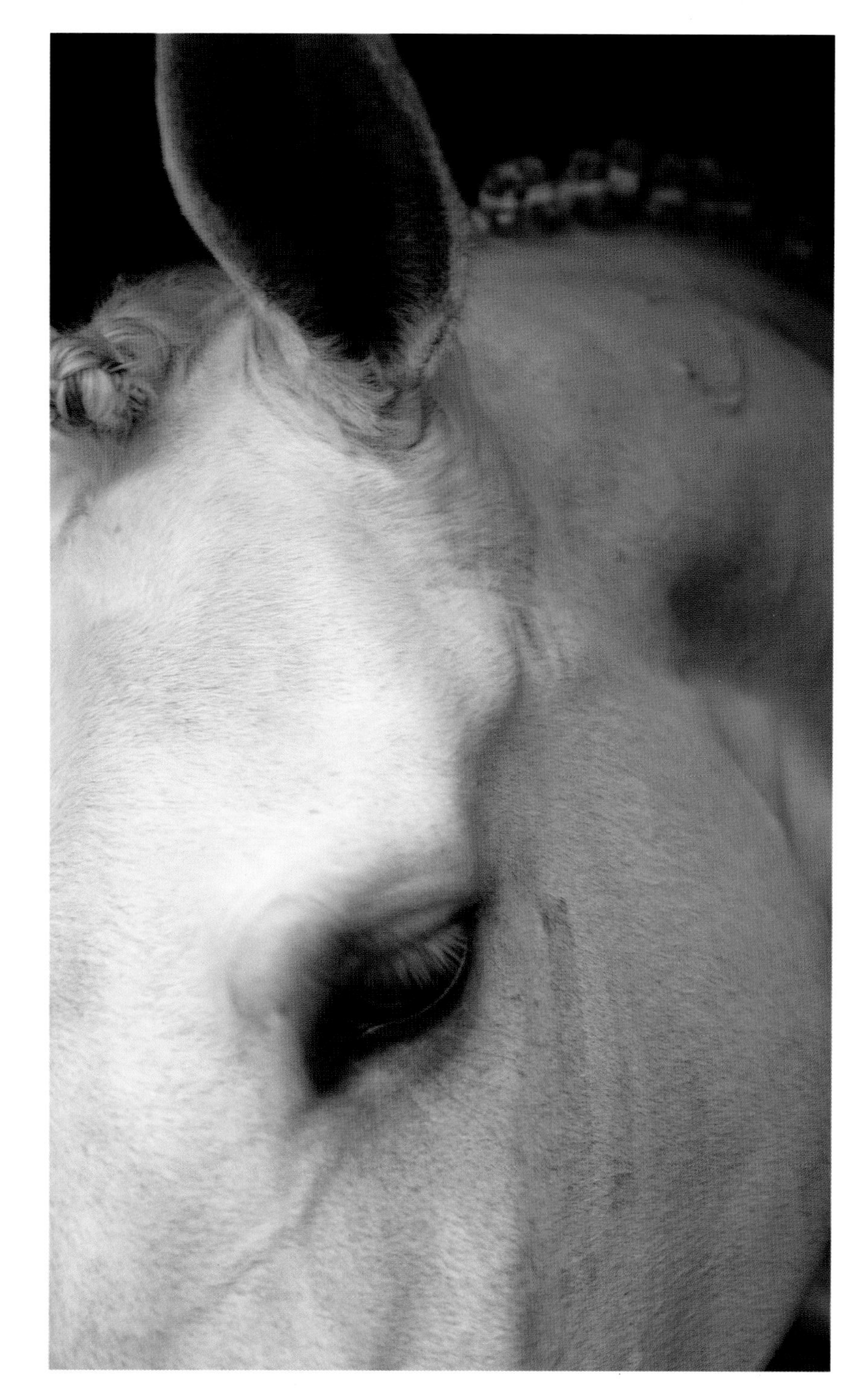

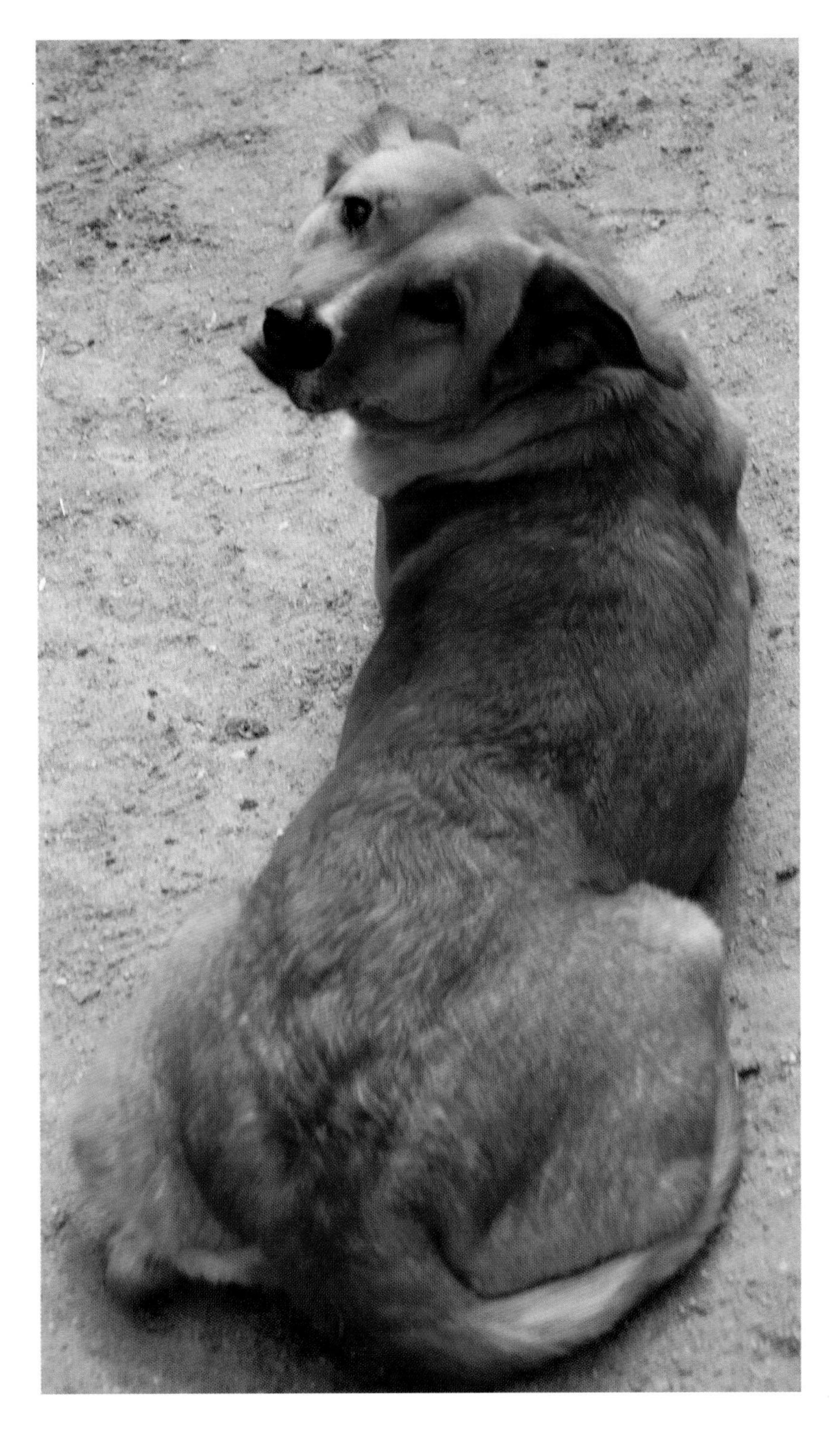

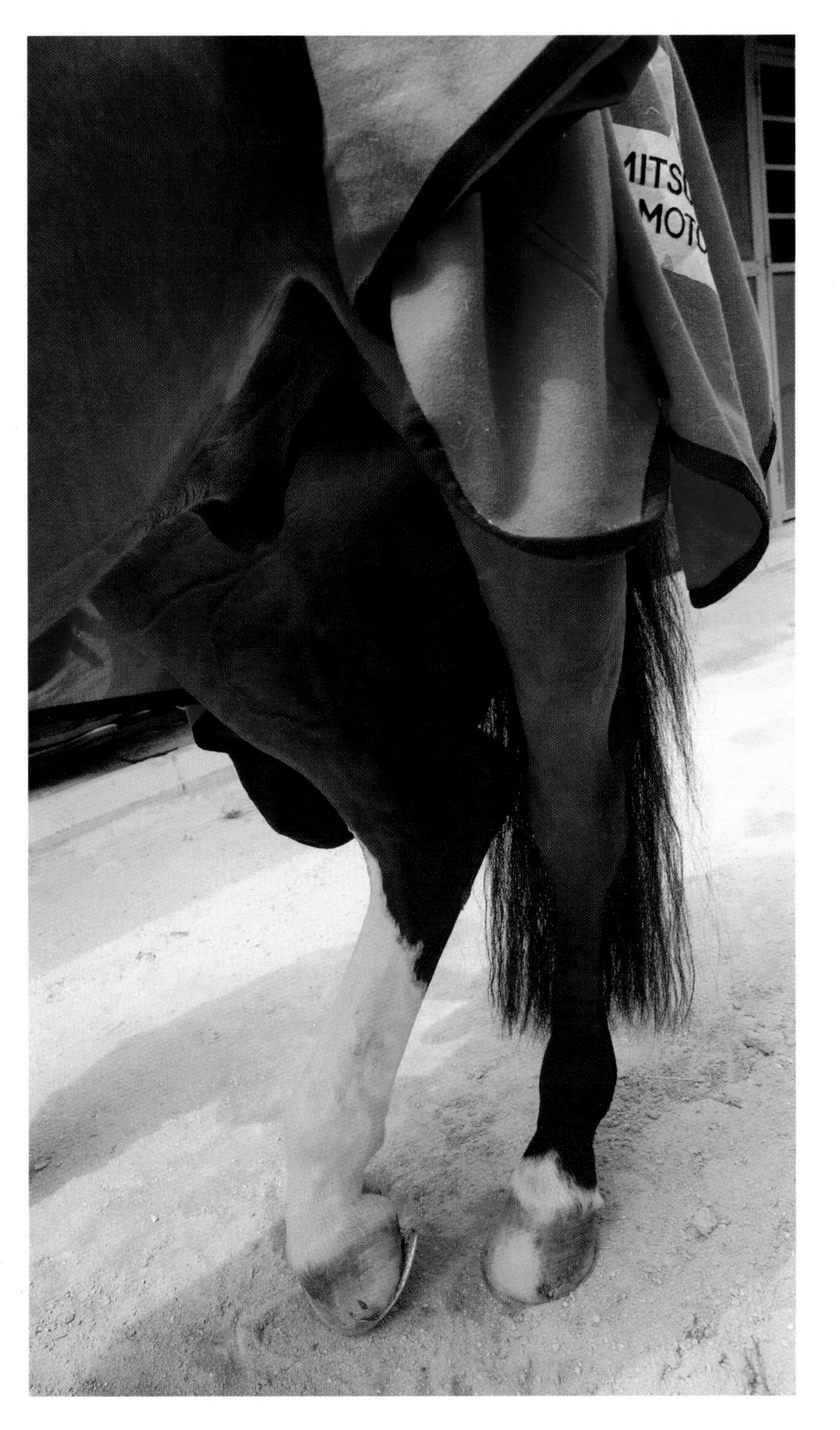

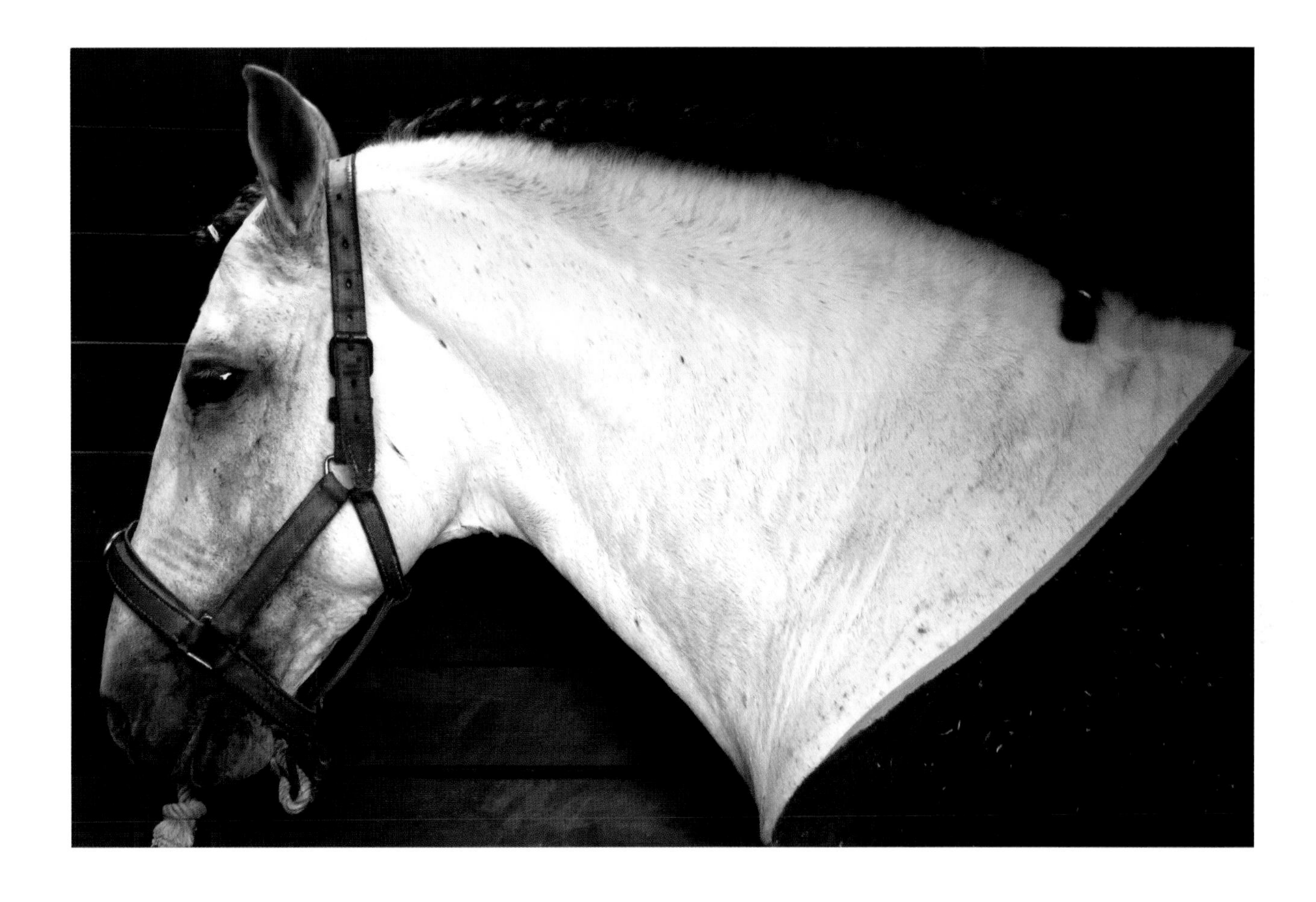

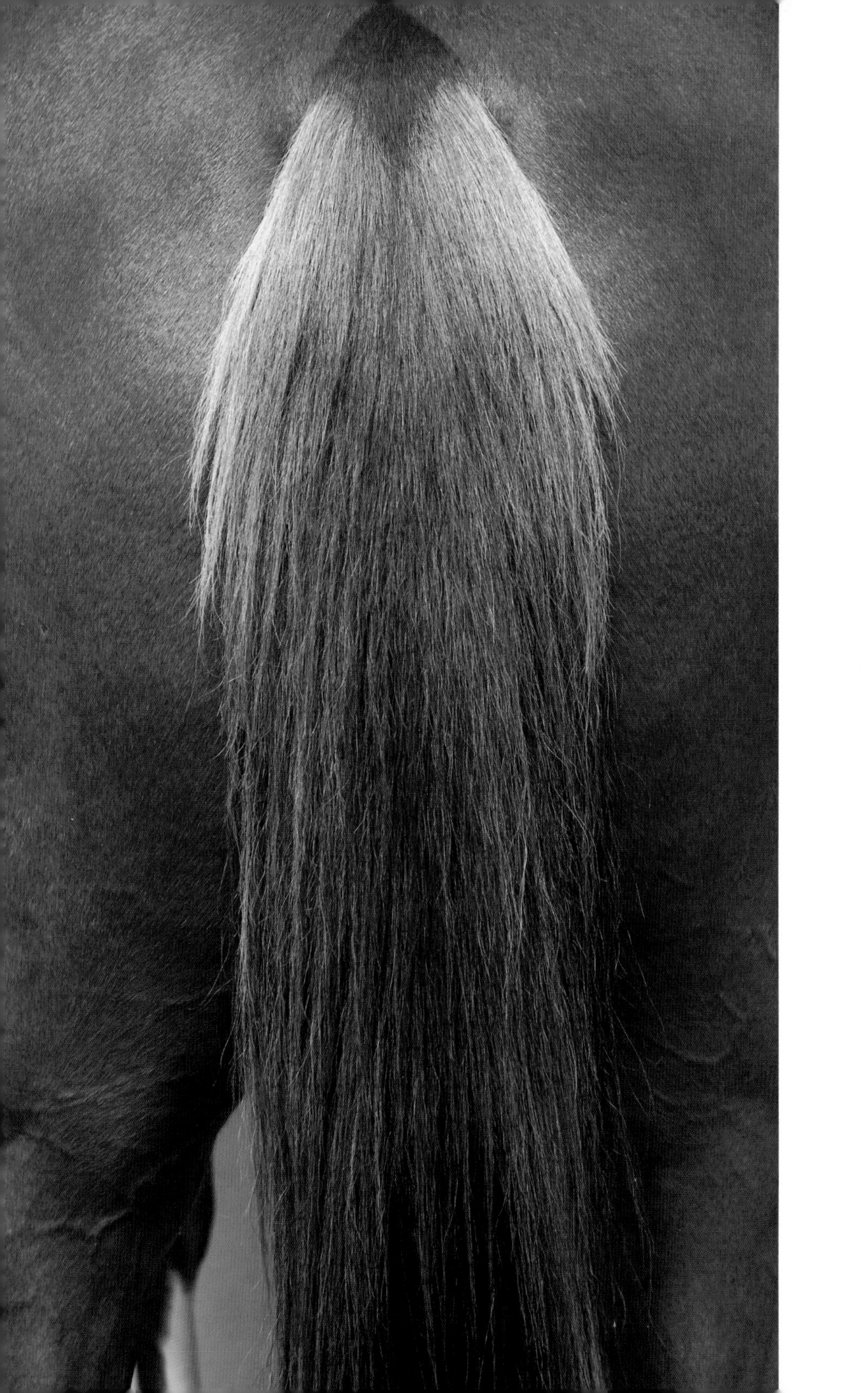

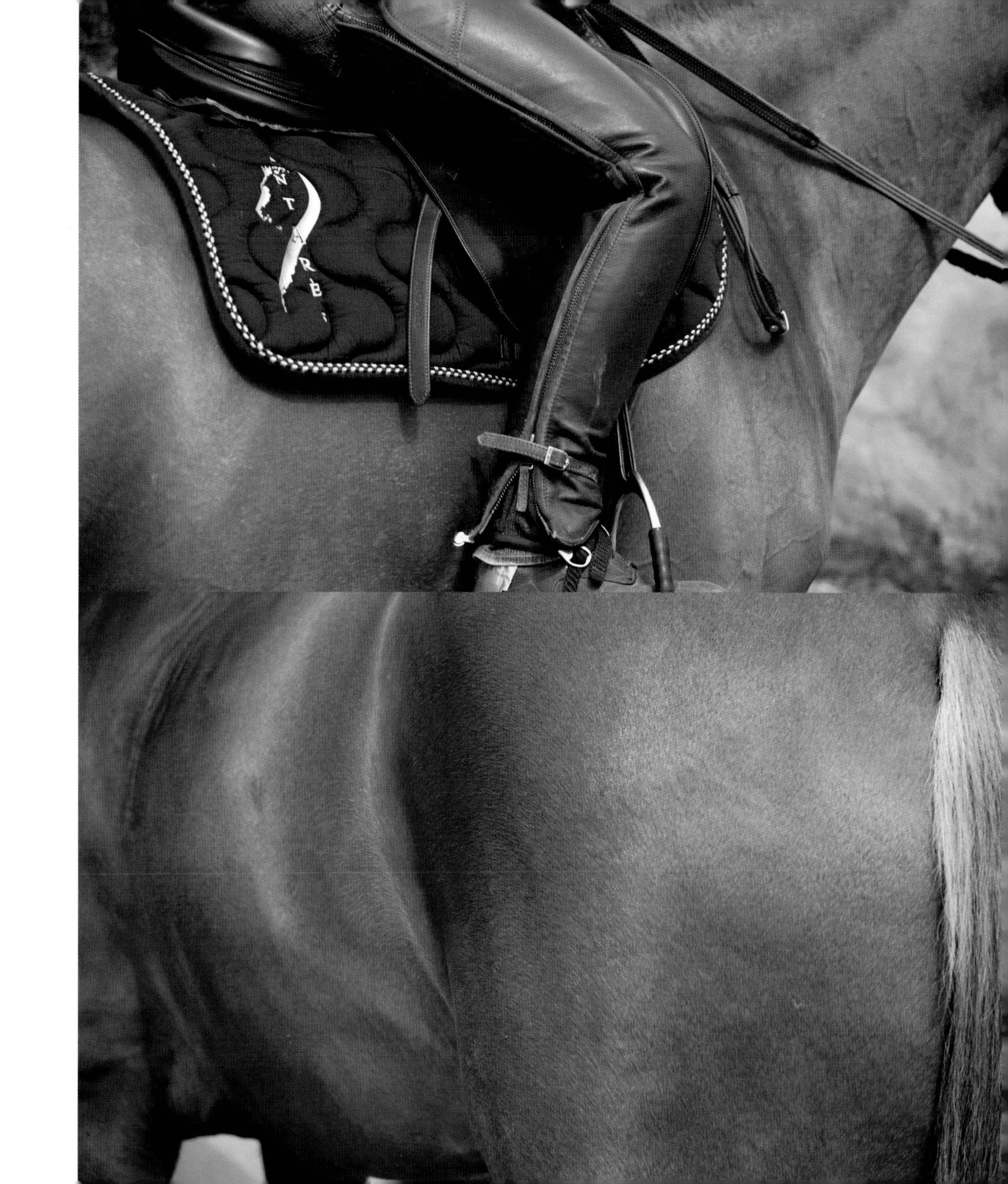

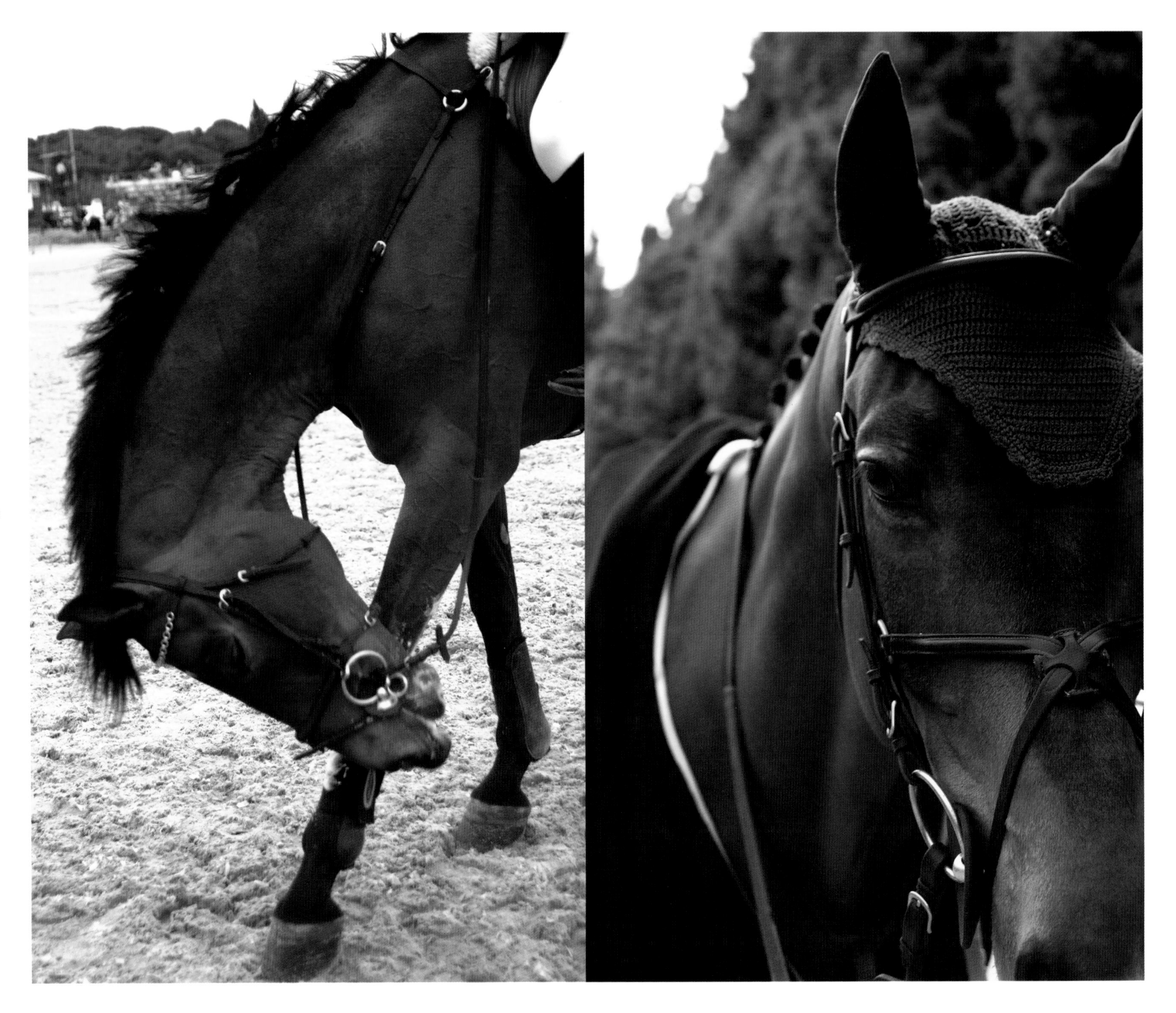

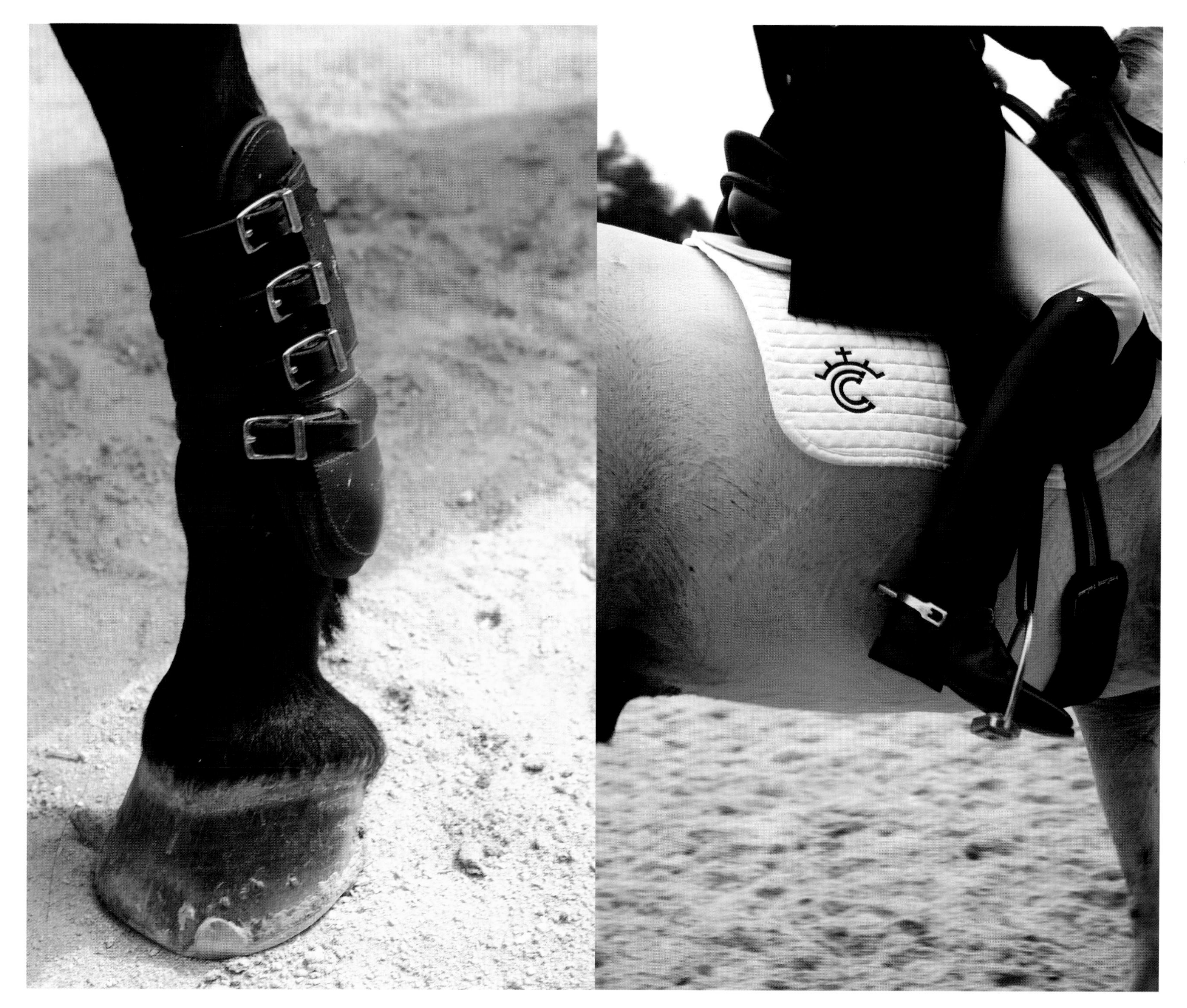

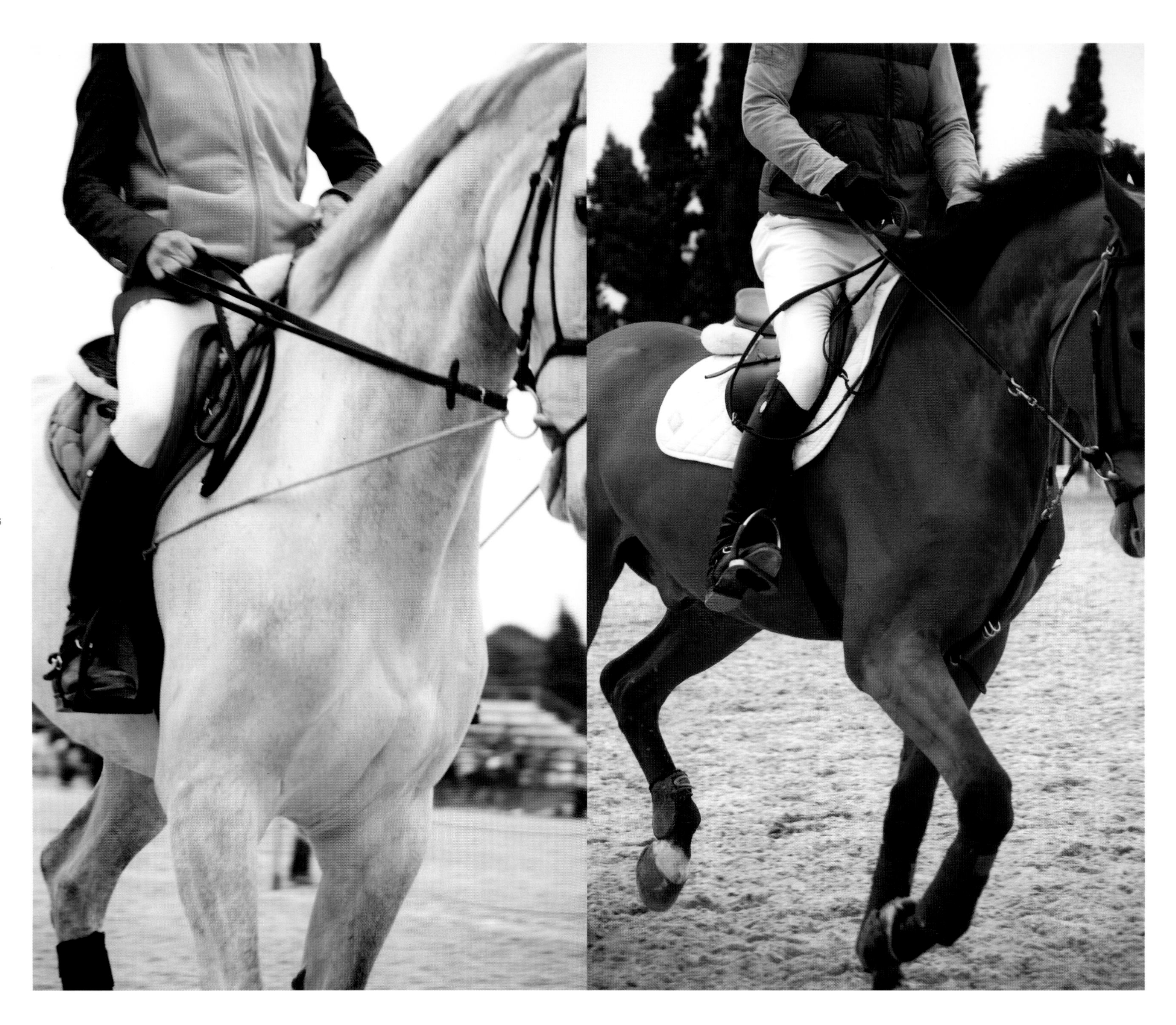

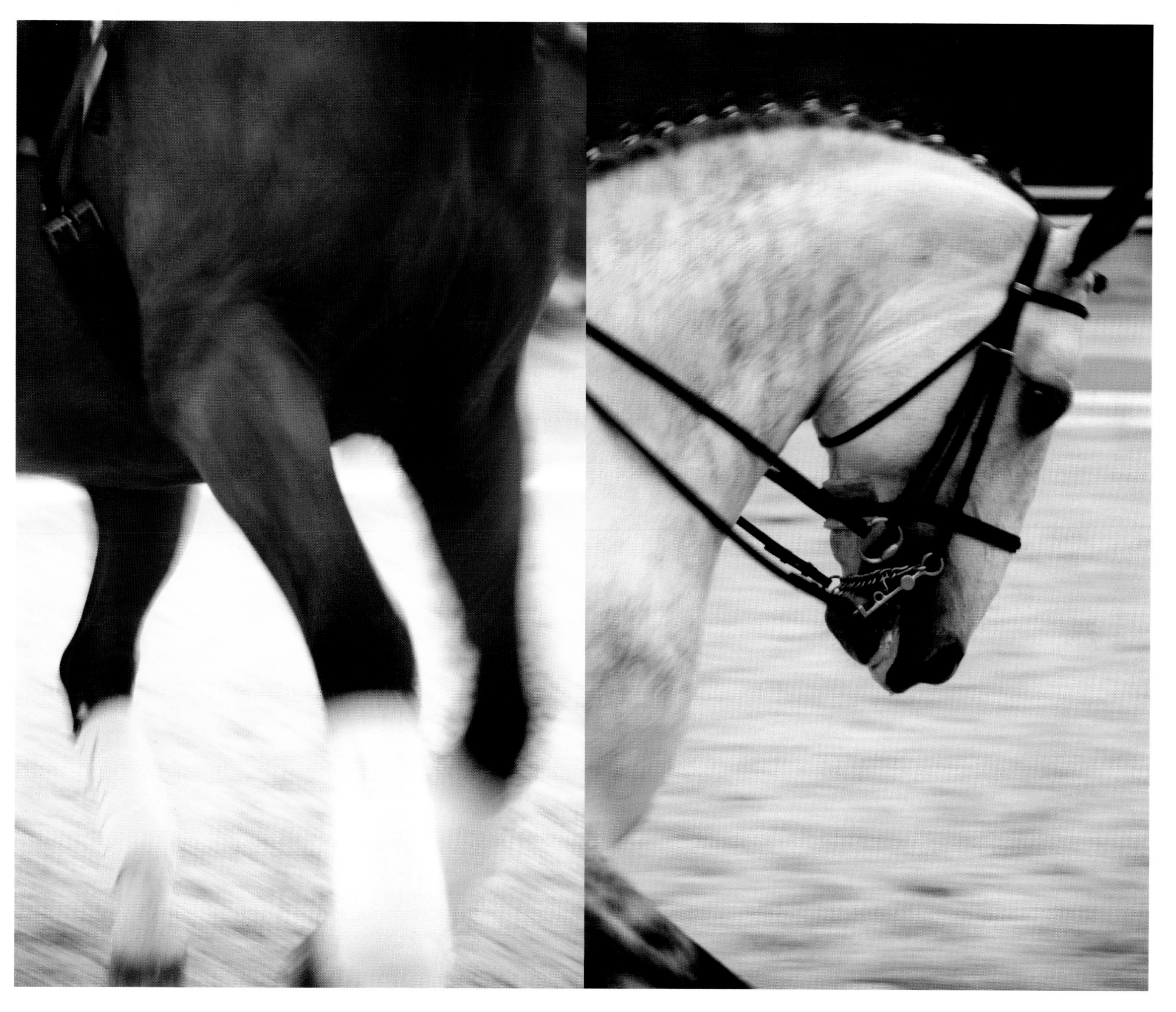

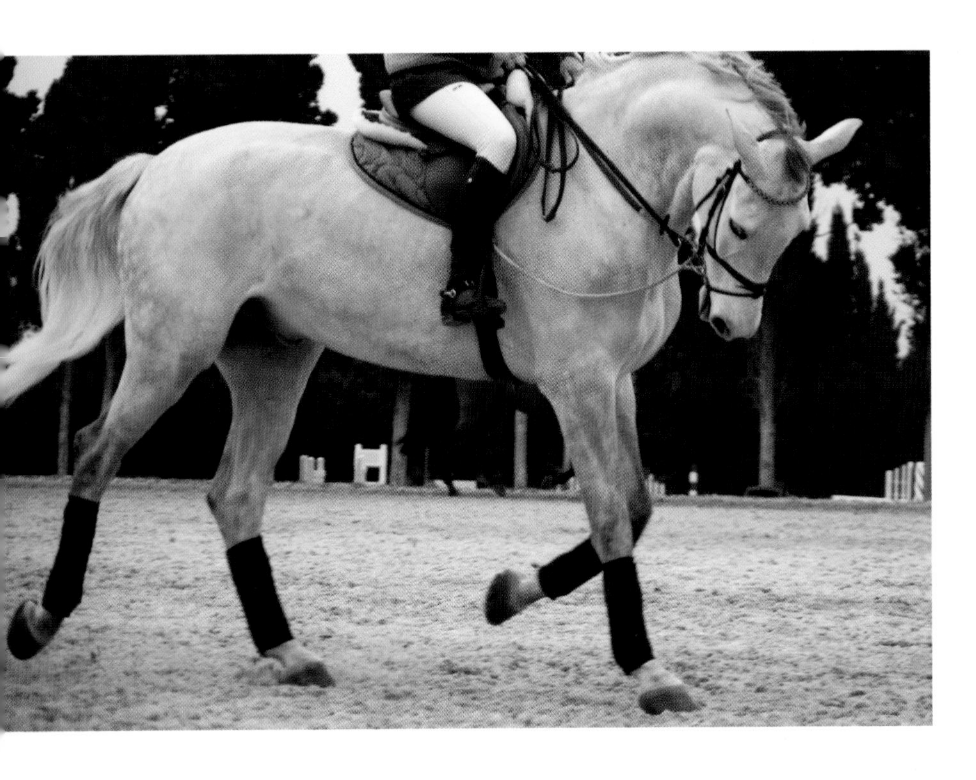

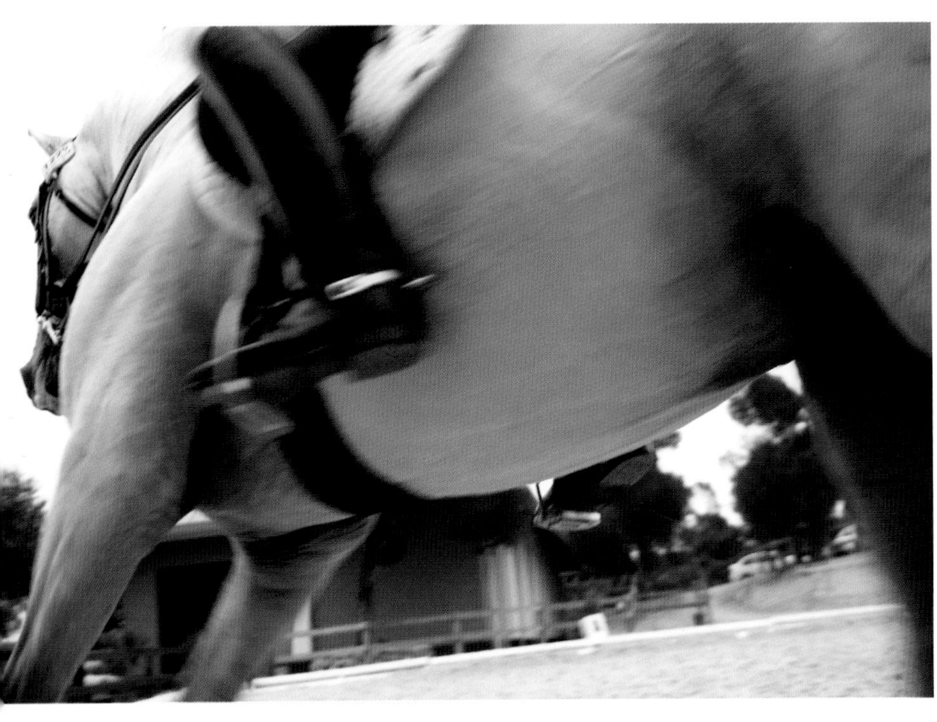

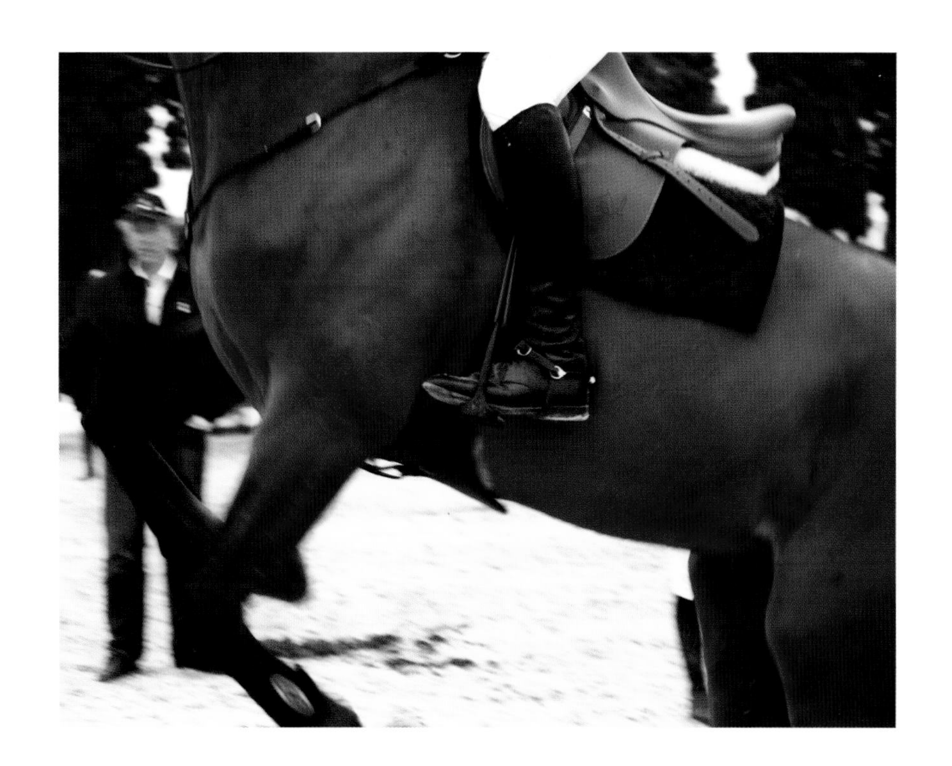

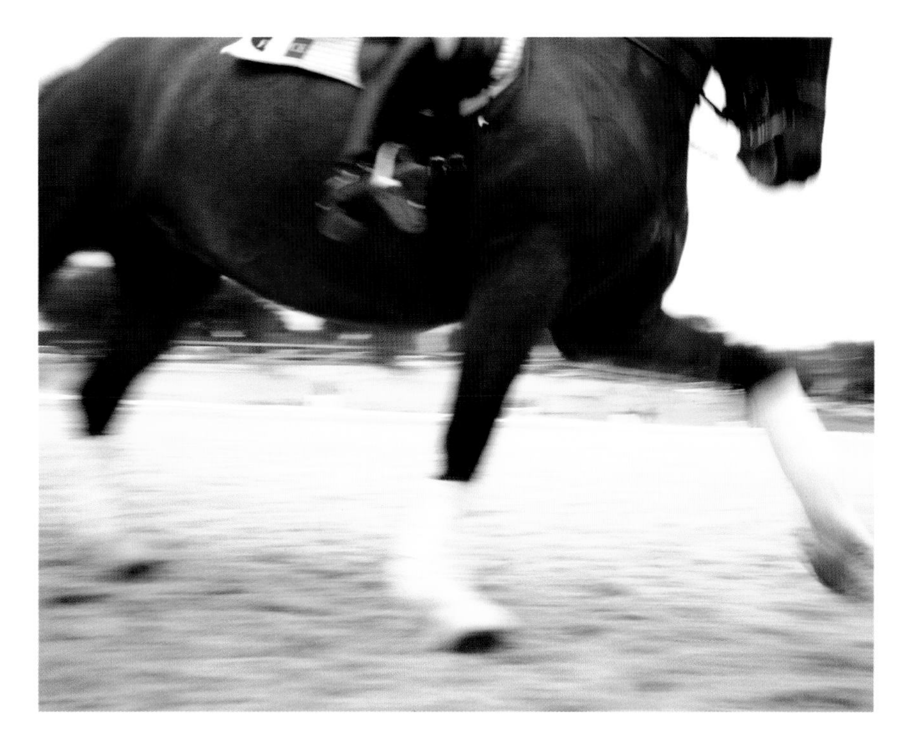

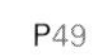

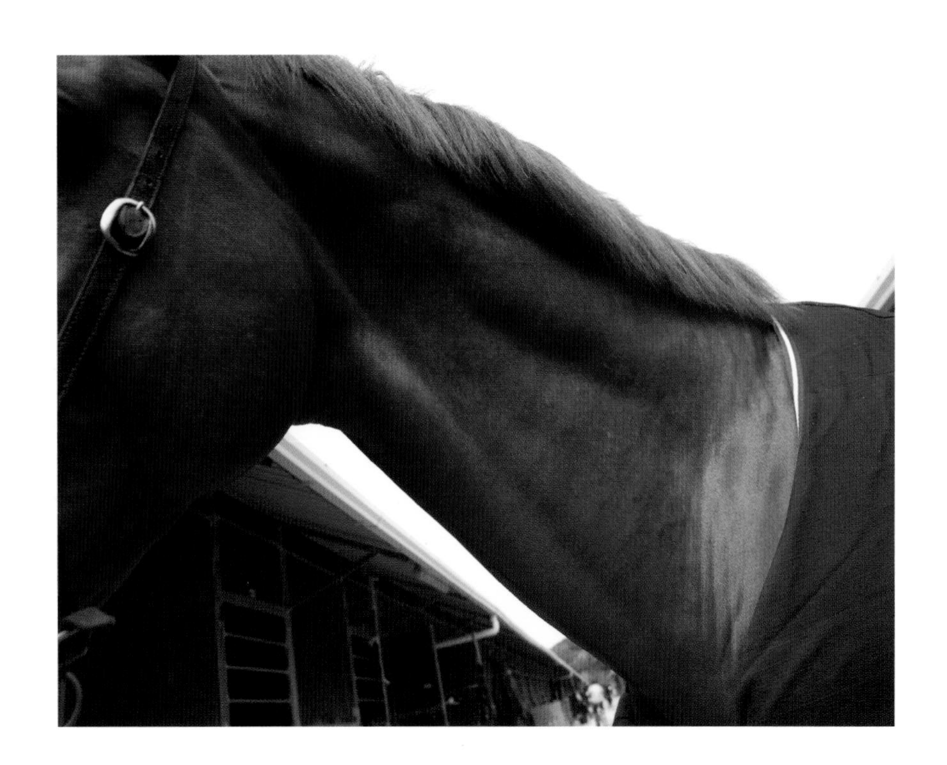

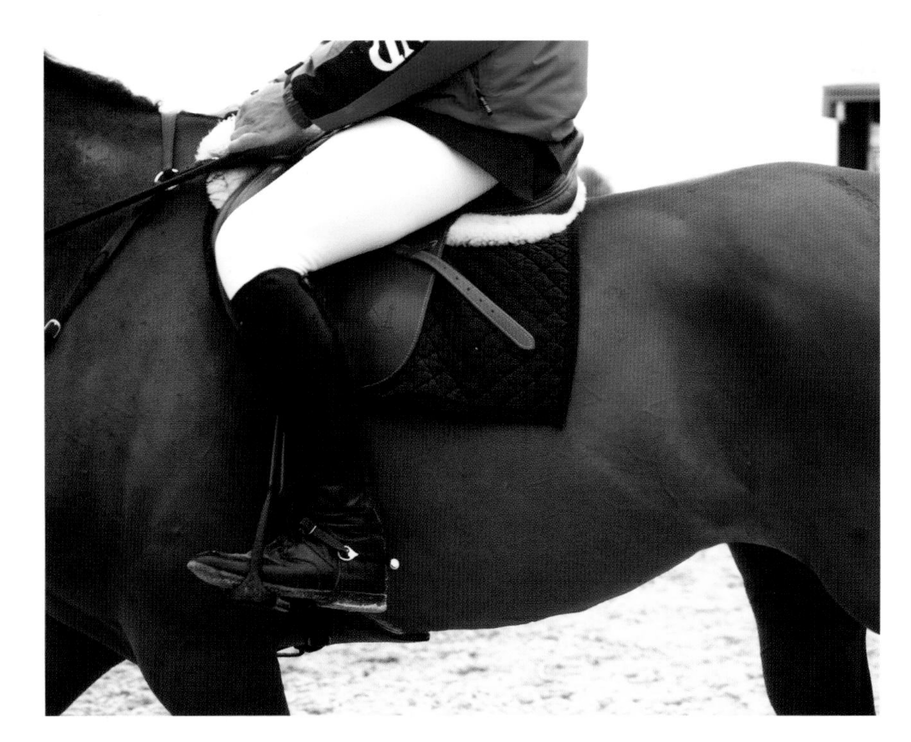

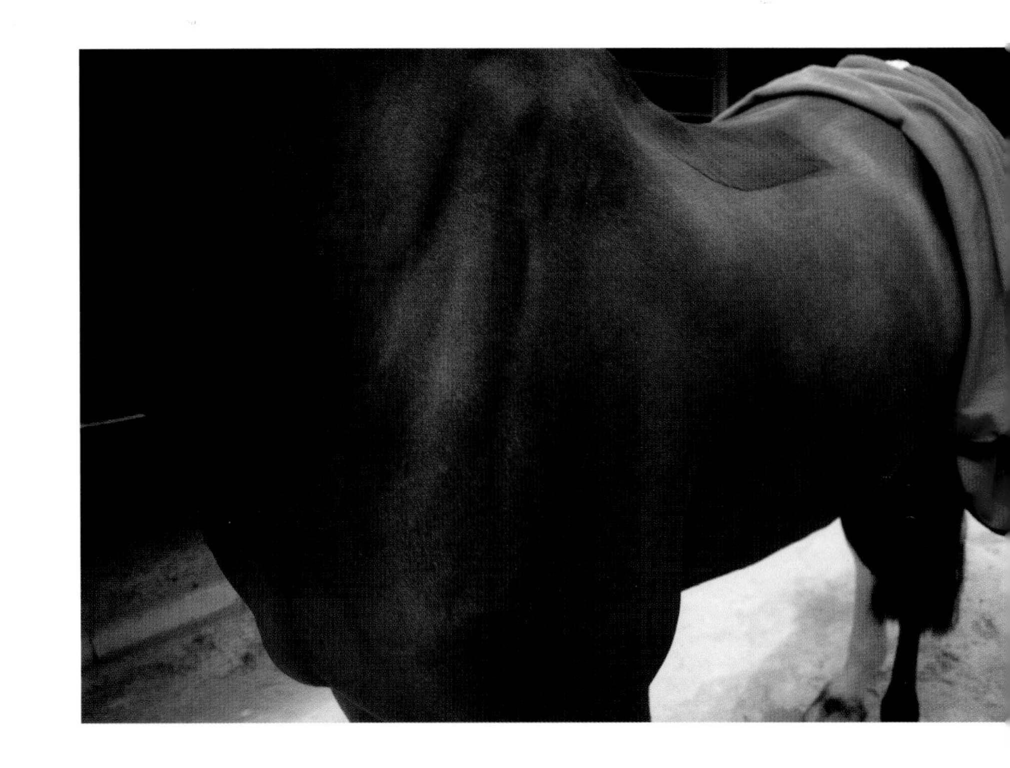

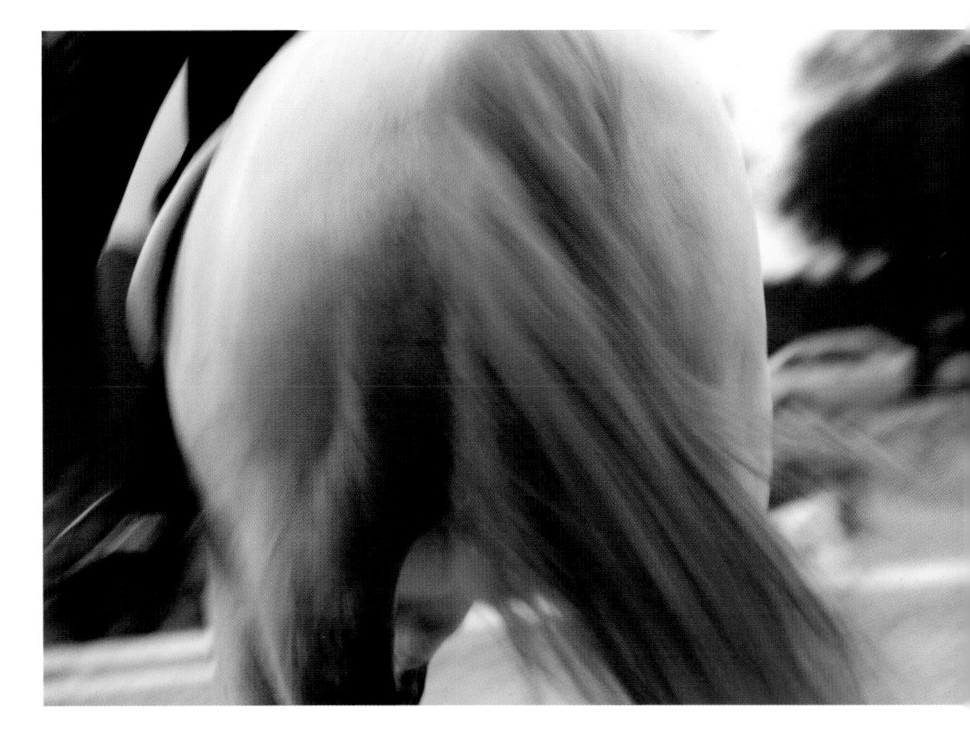

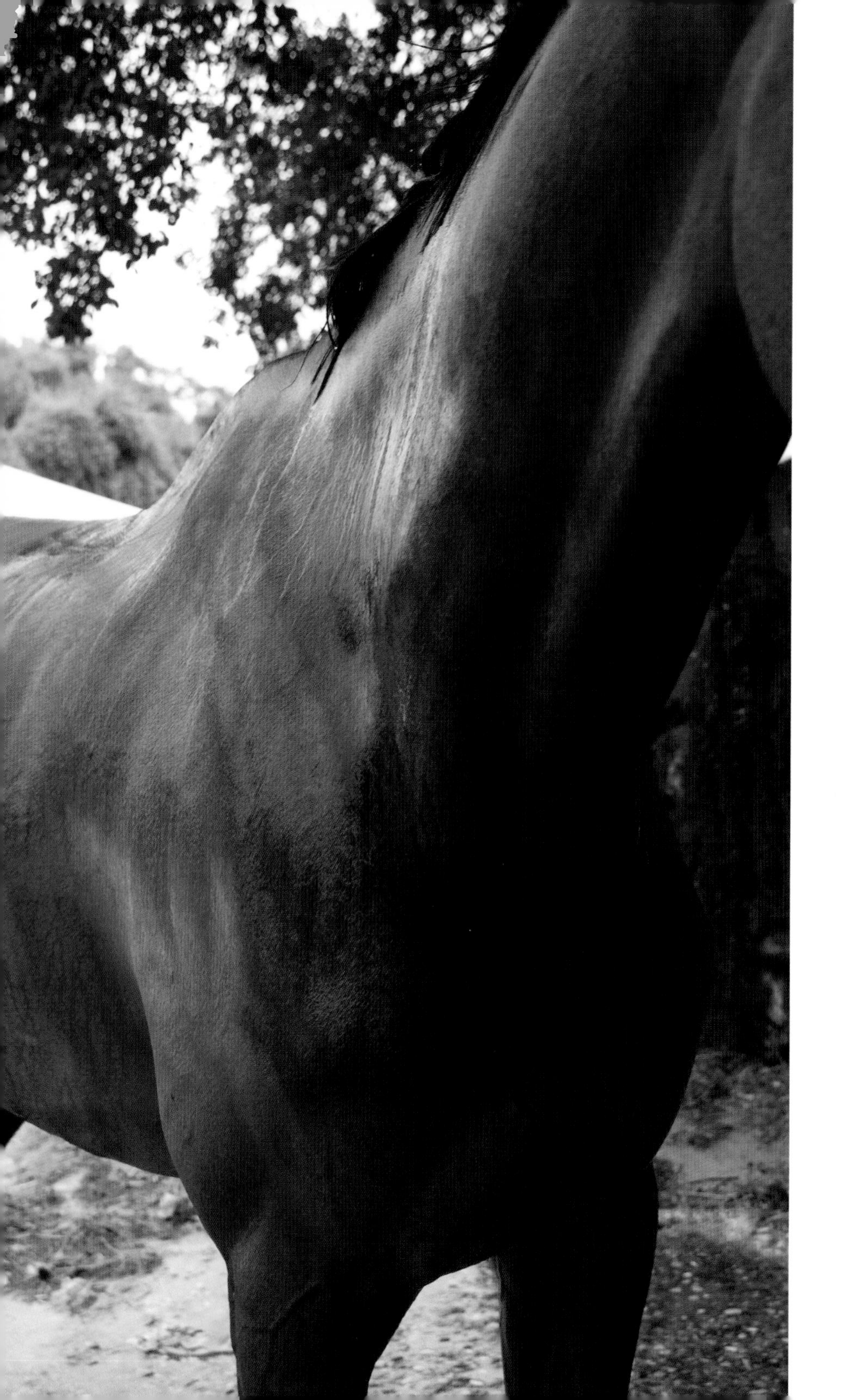

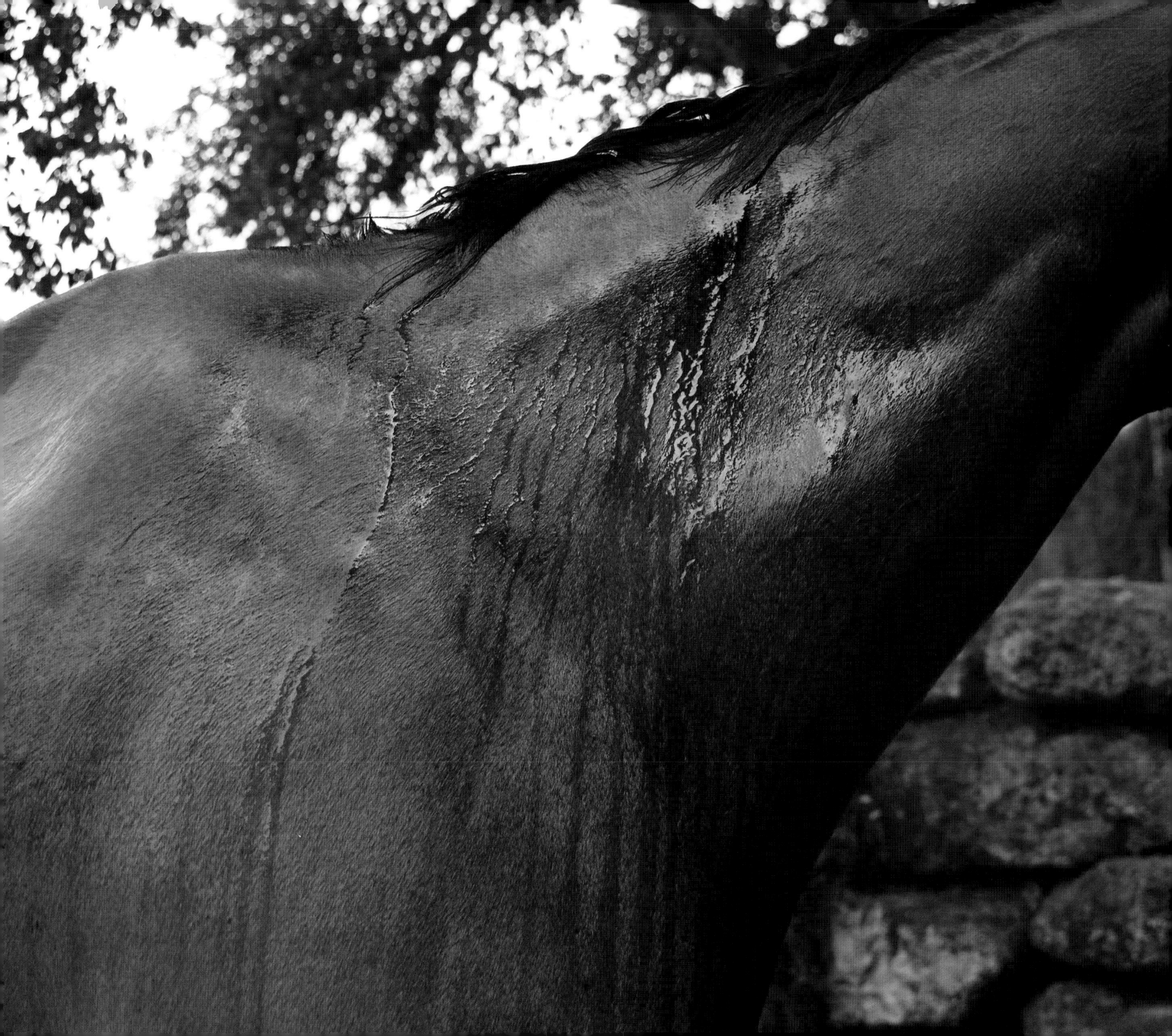

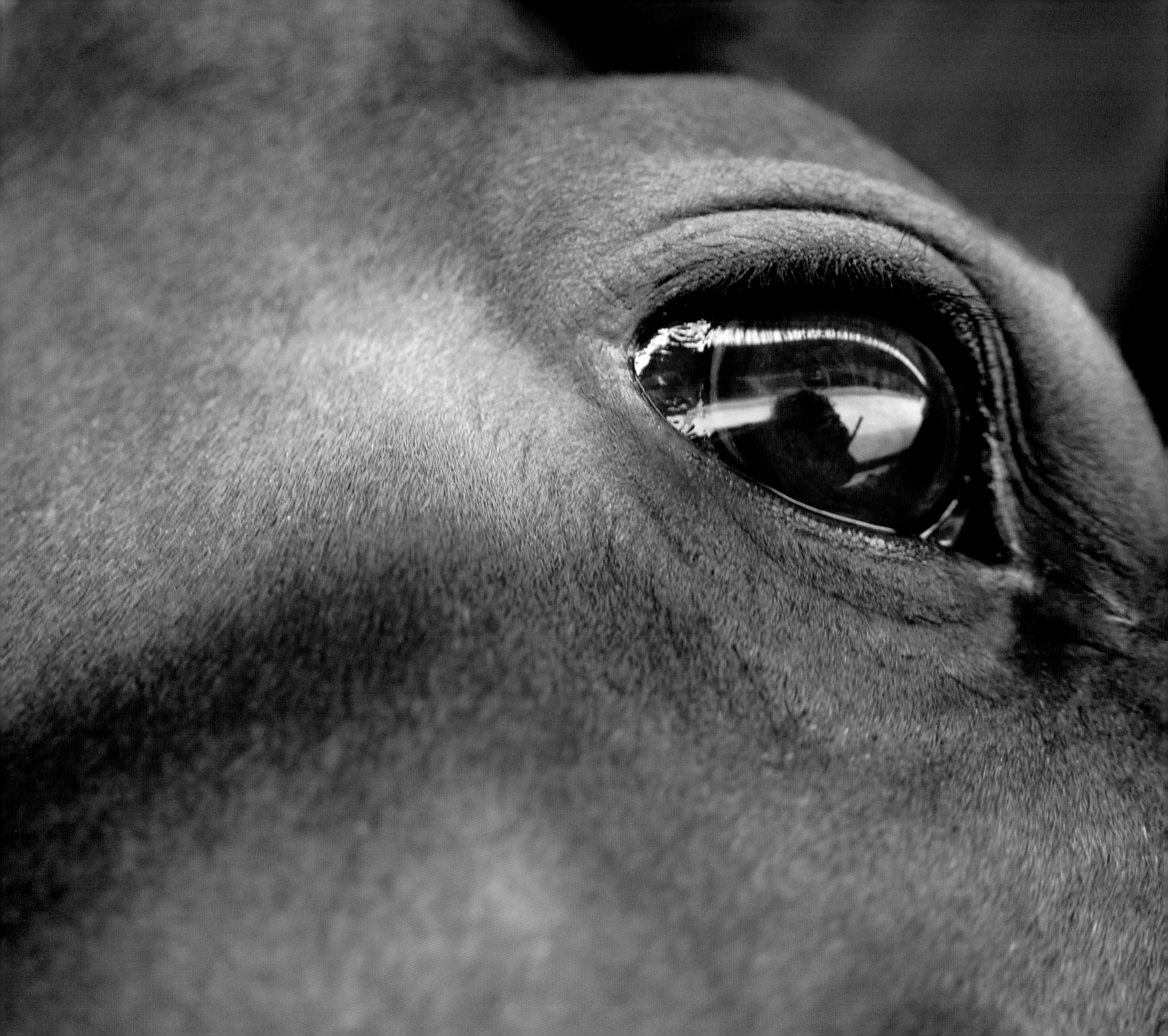

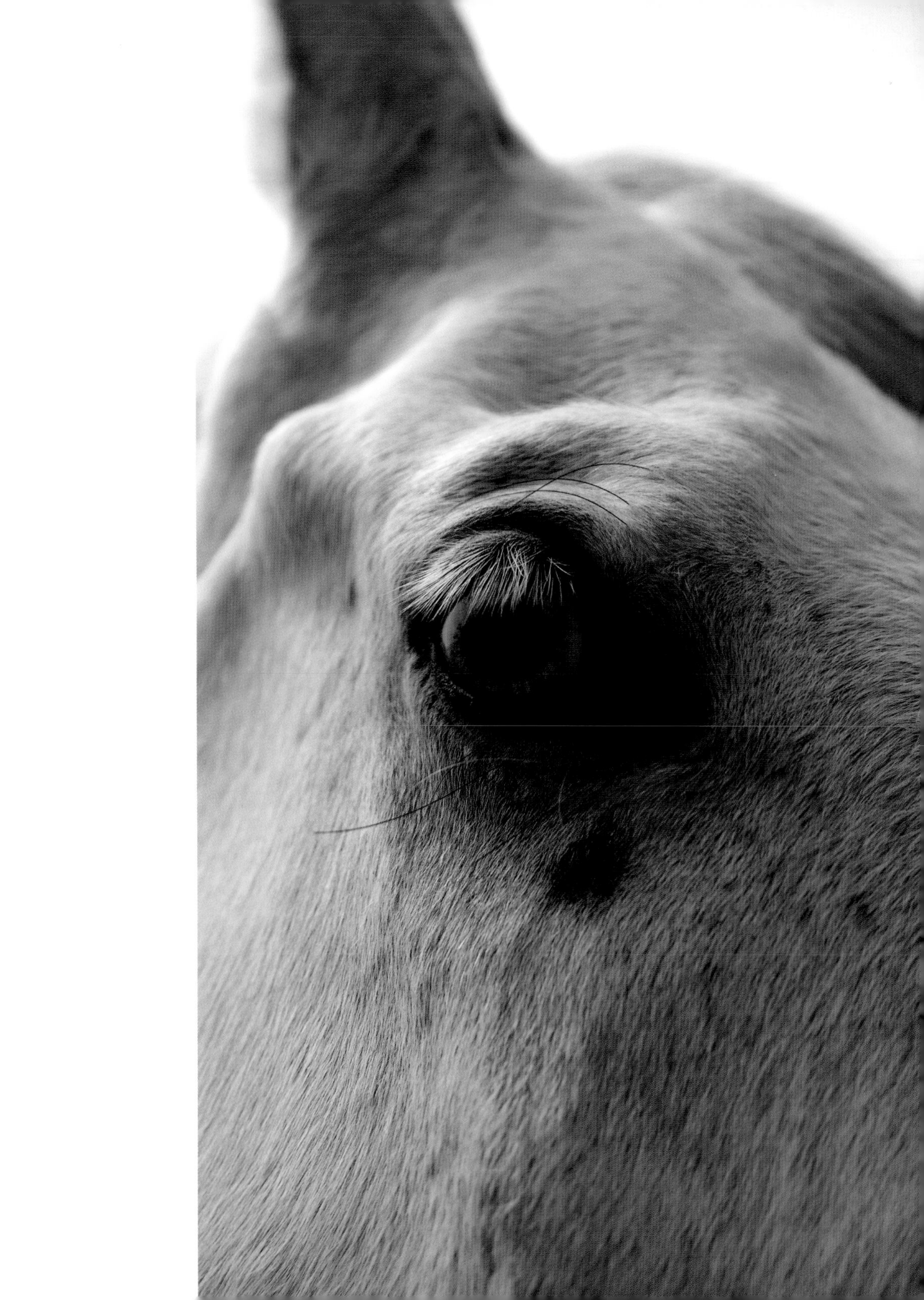

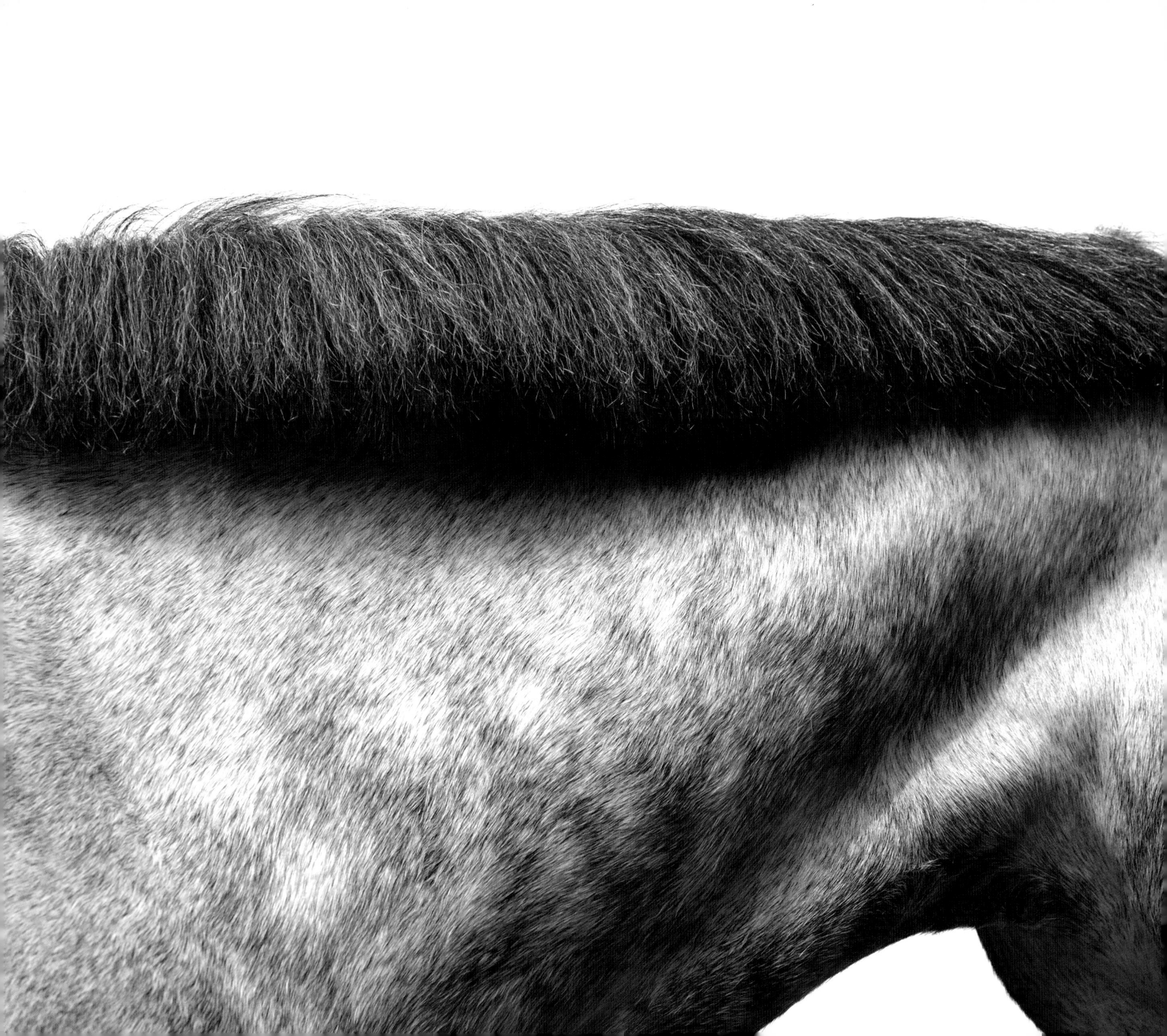

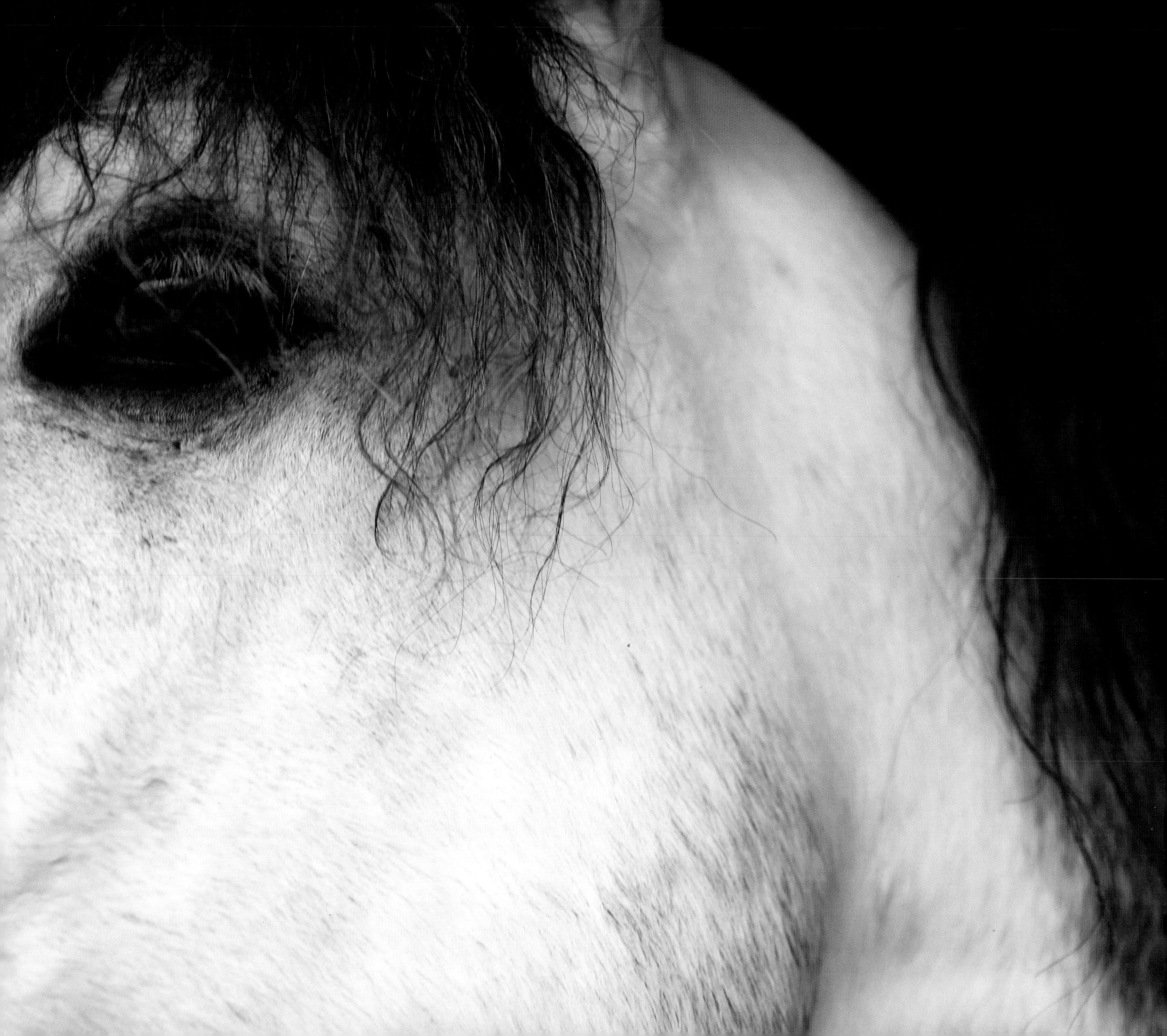

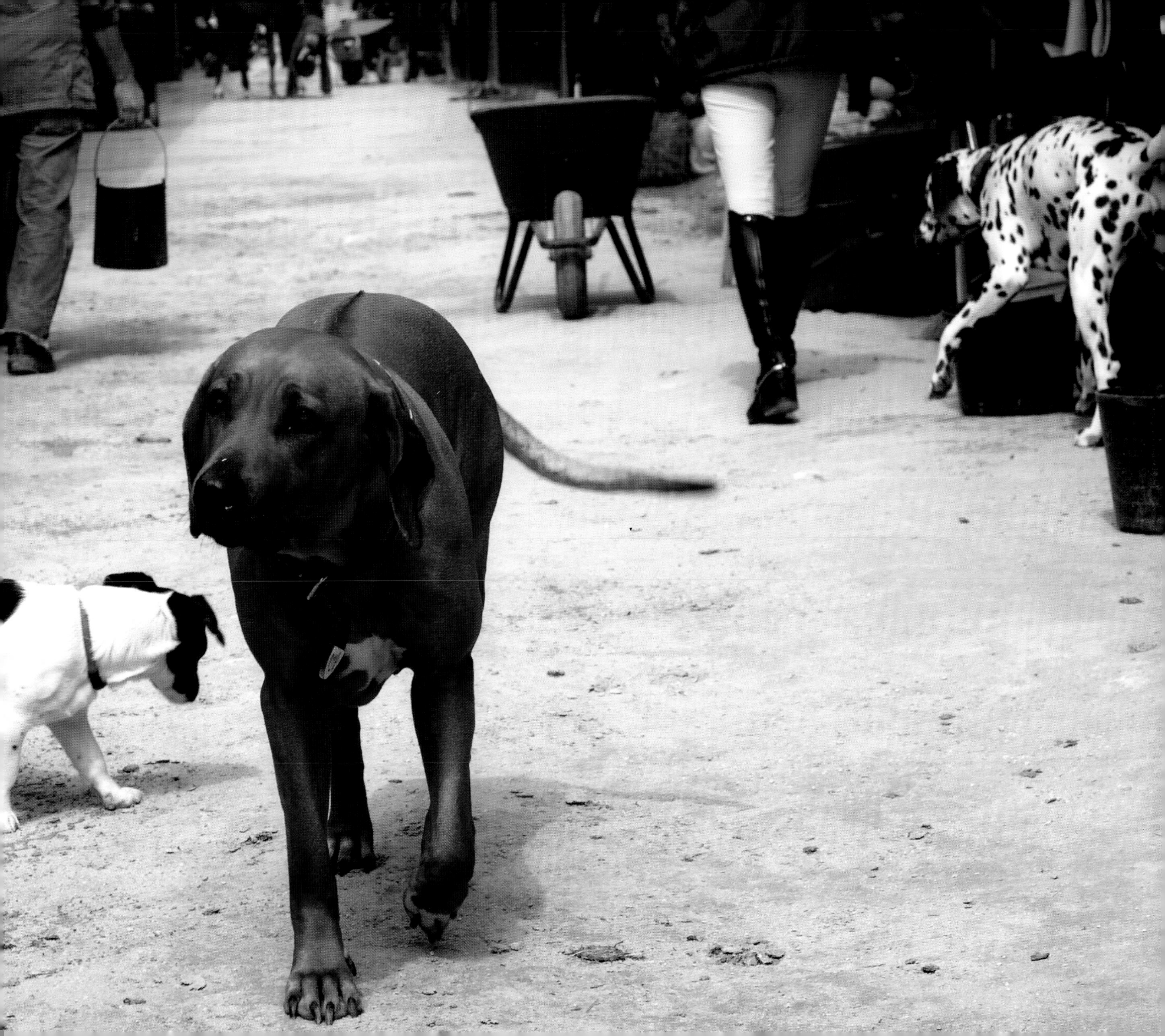

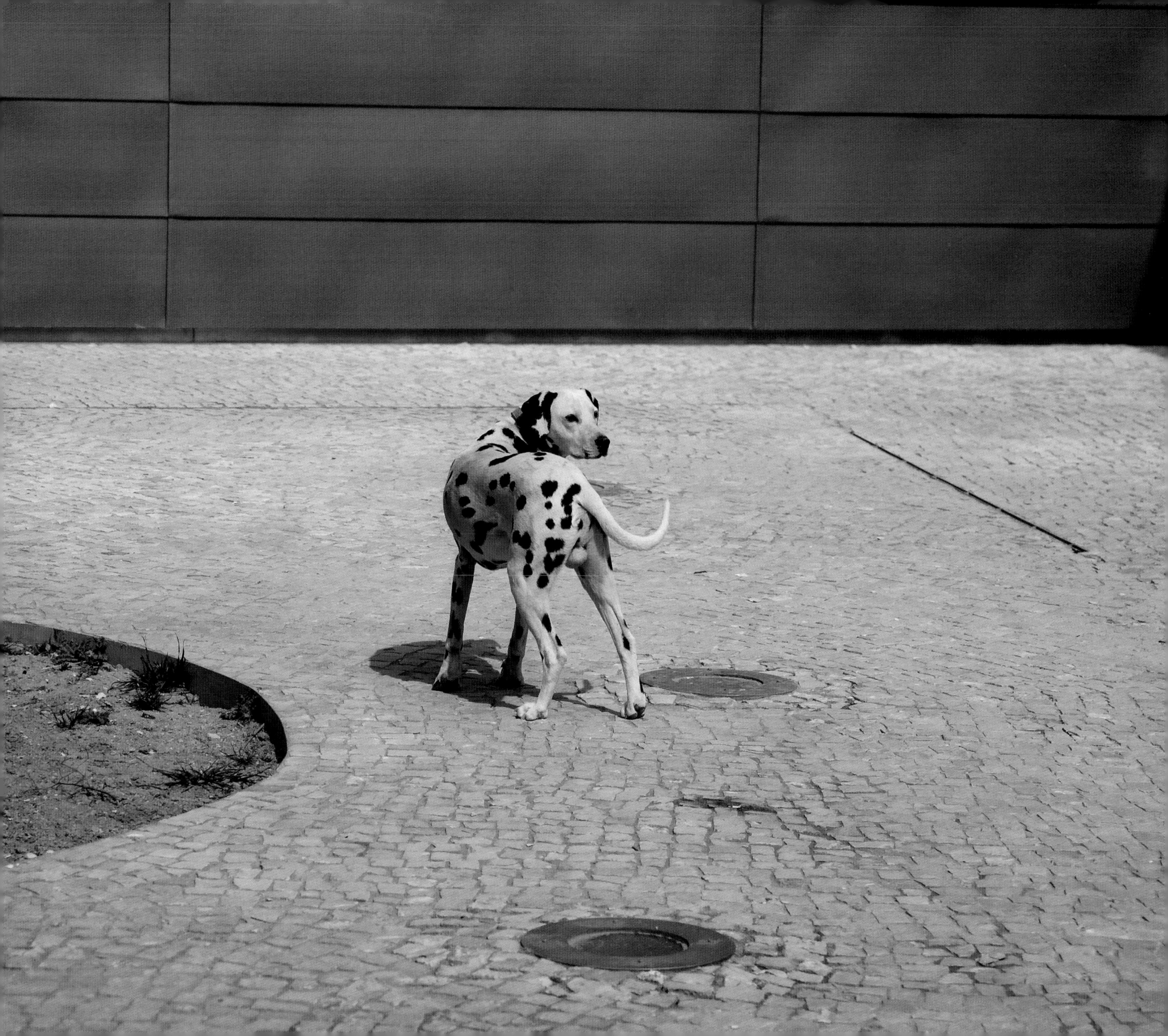

P62

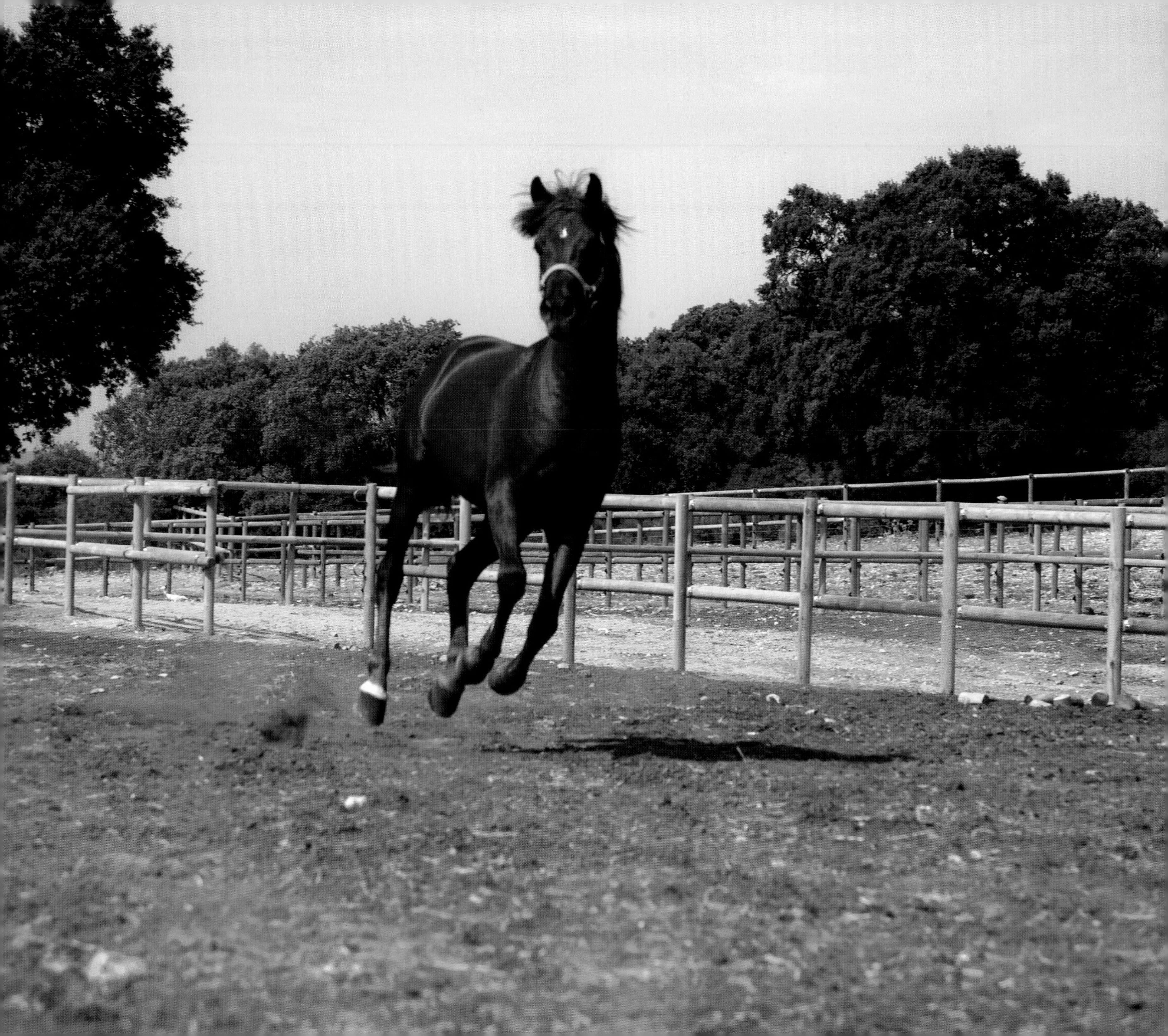

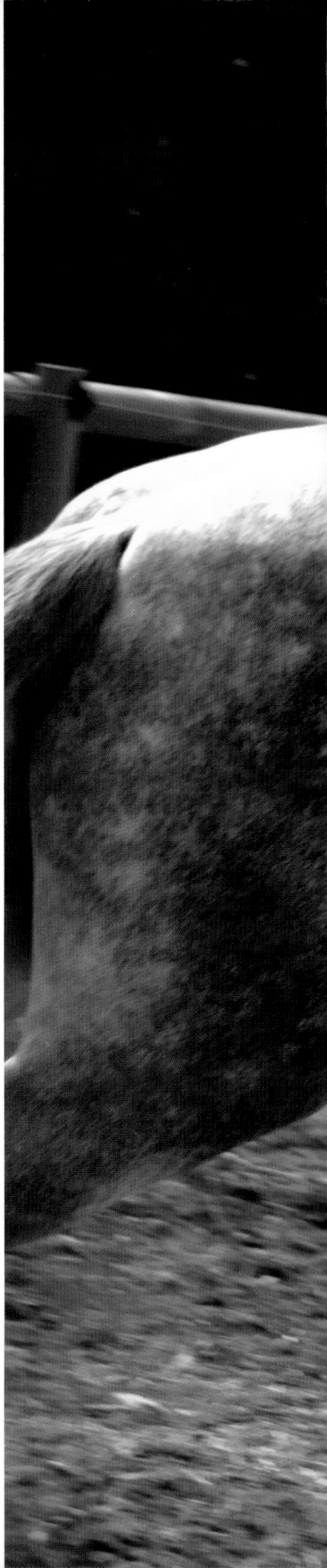

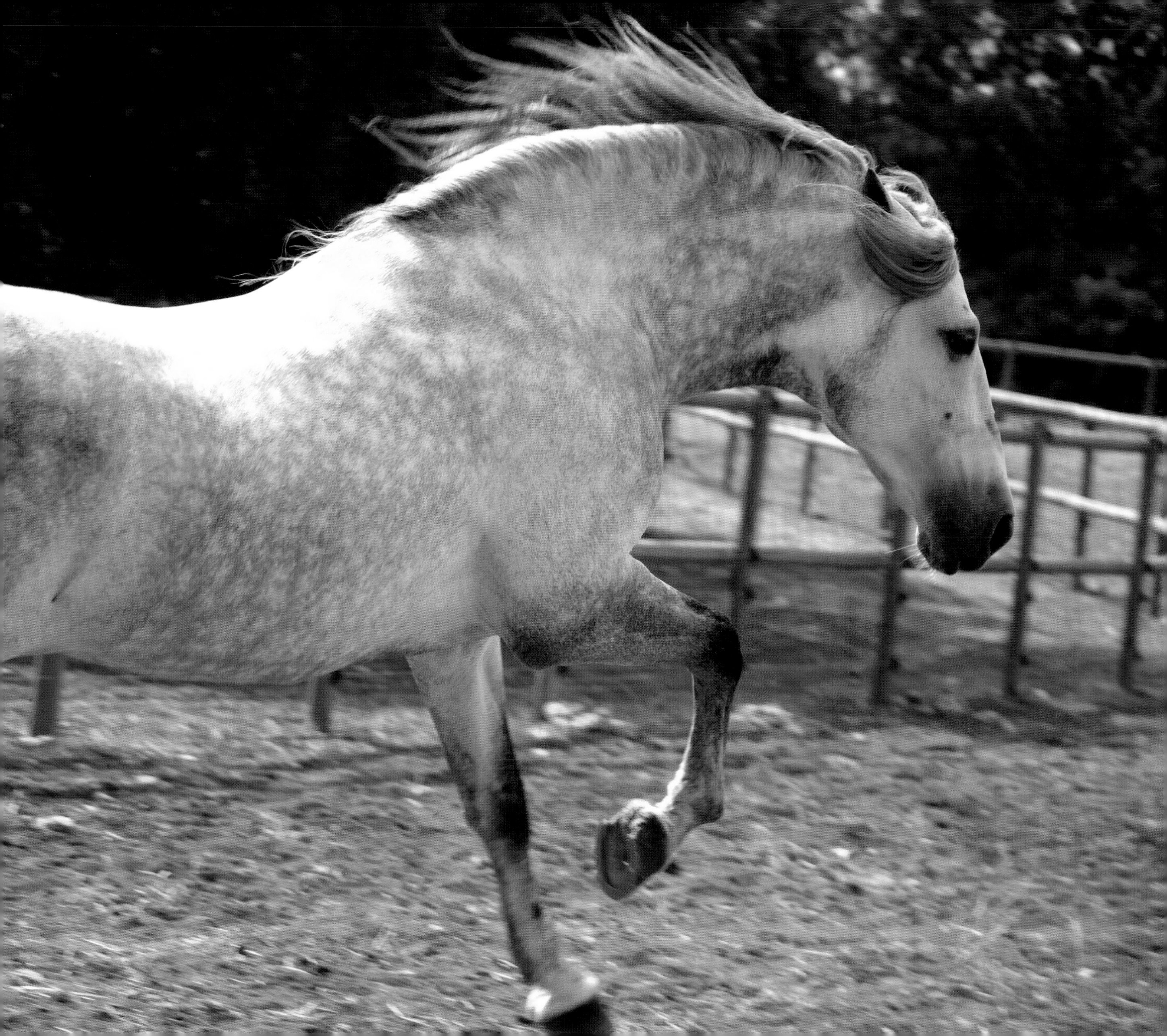

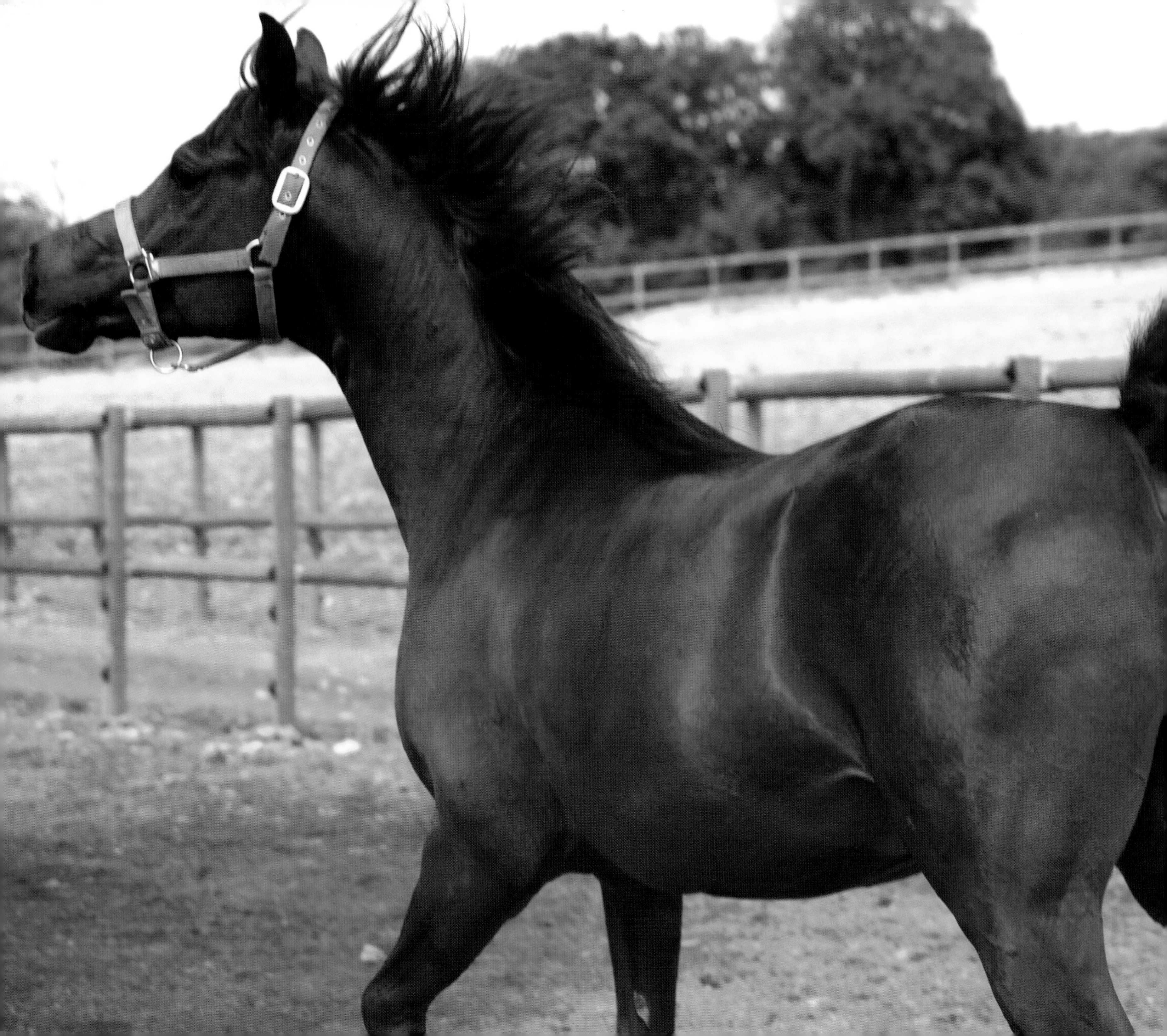

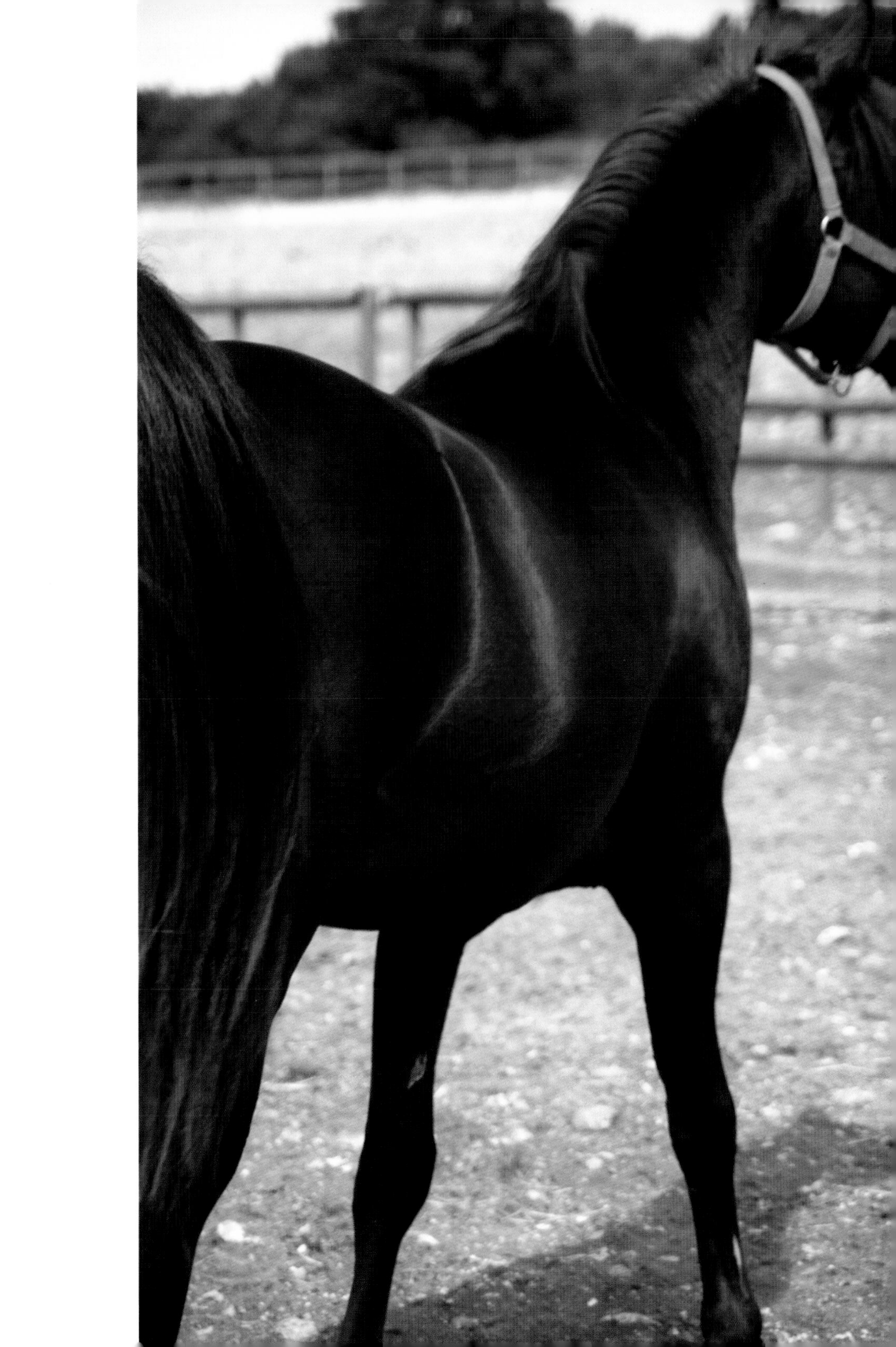

P68

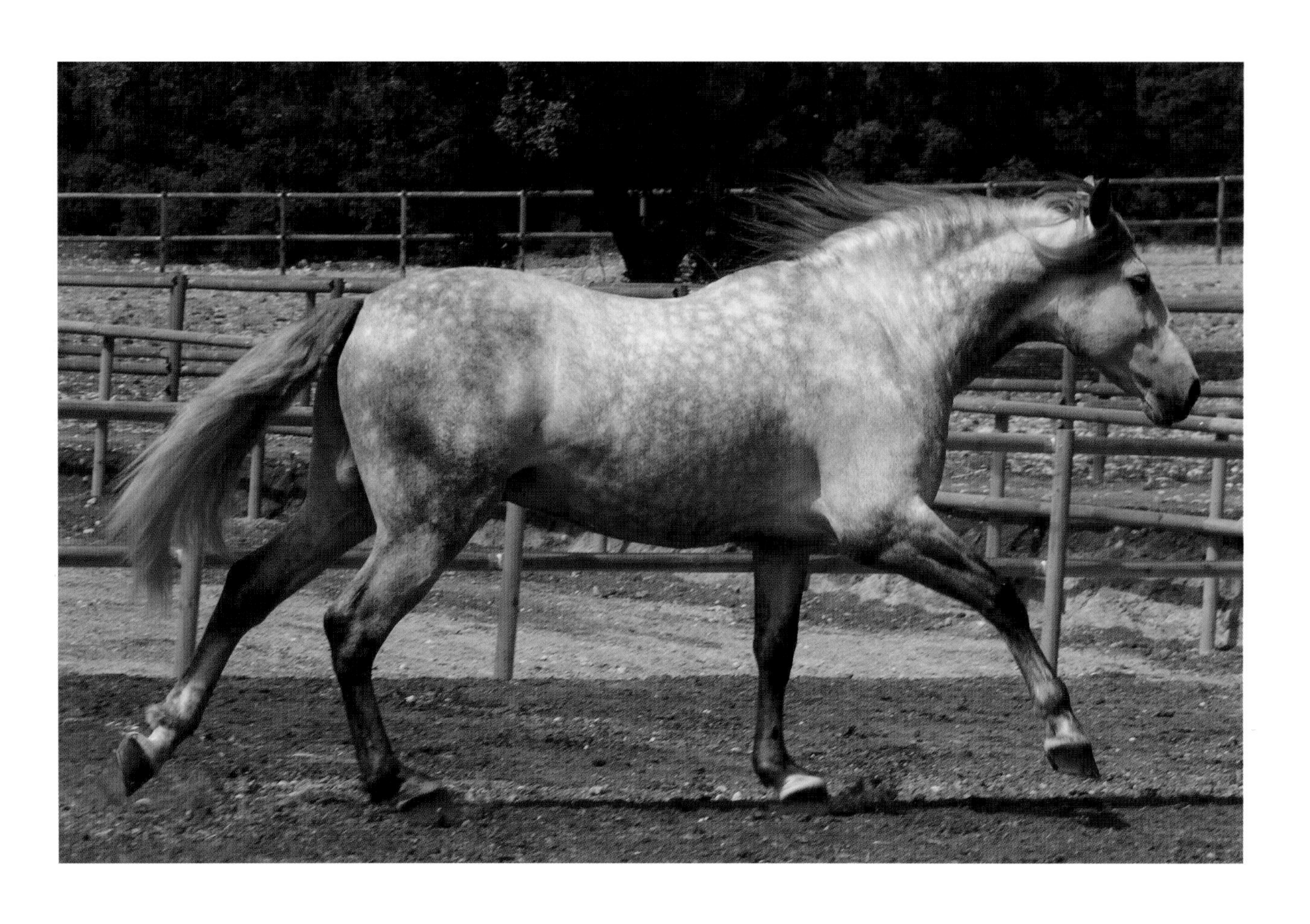

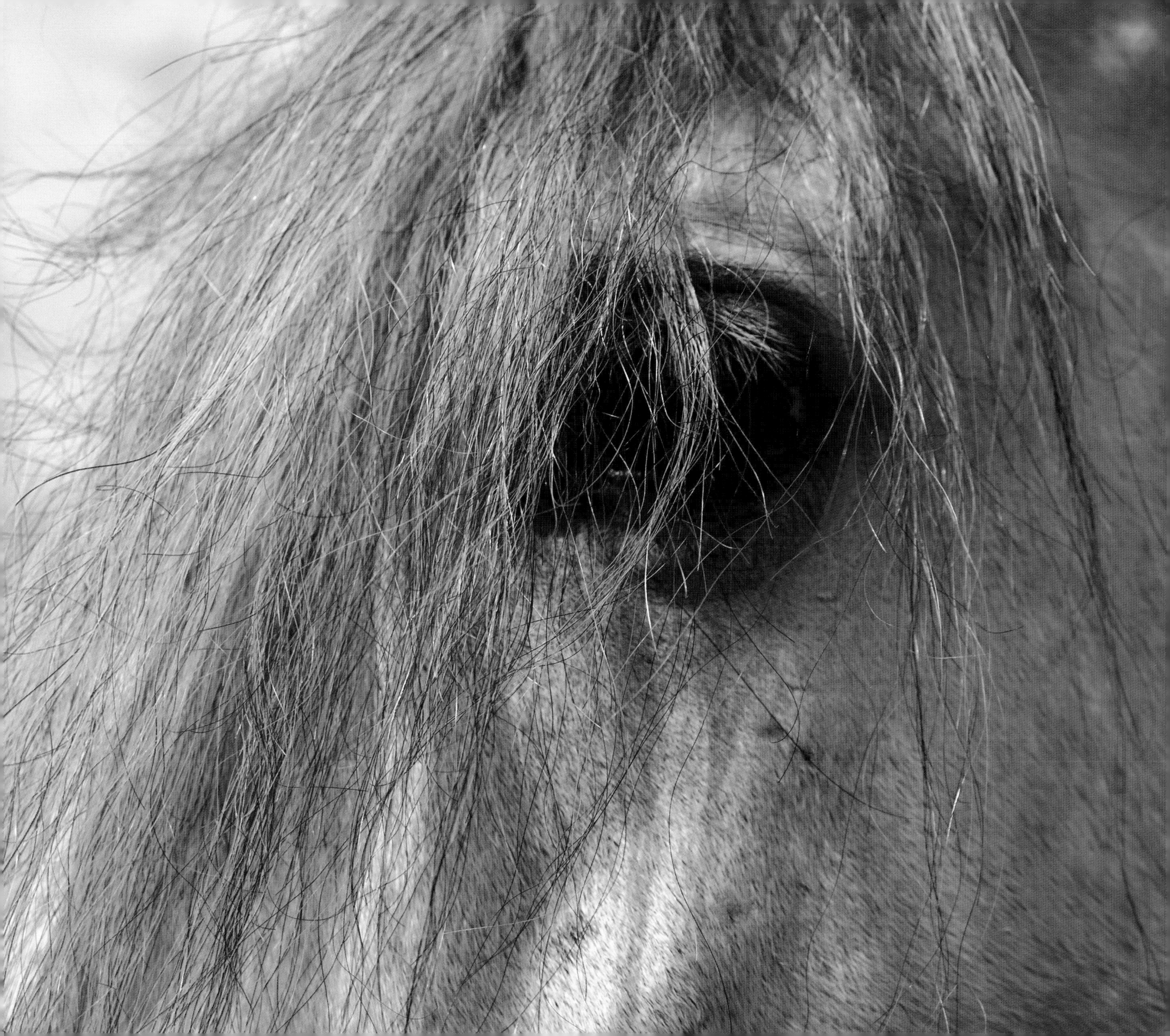

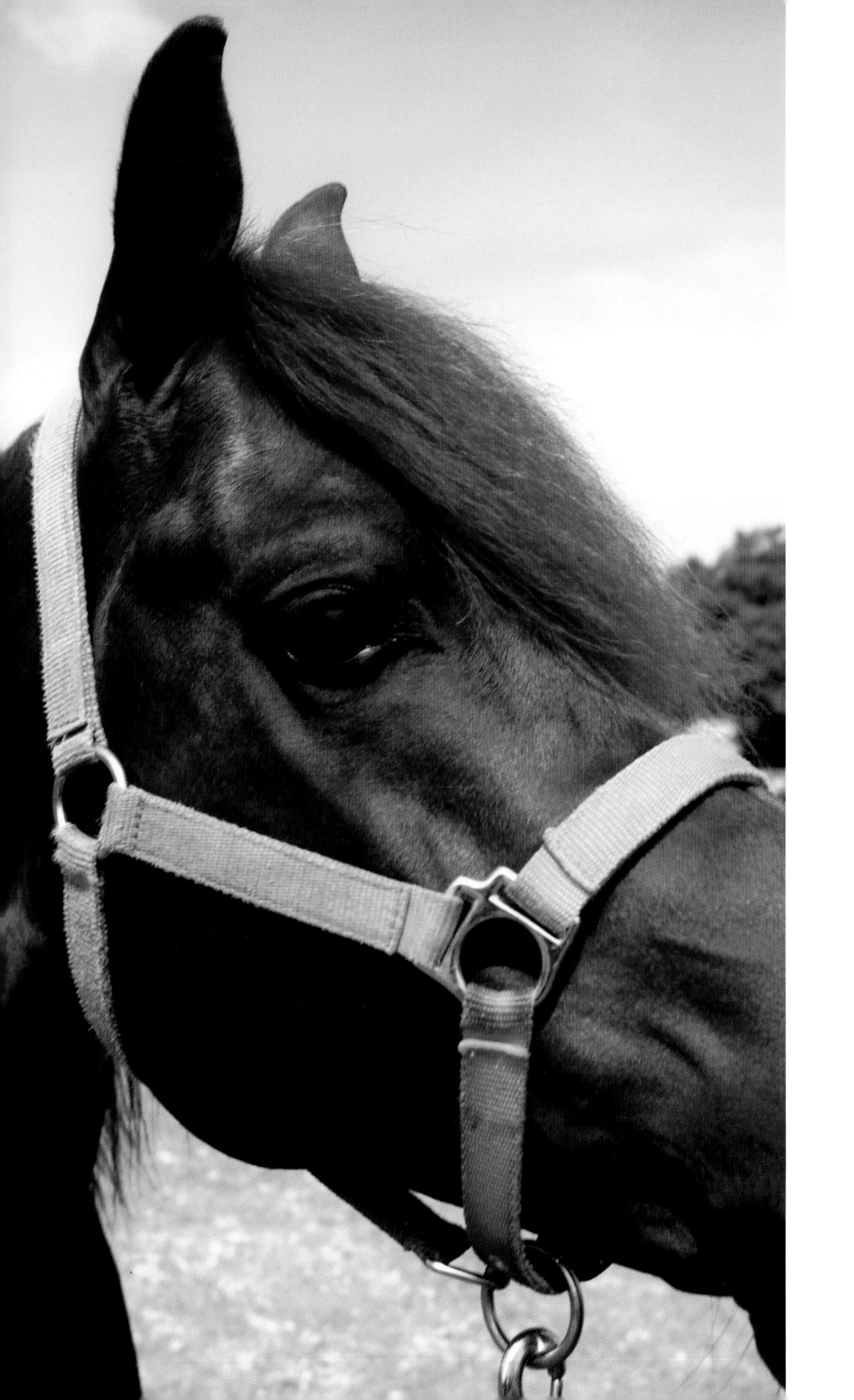

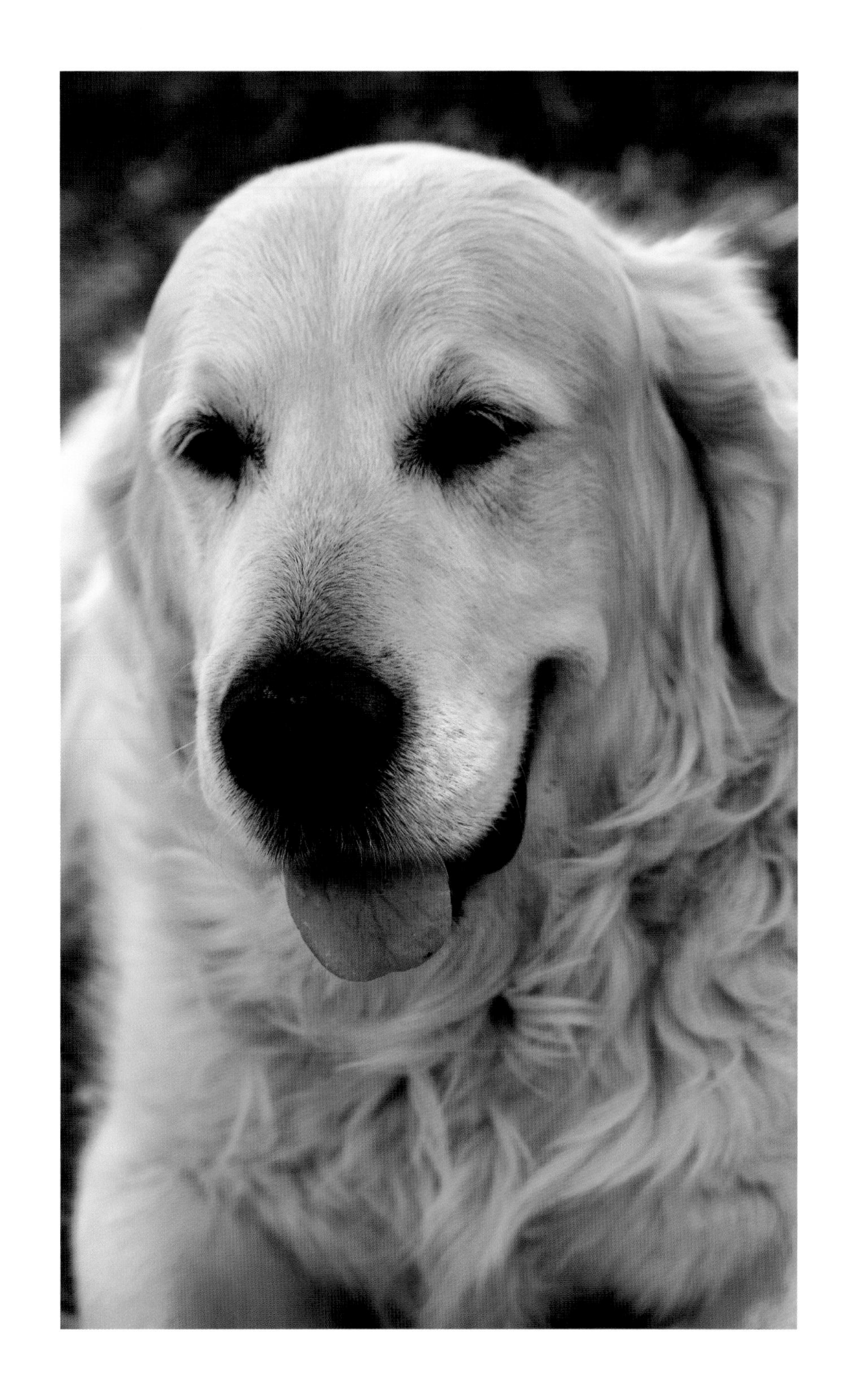

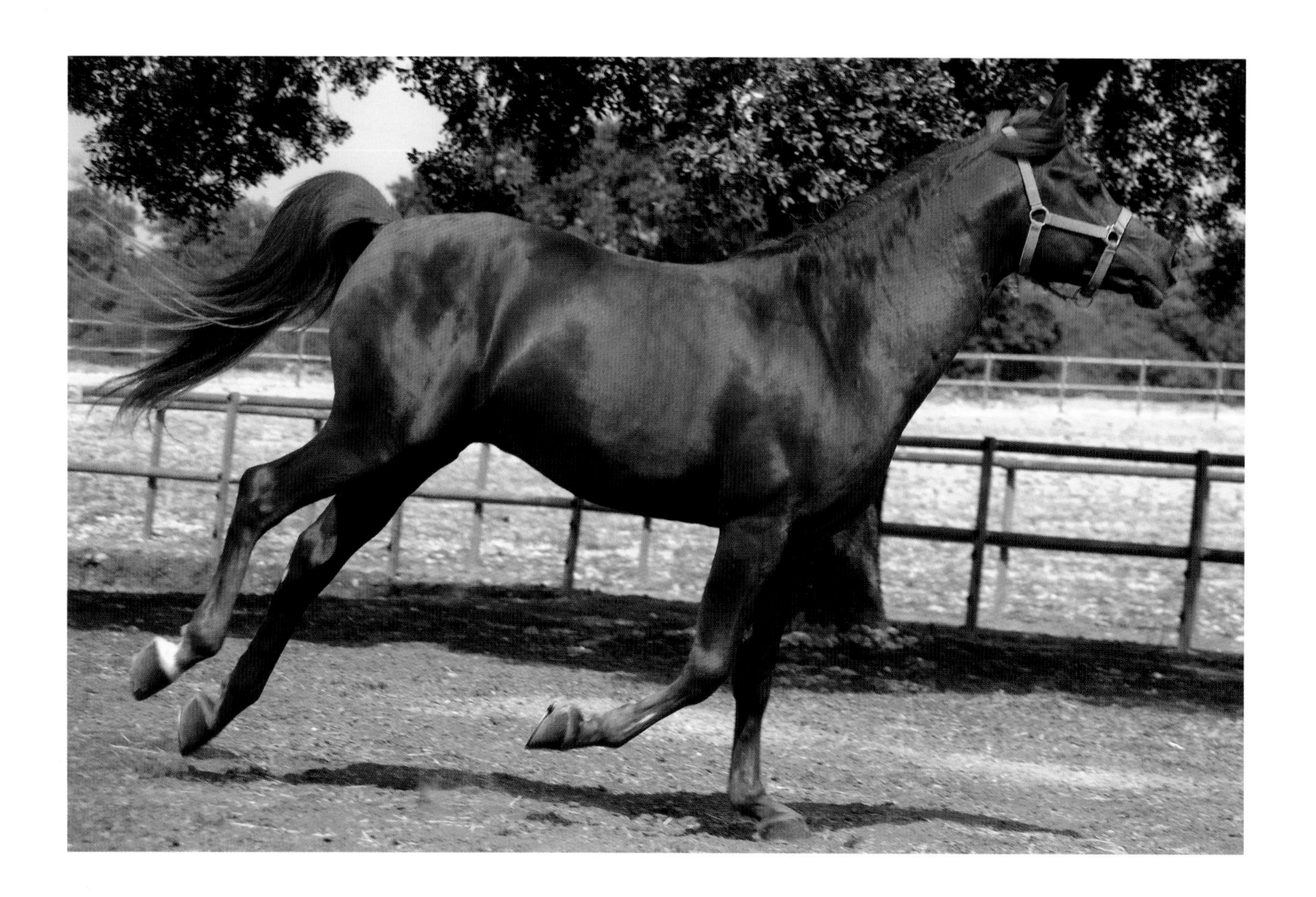

P72

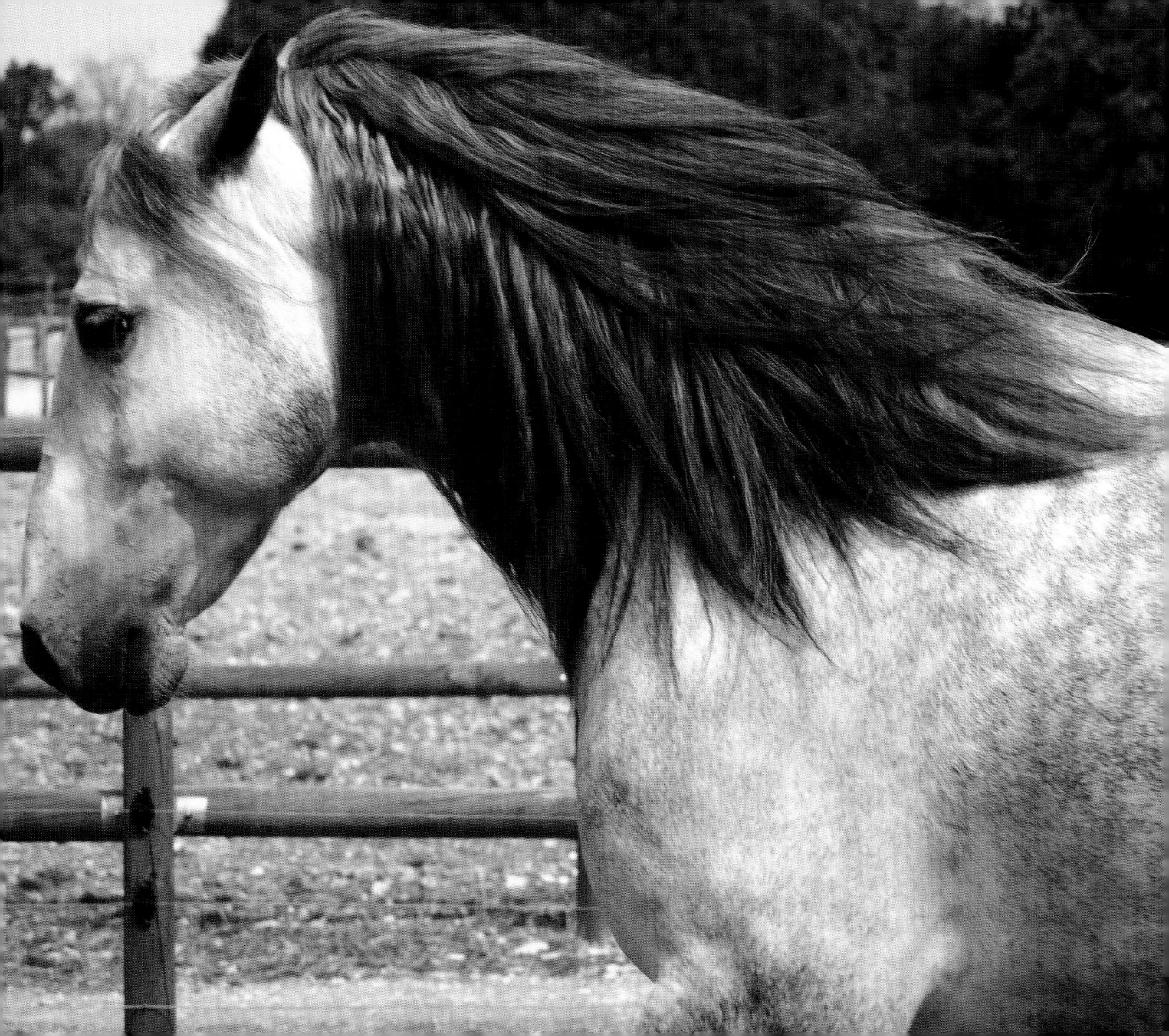

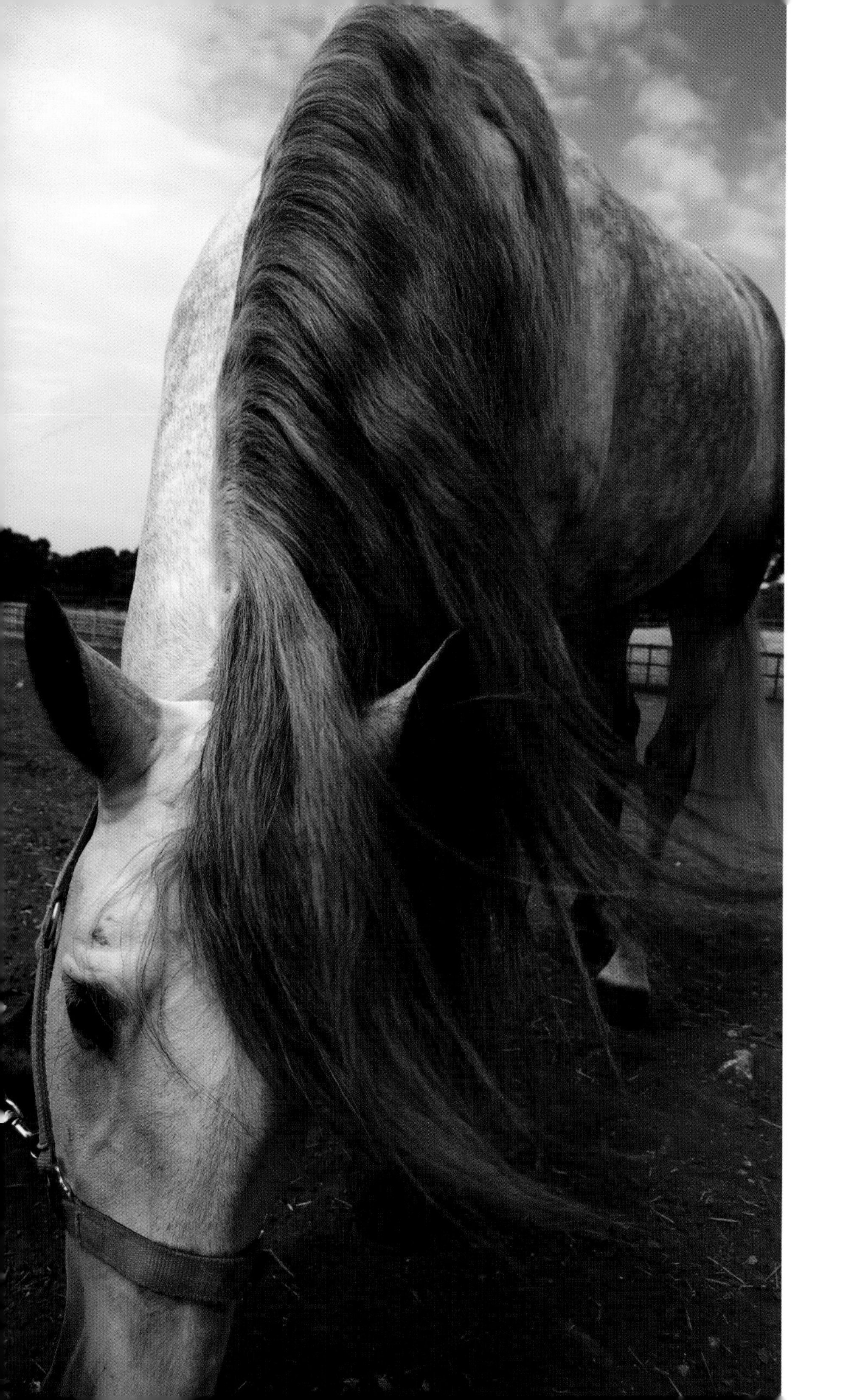

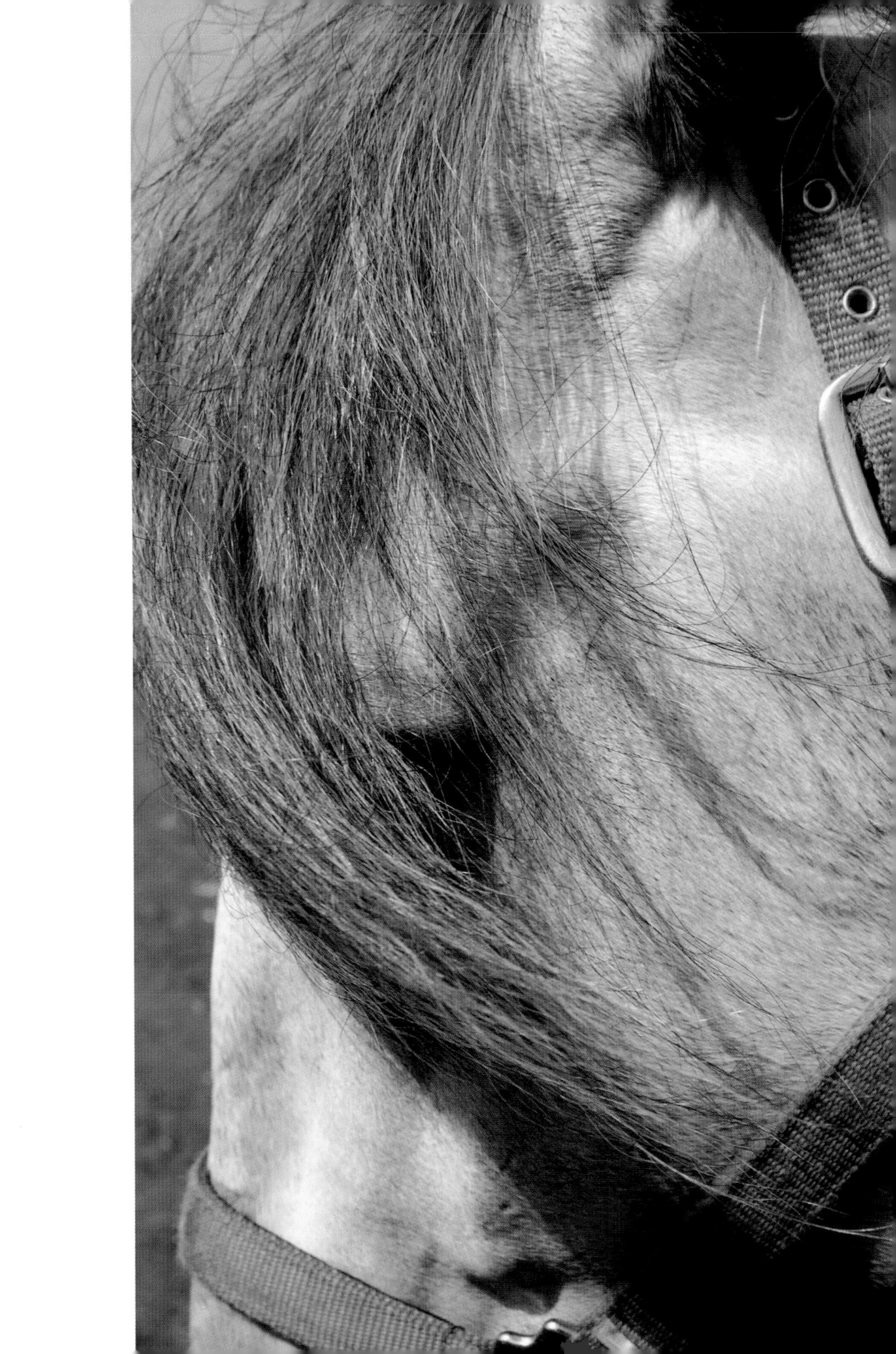

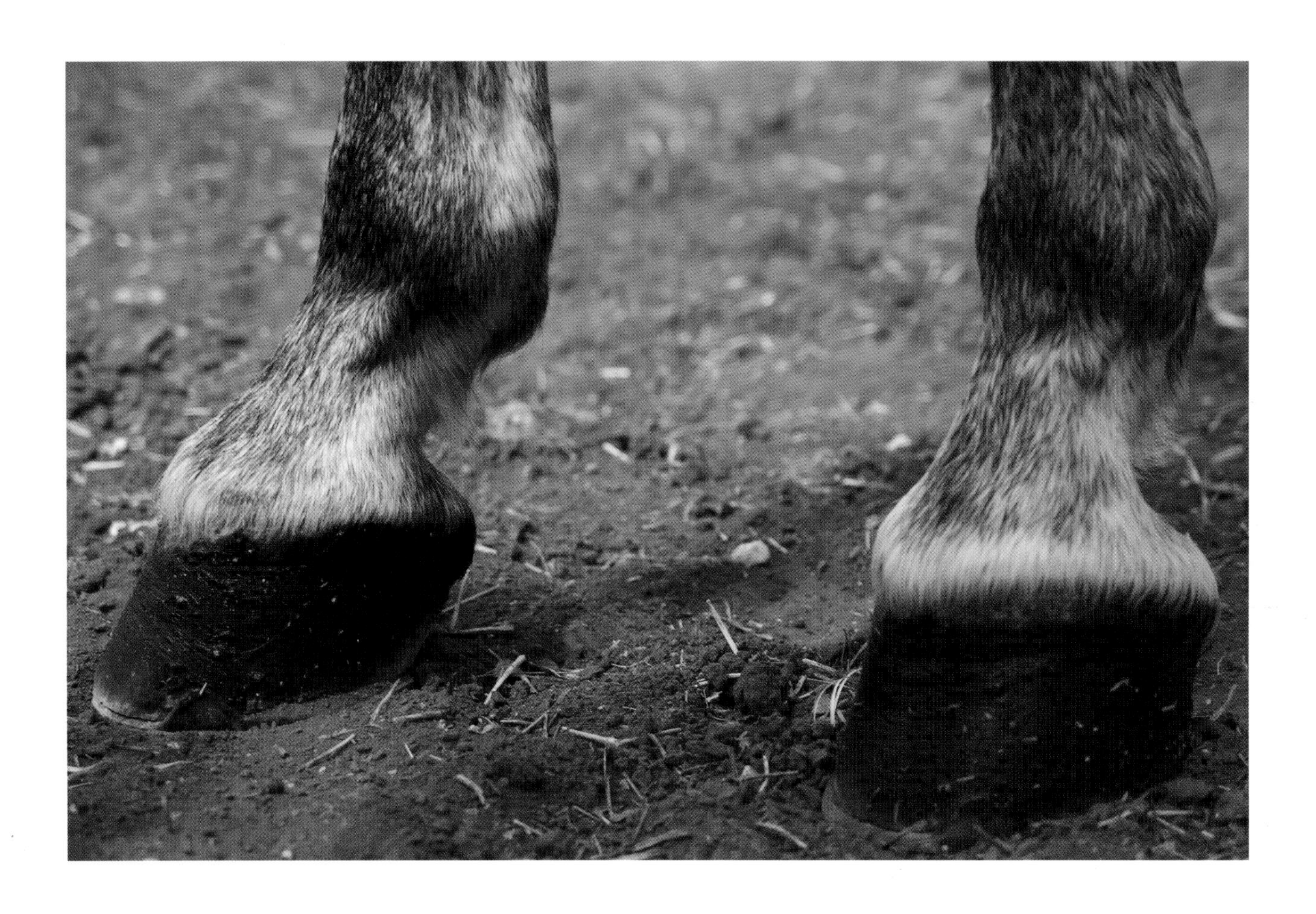

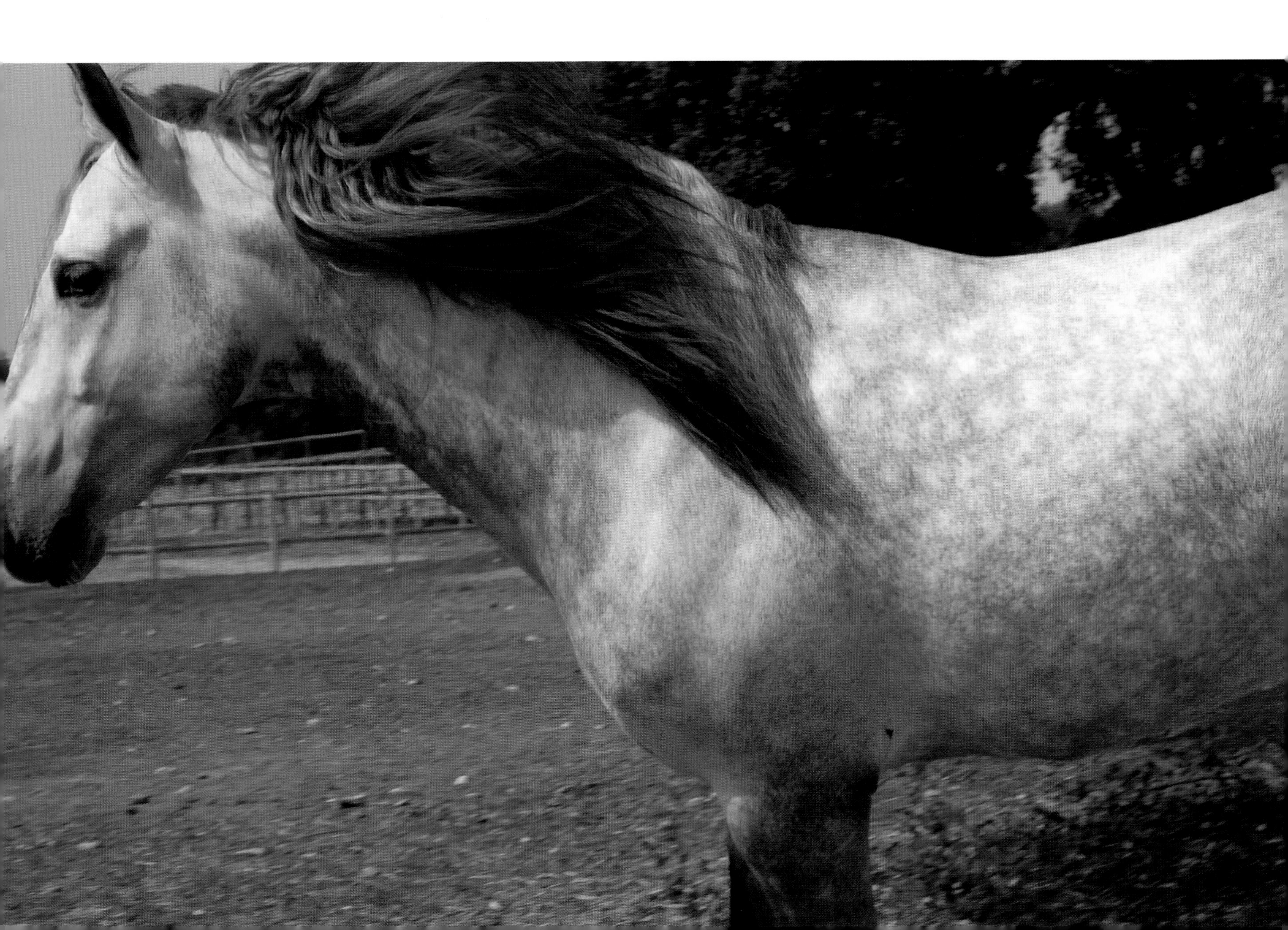

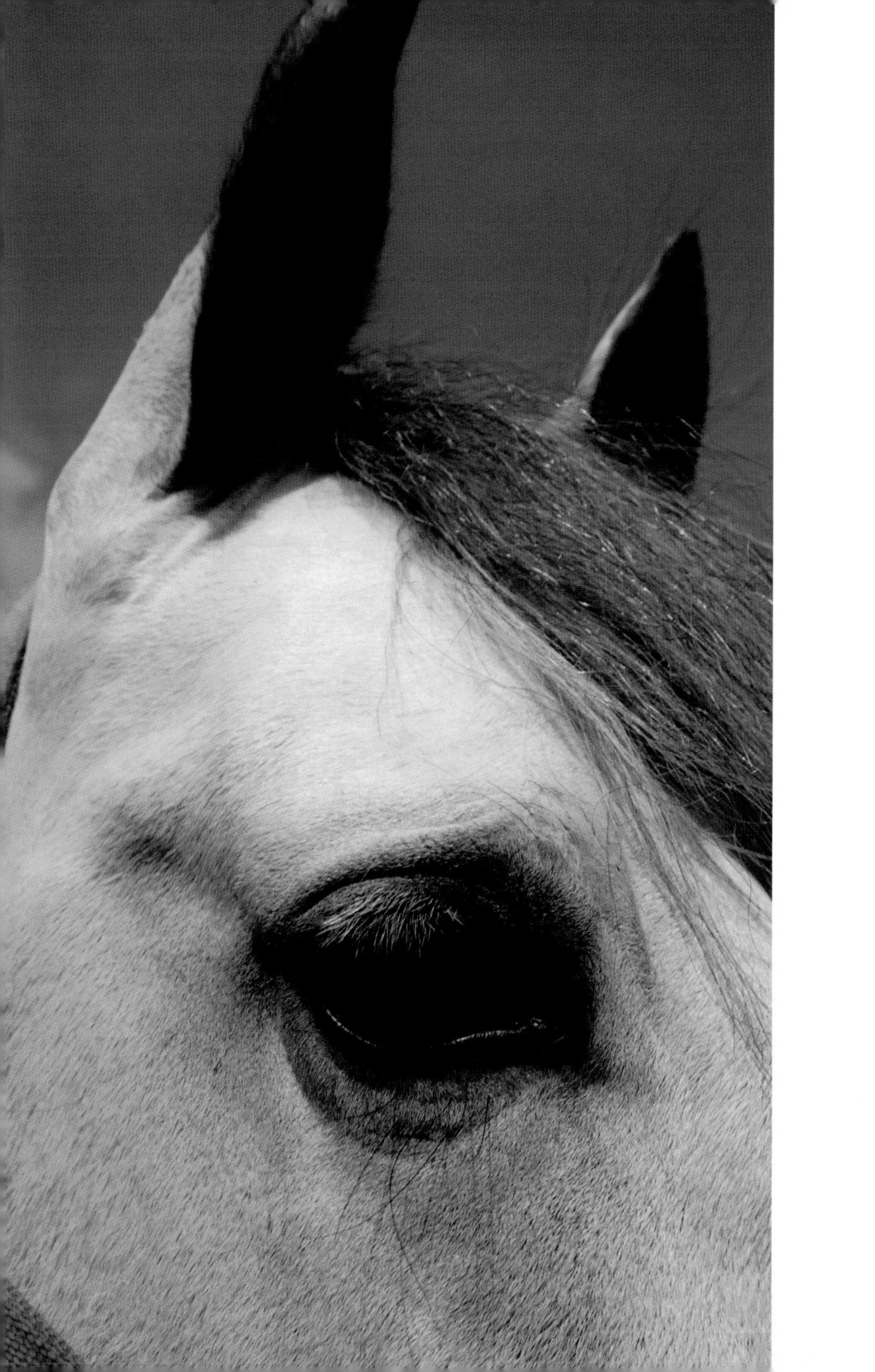

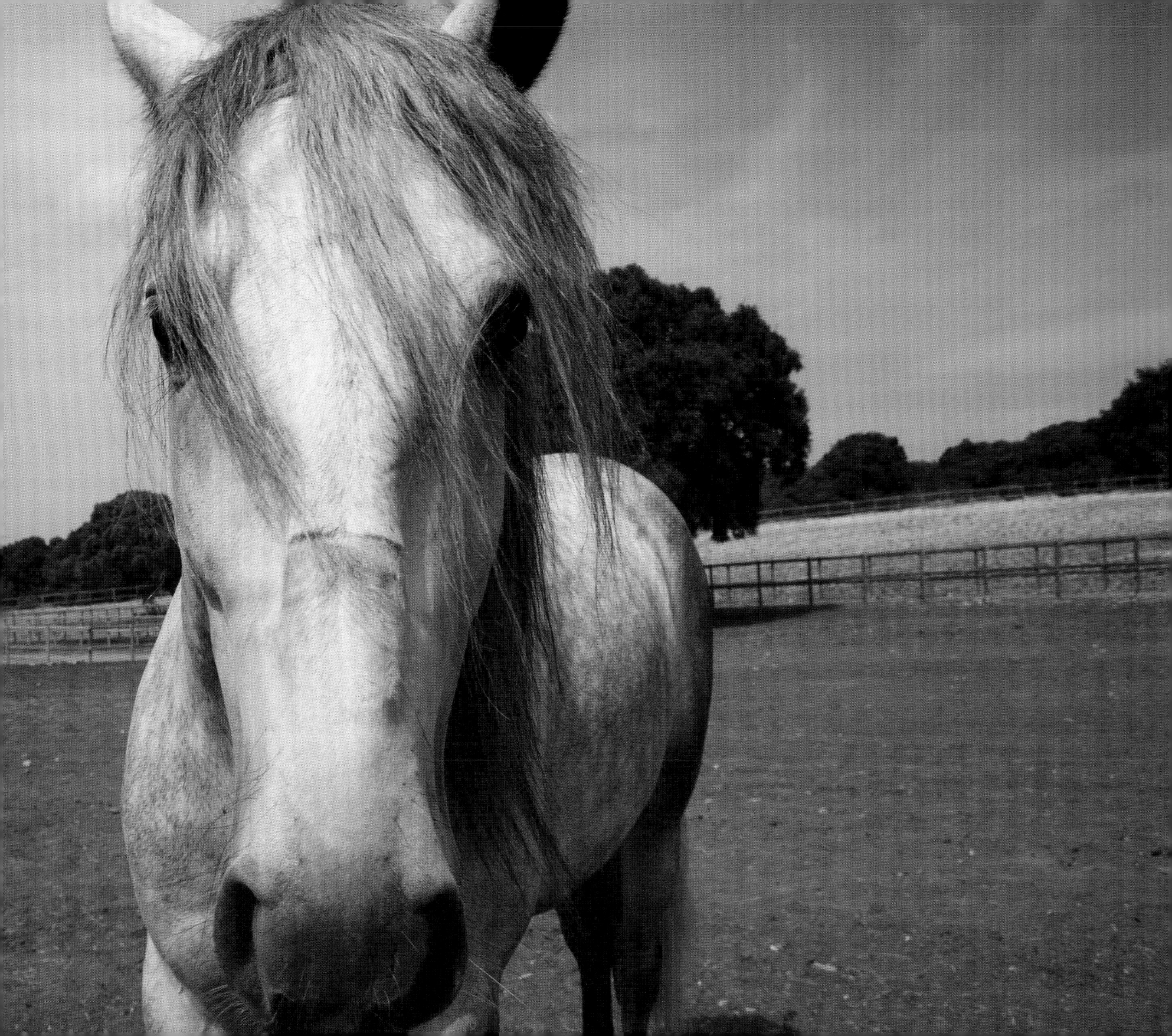

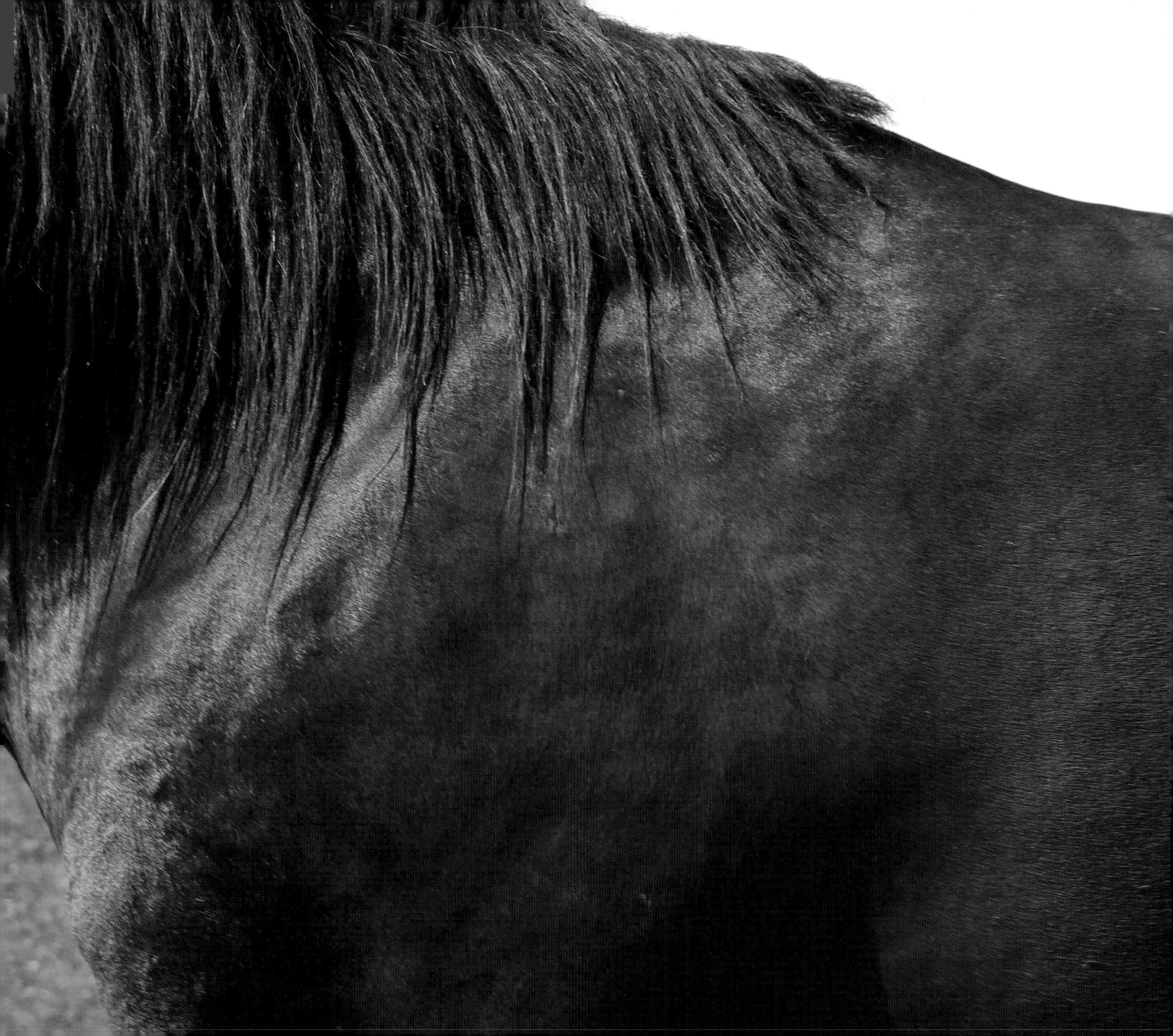

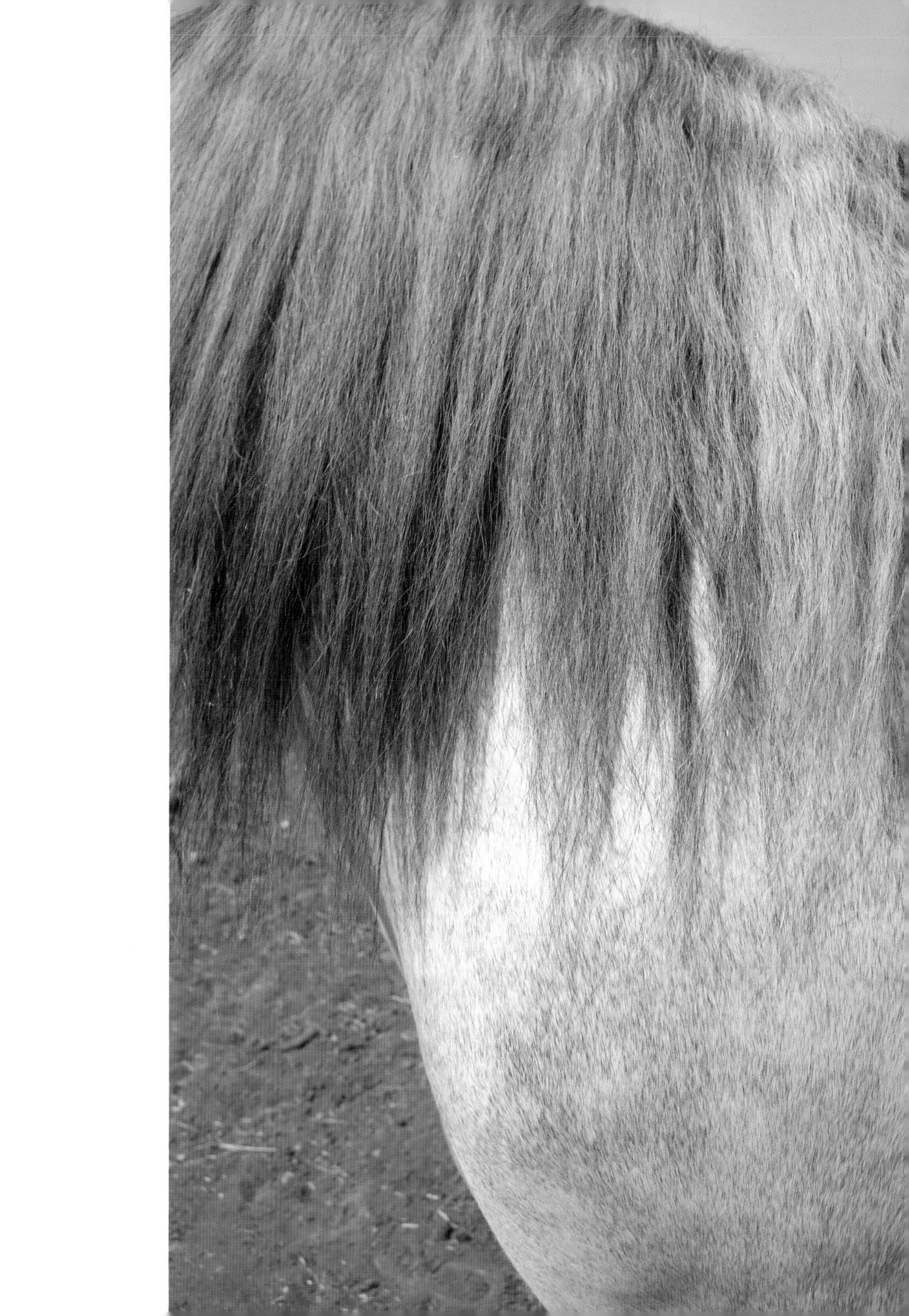

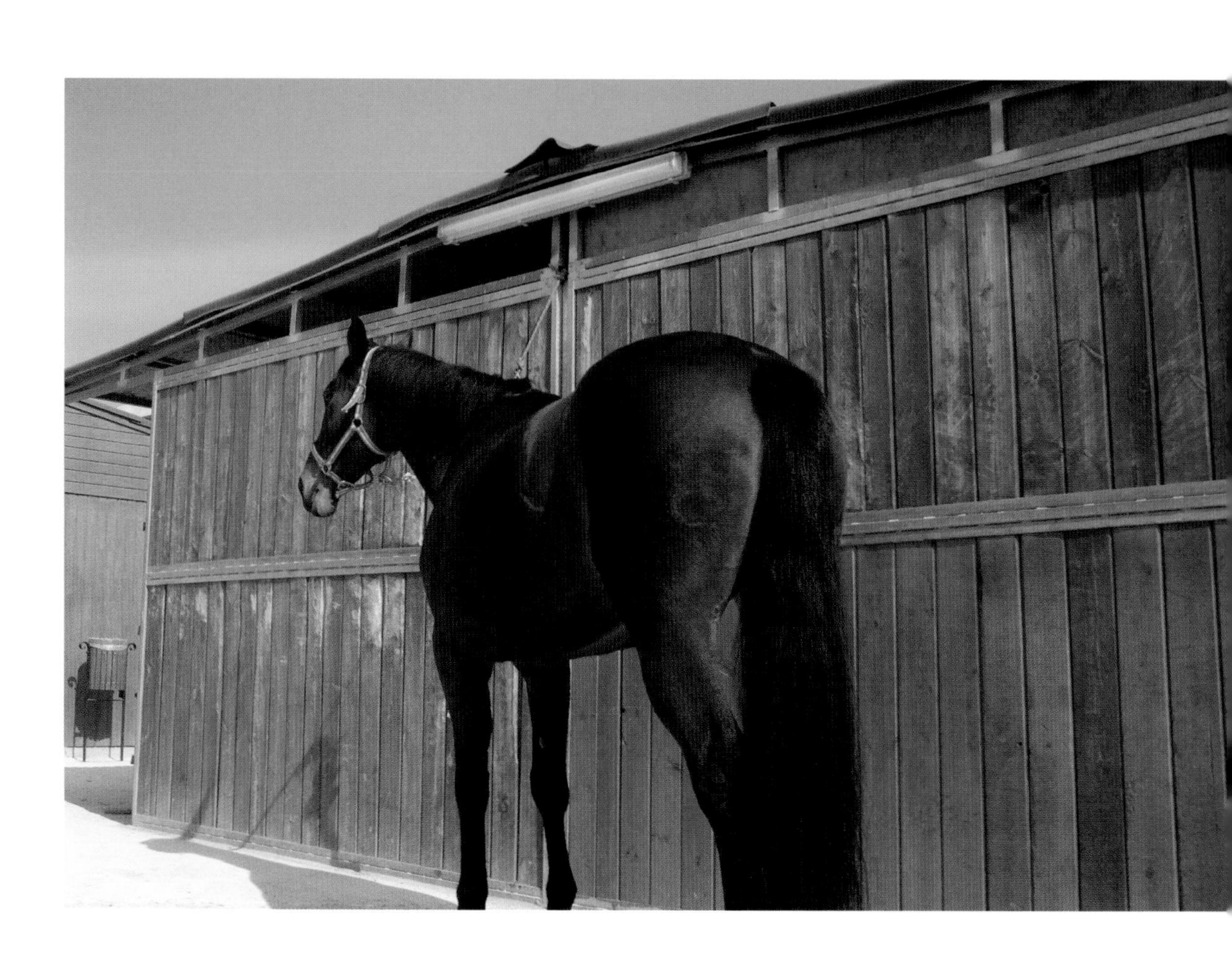

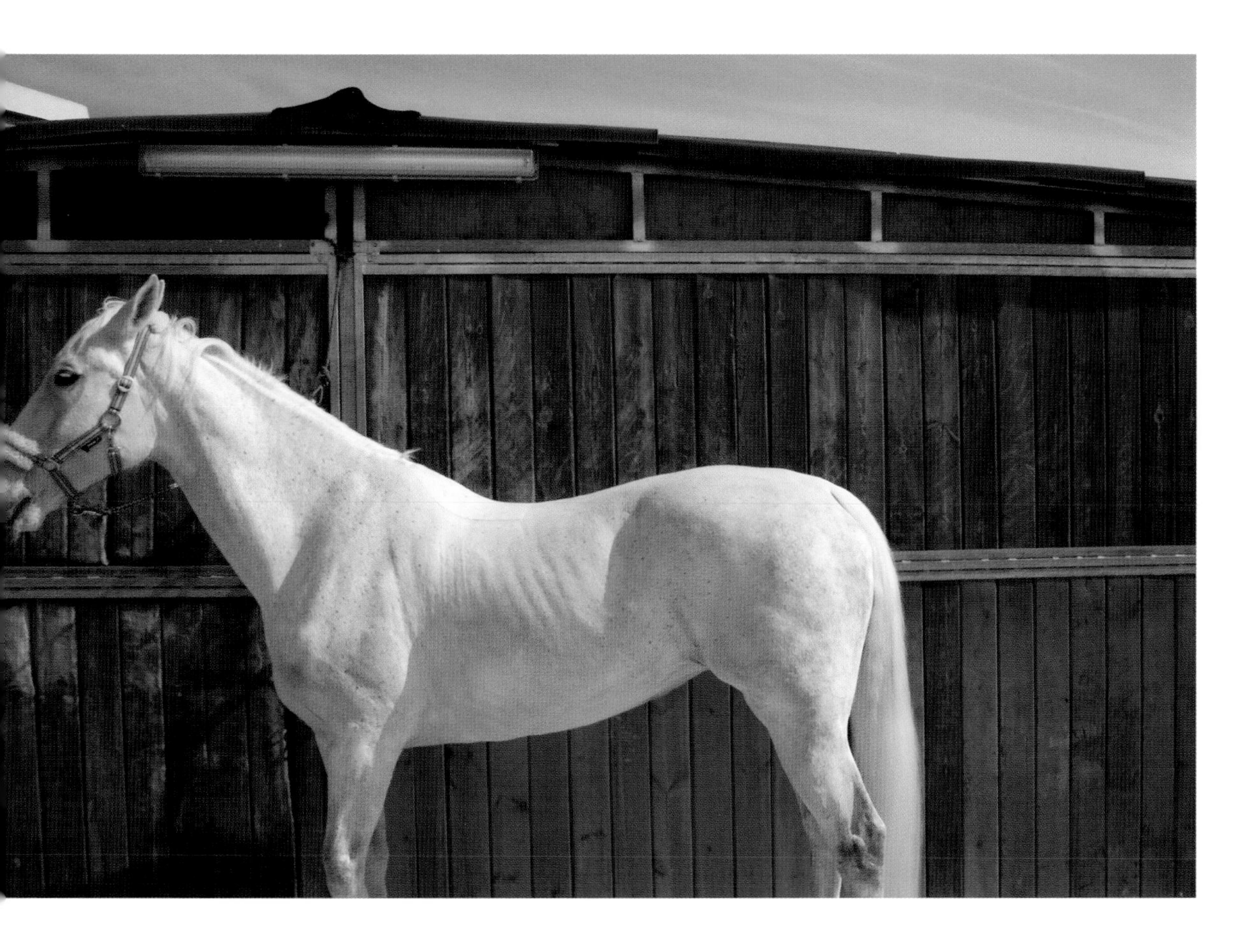

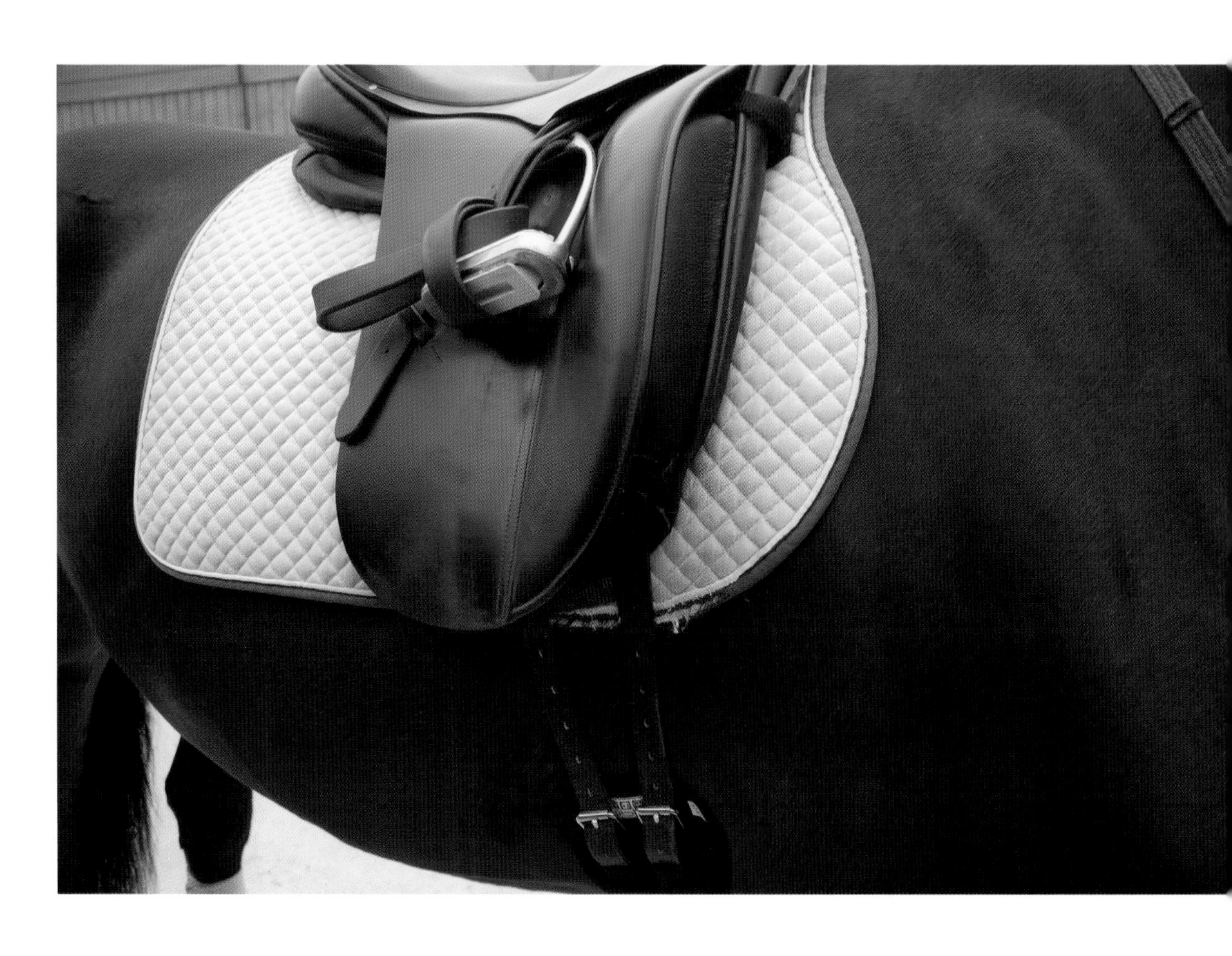

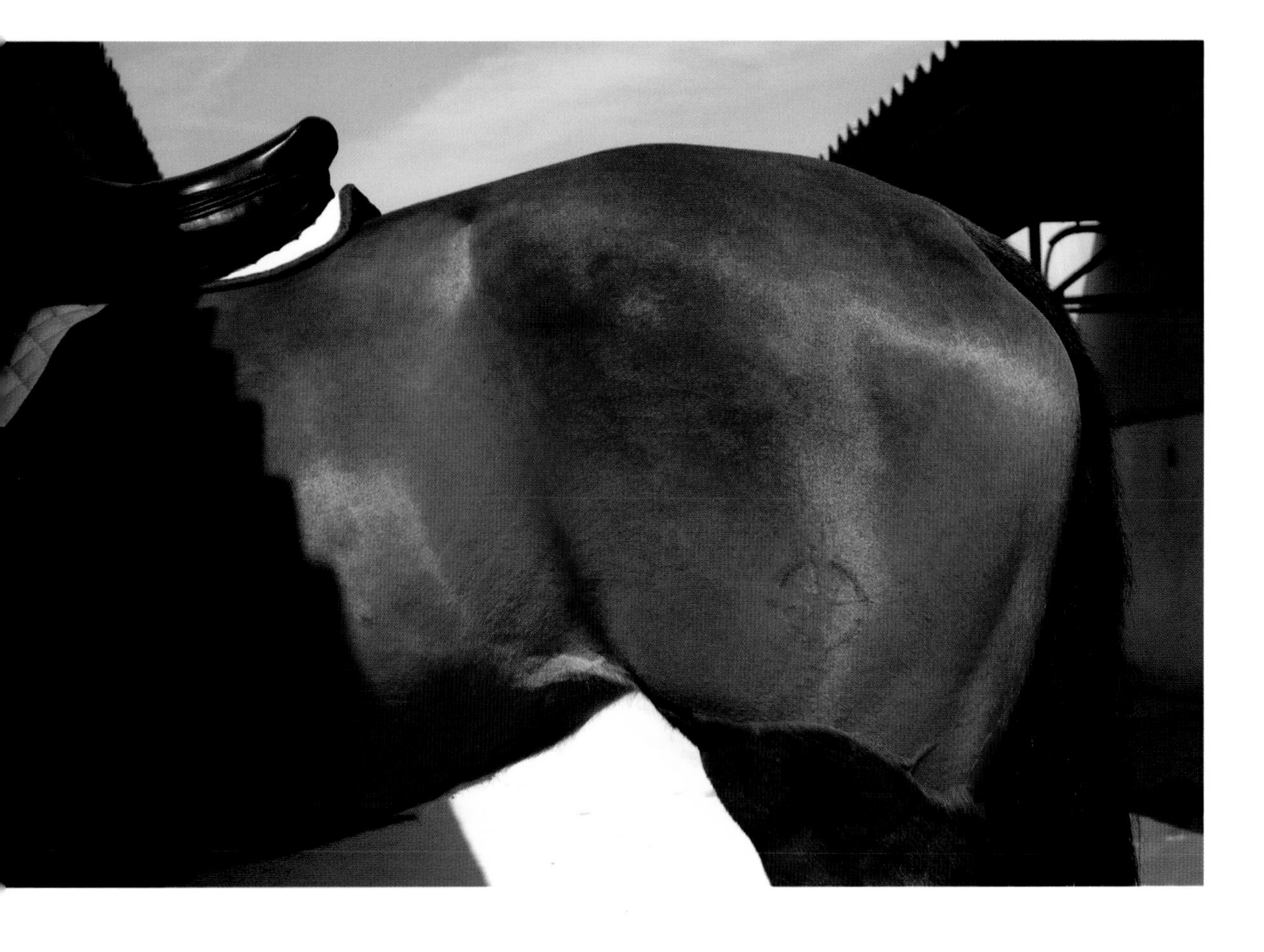

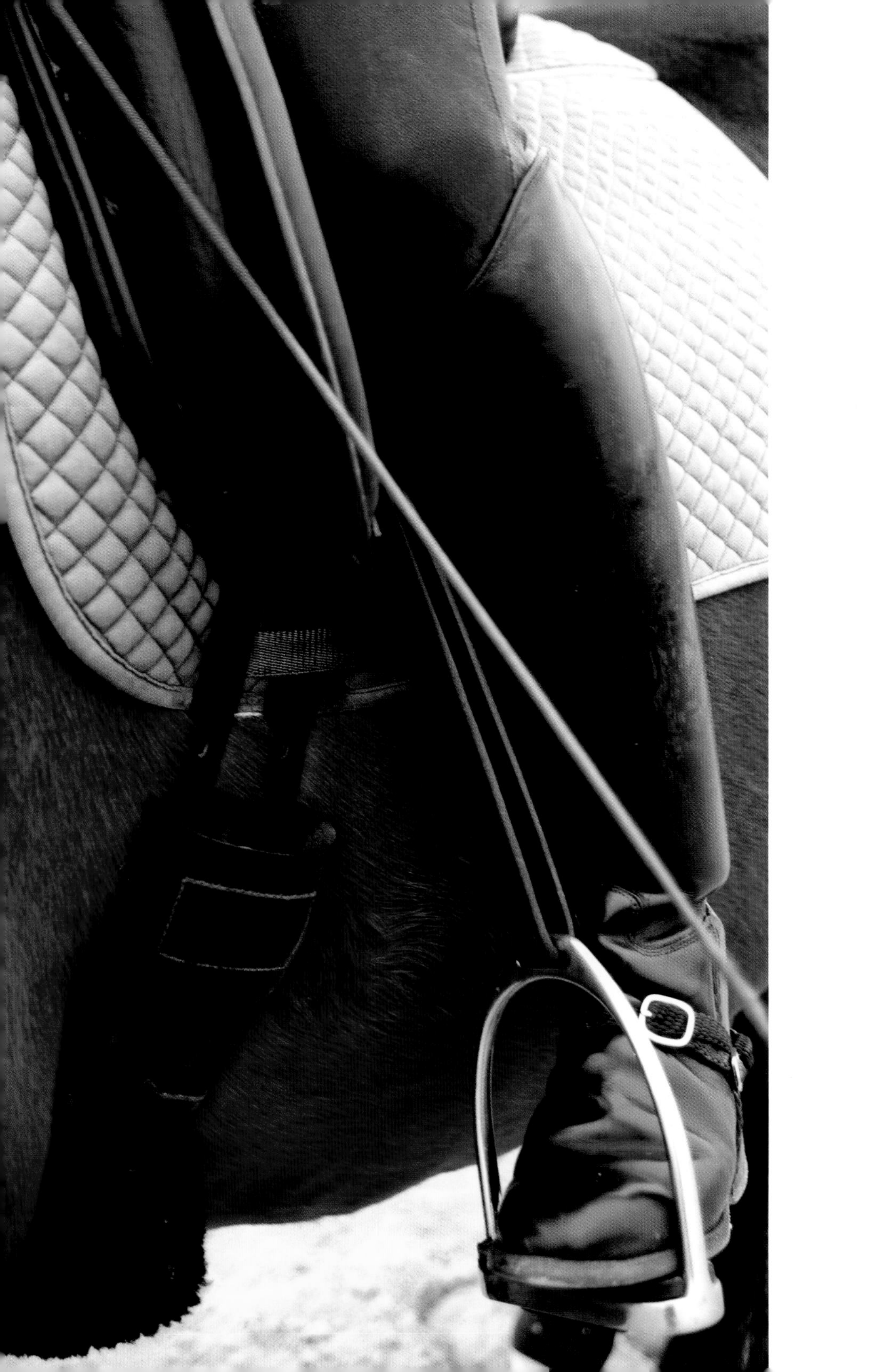

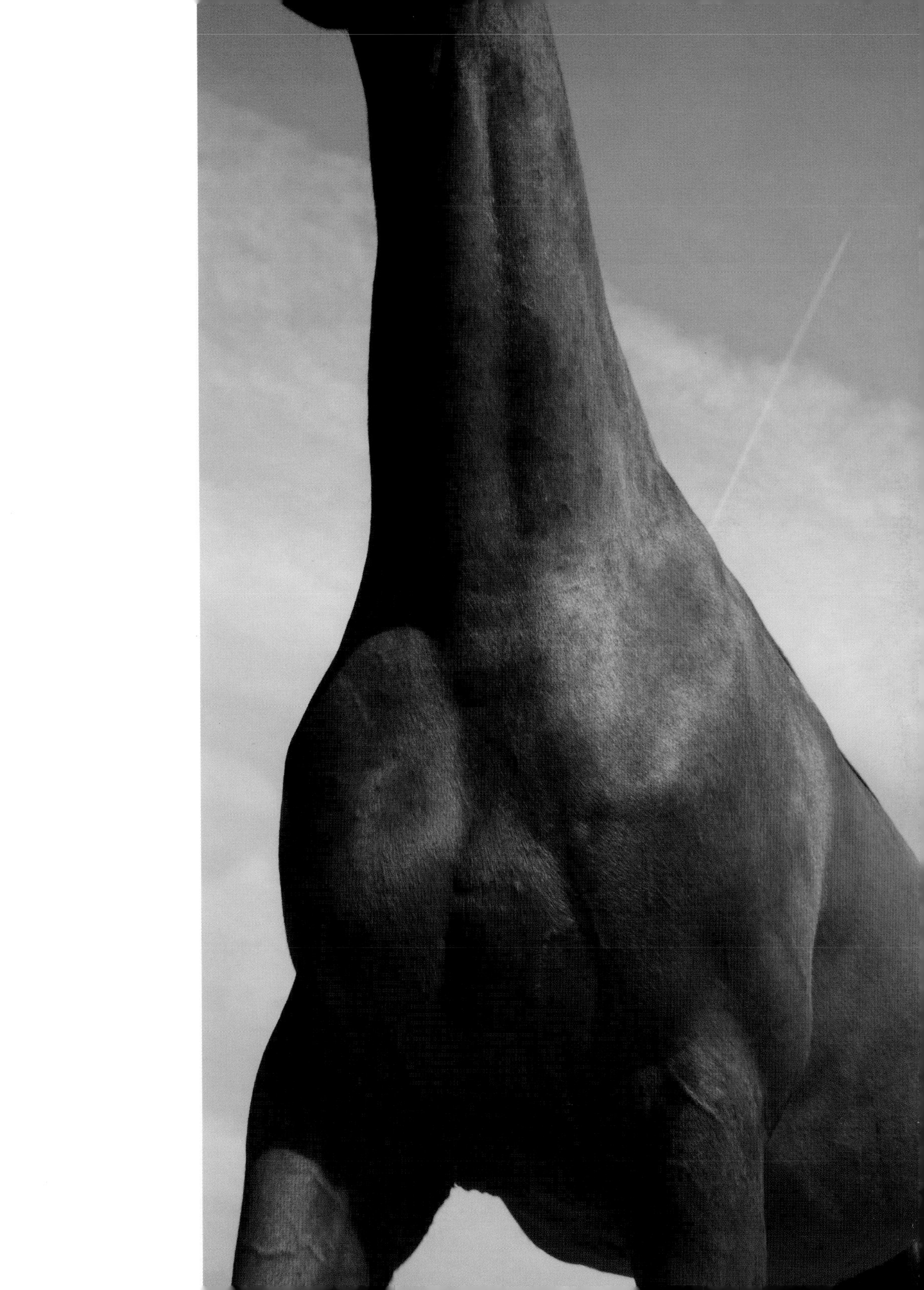

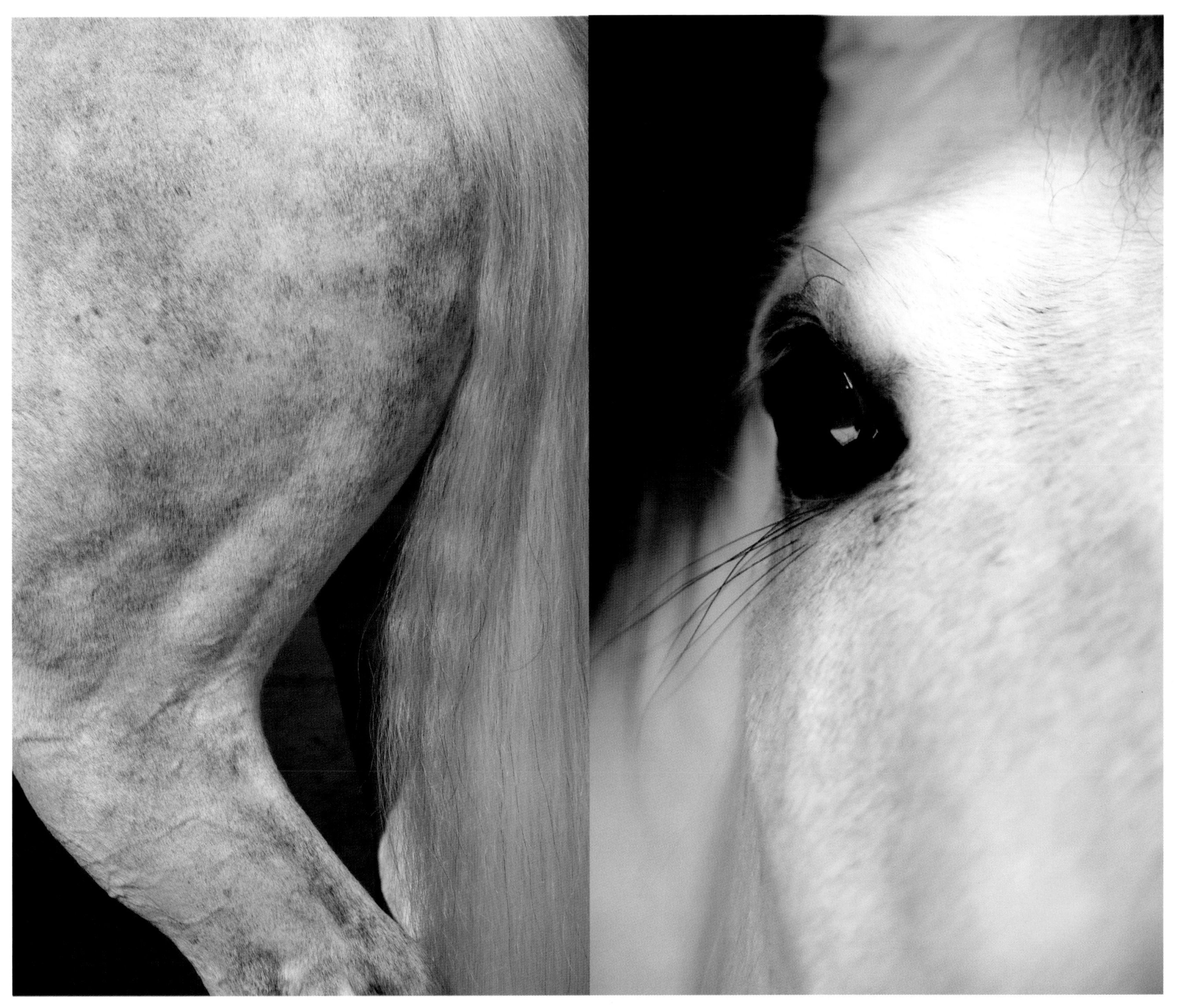

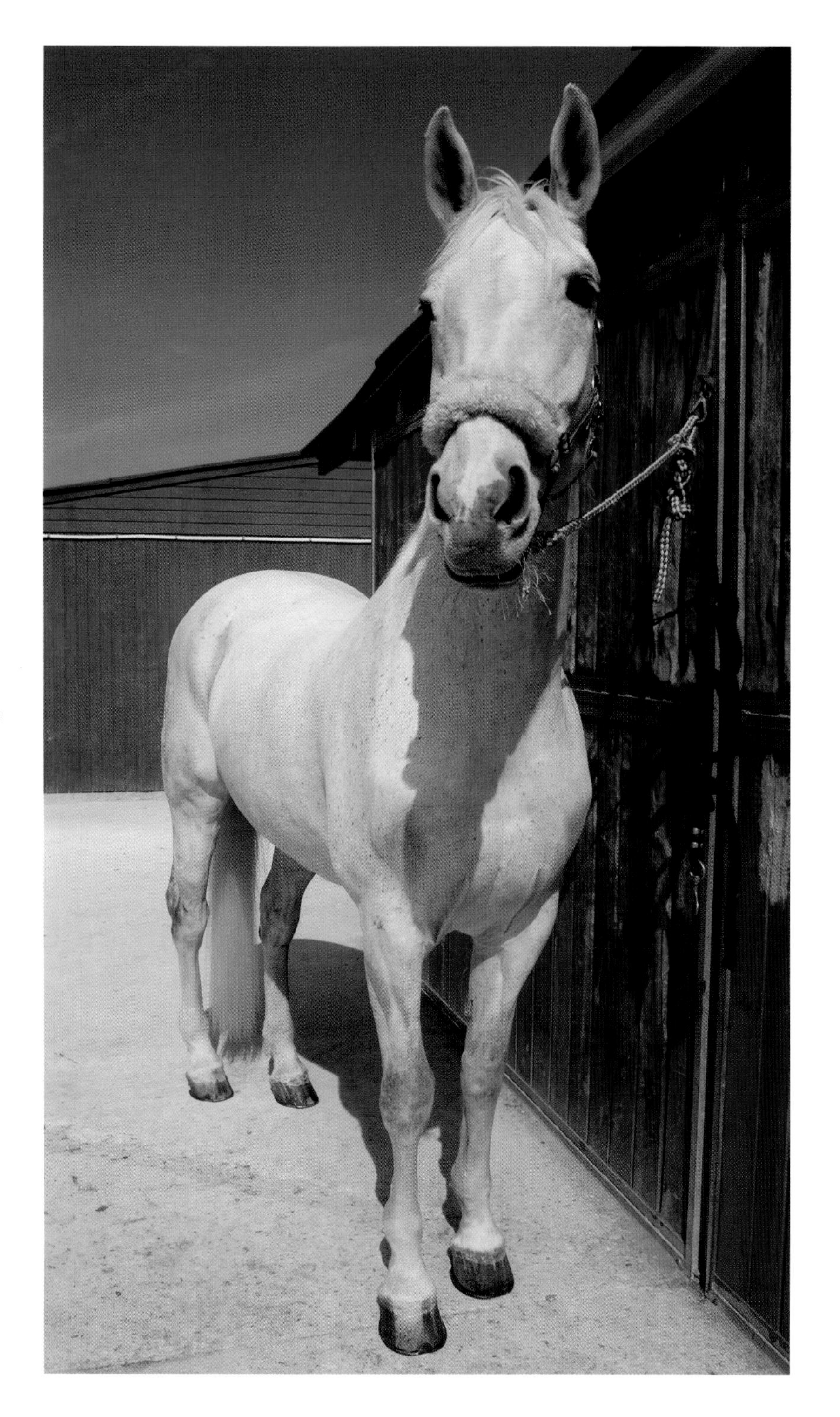

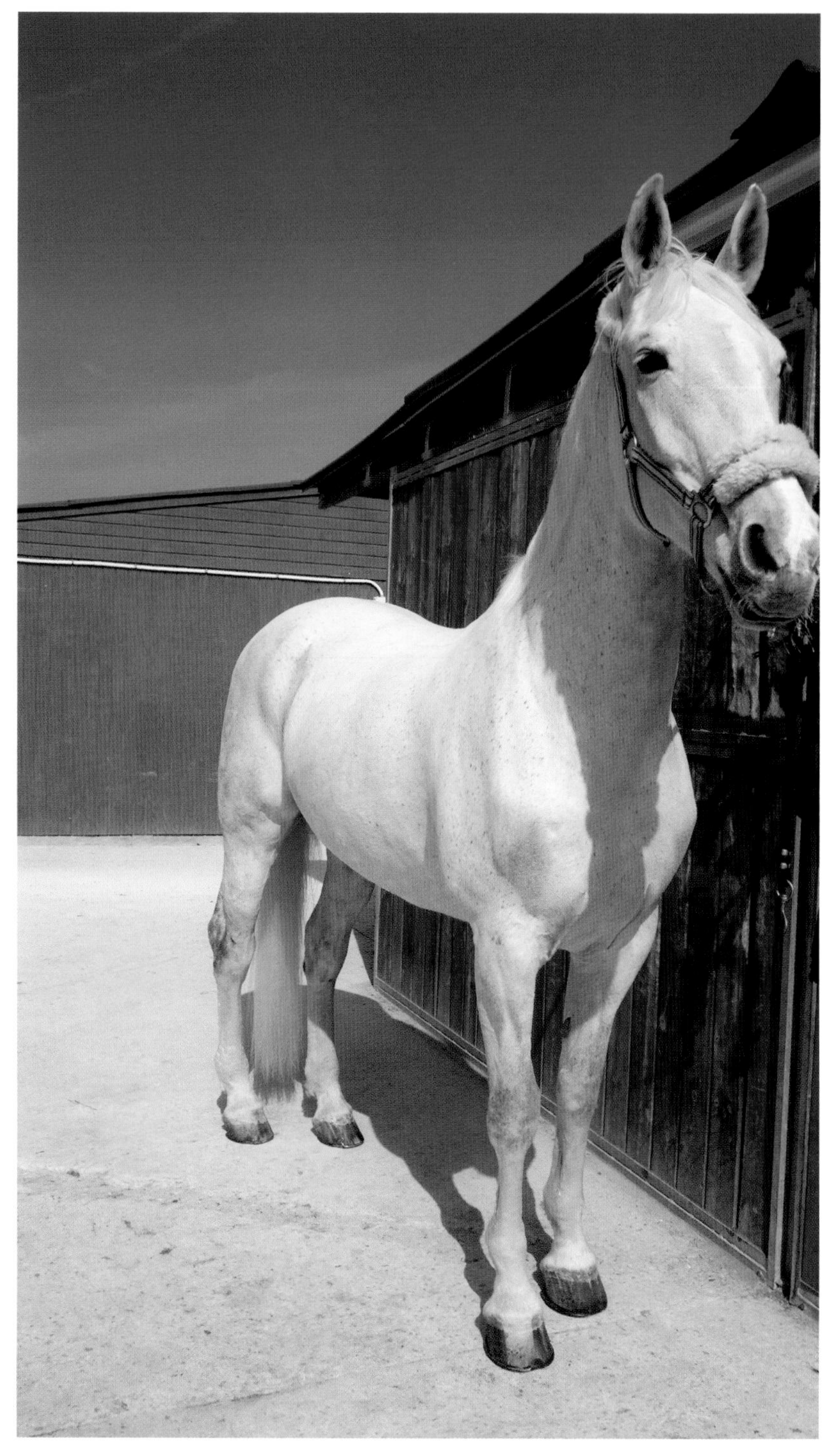

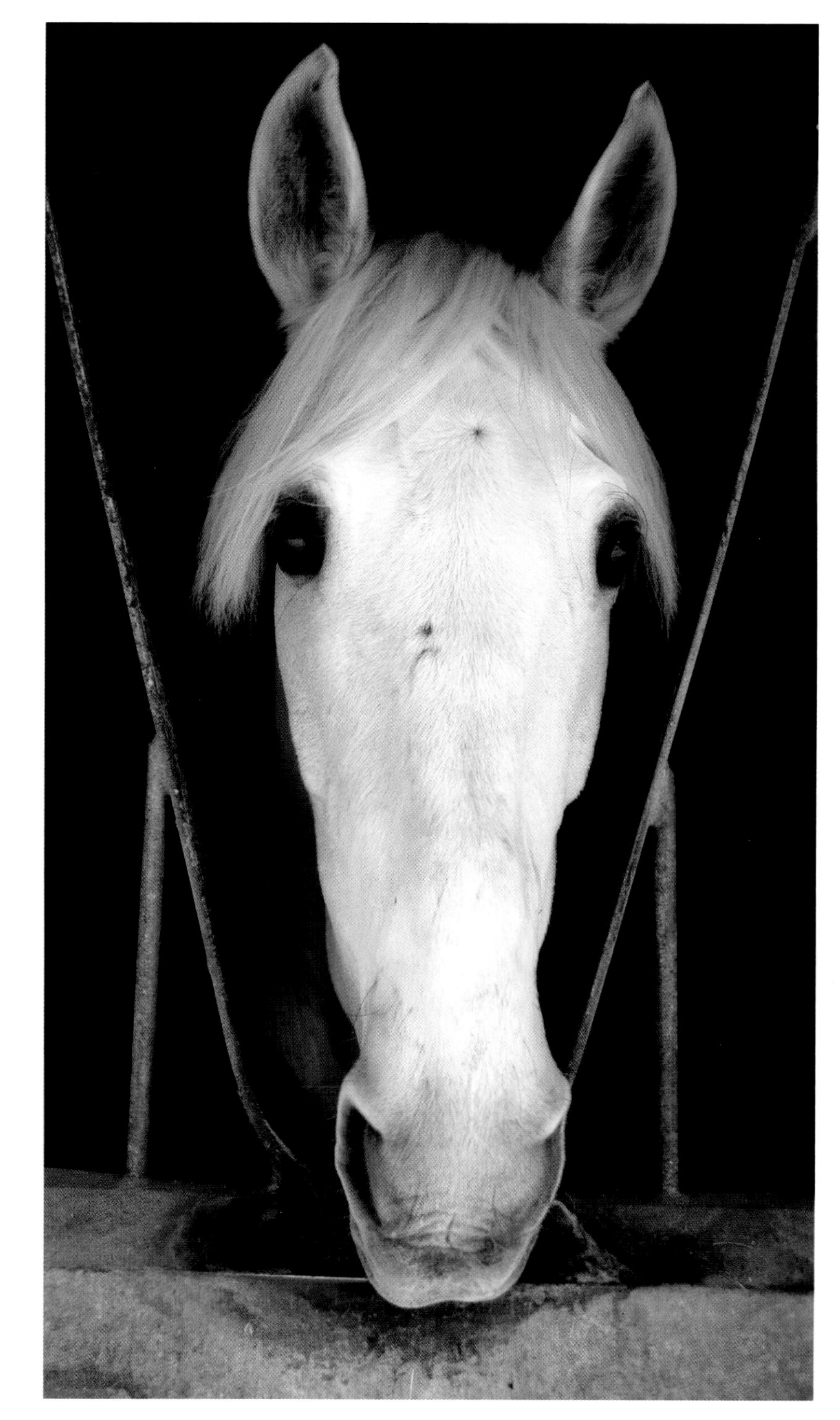

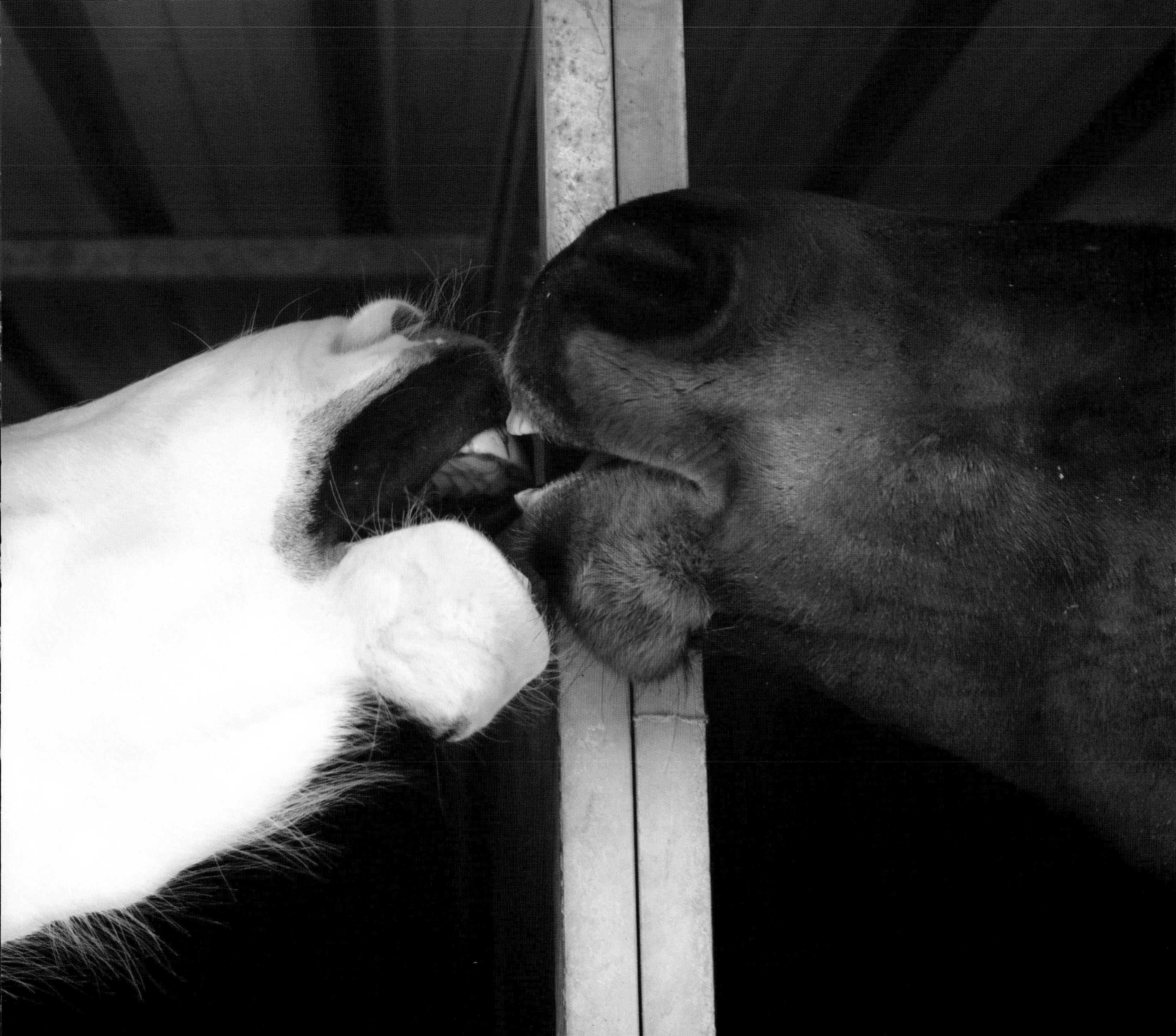

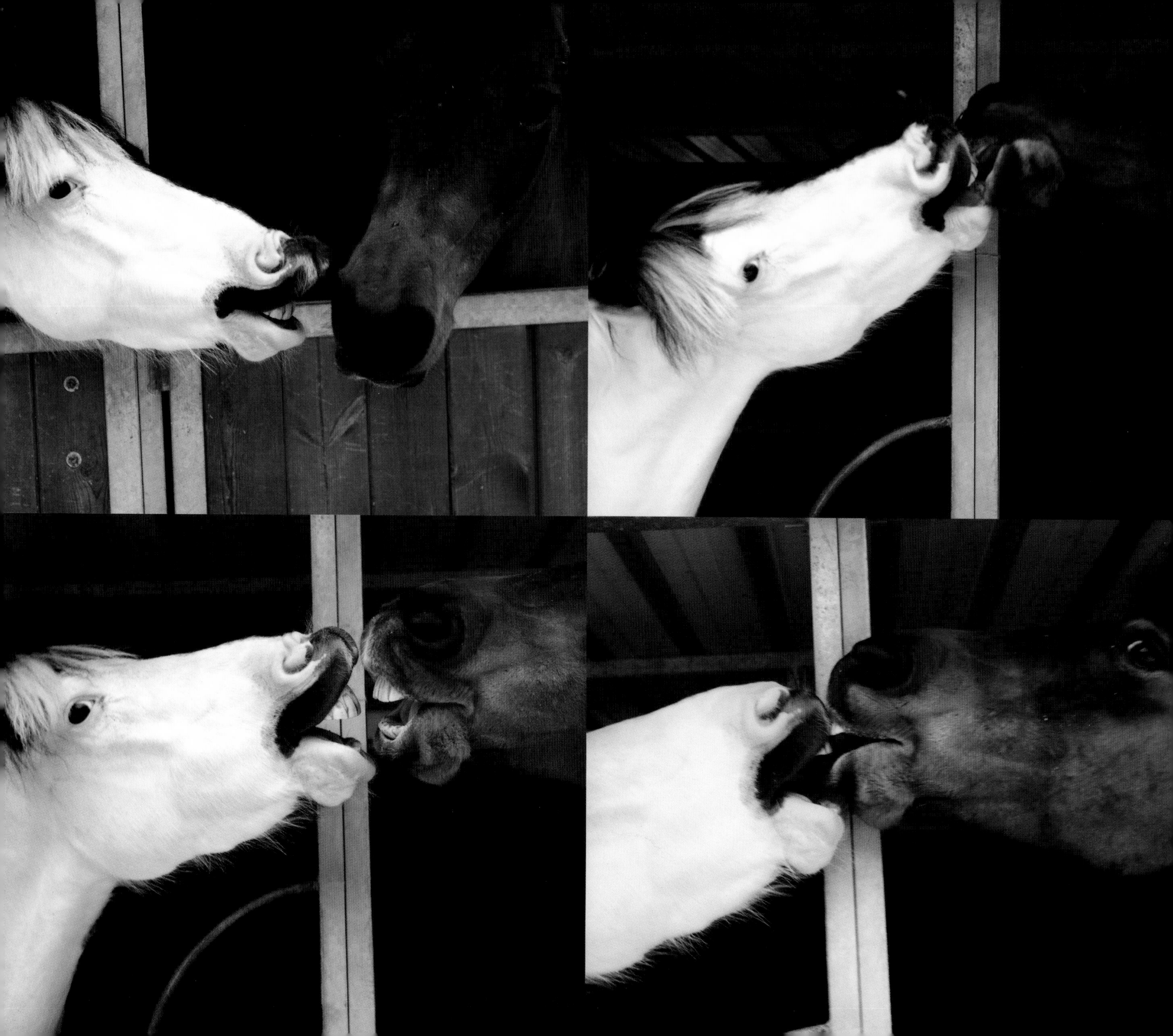

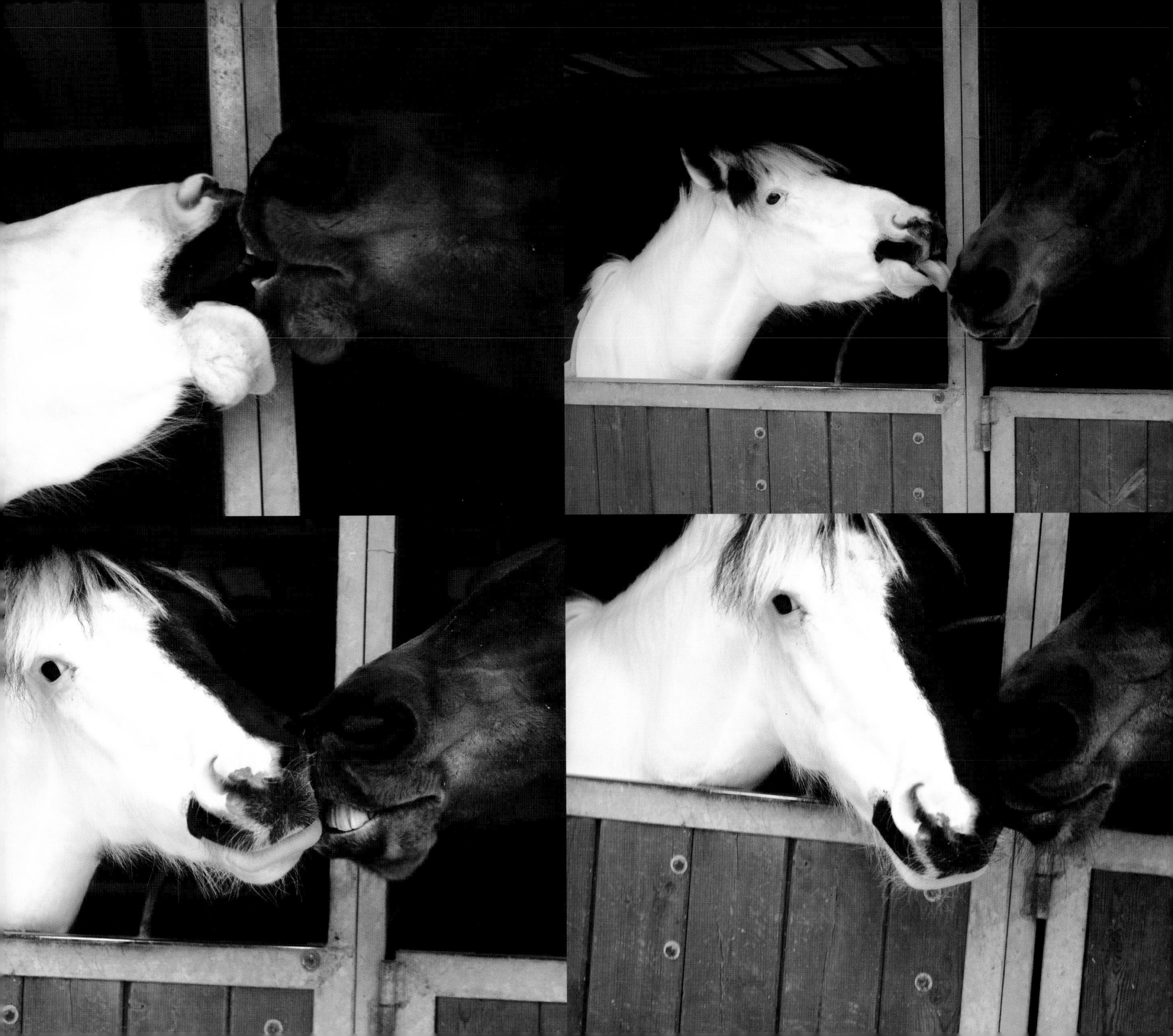

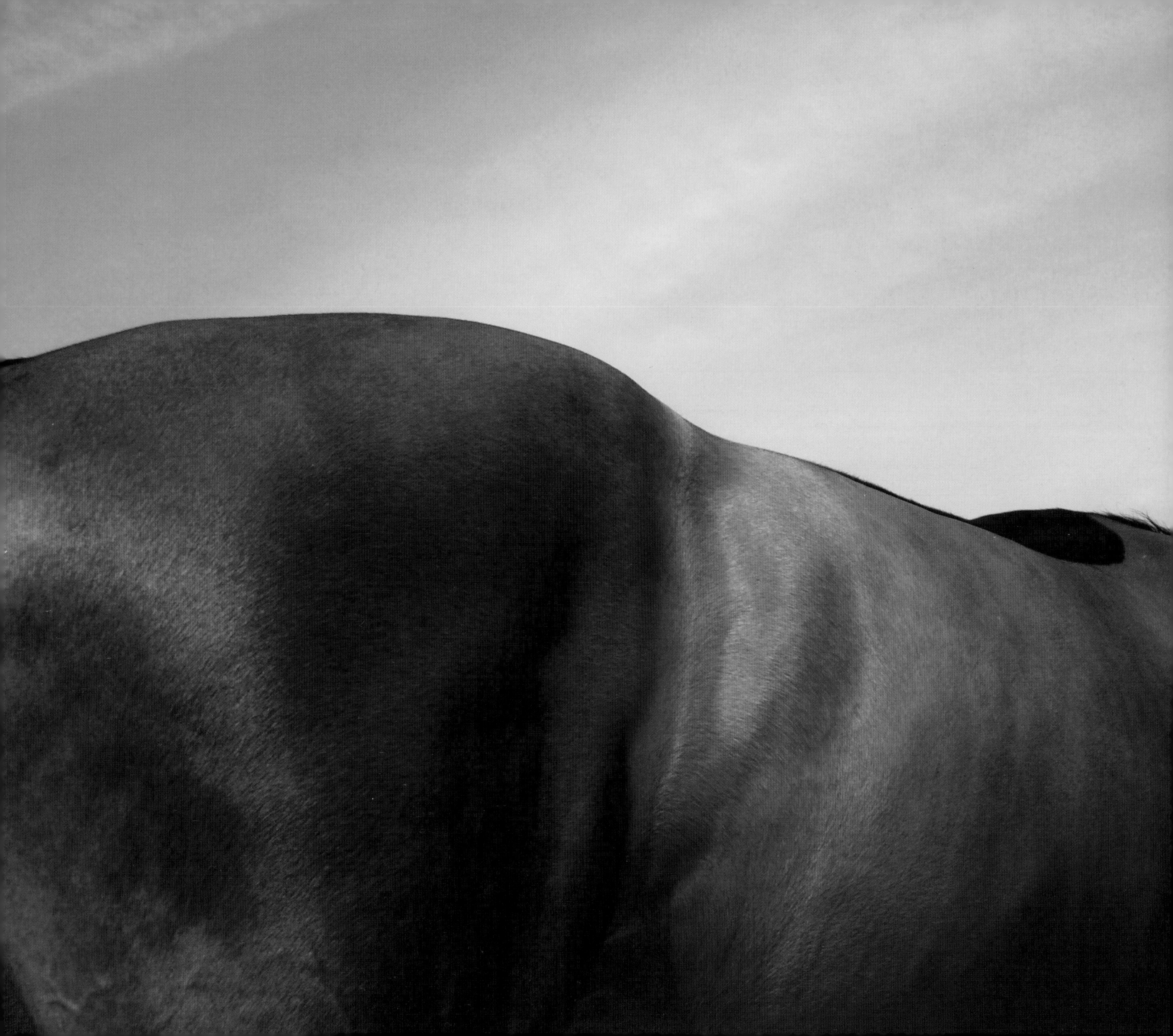

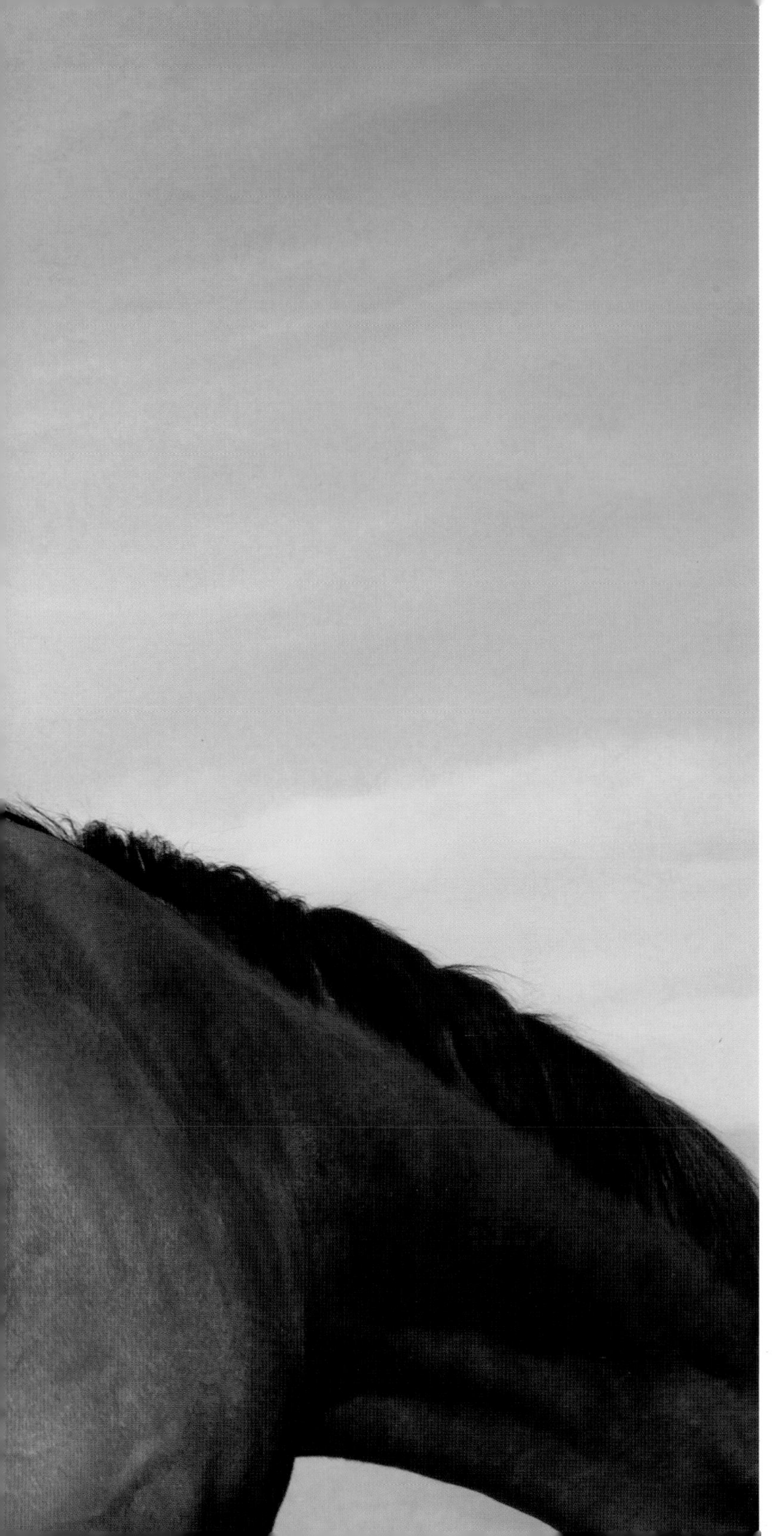

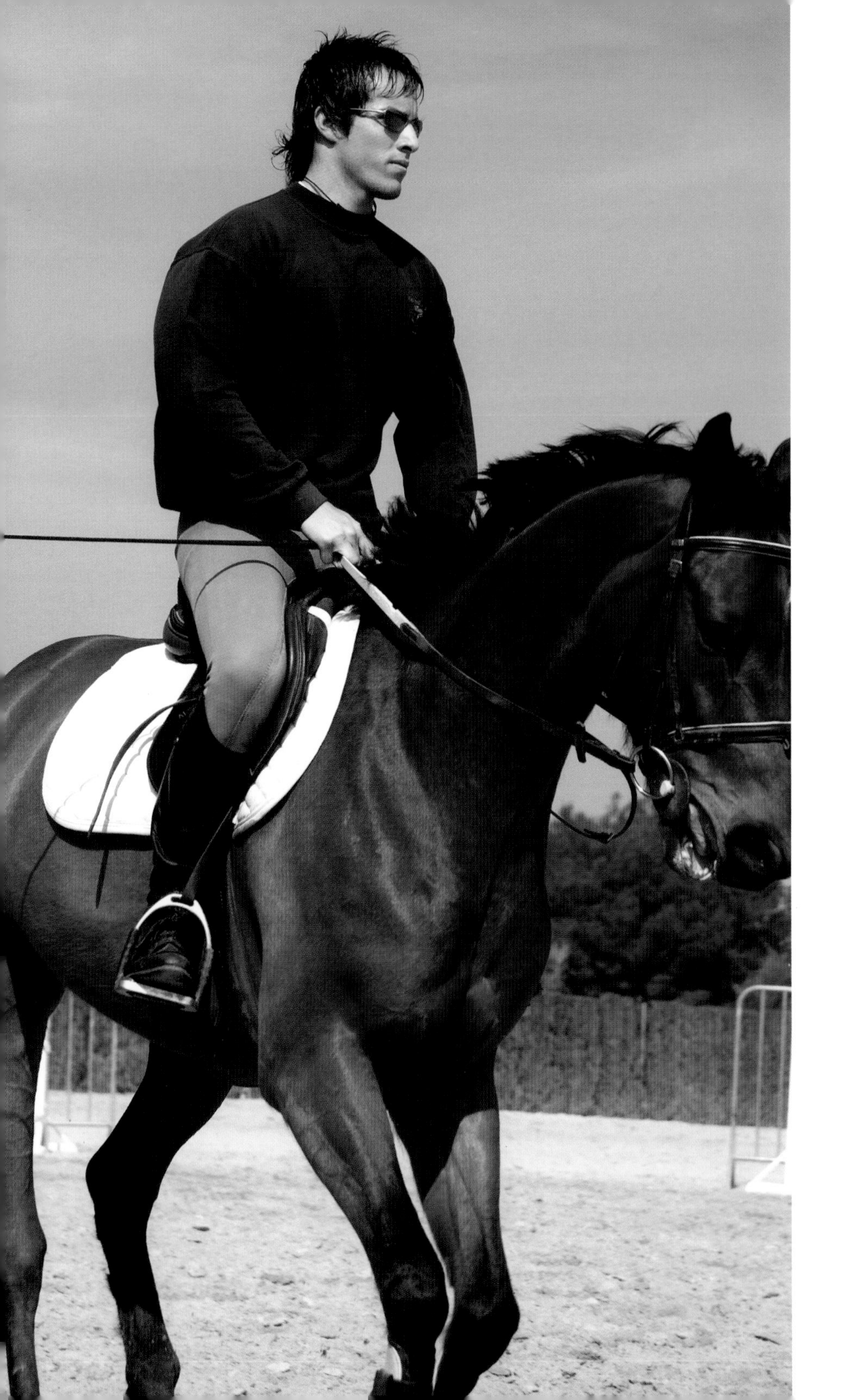

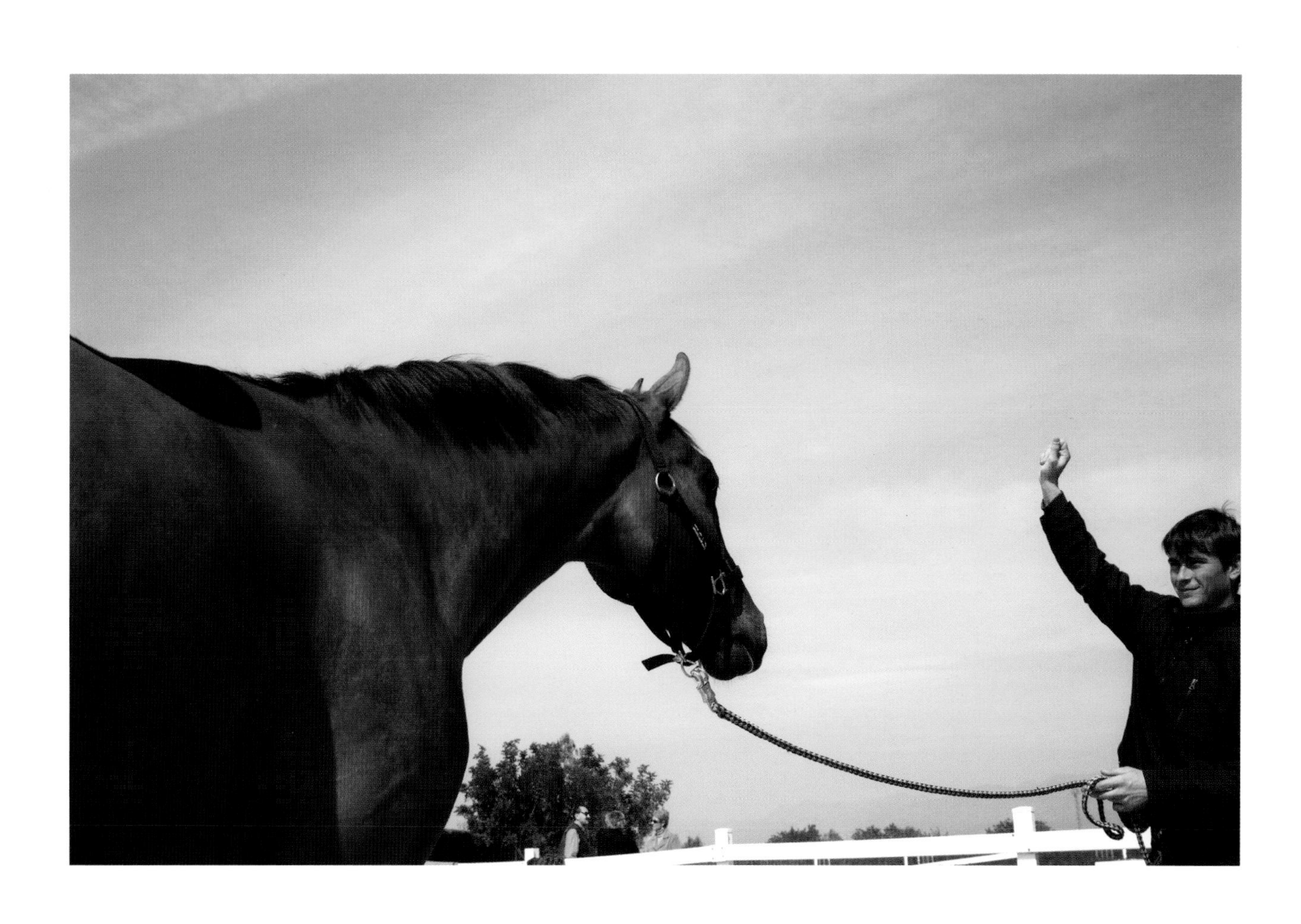

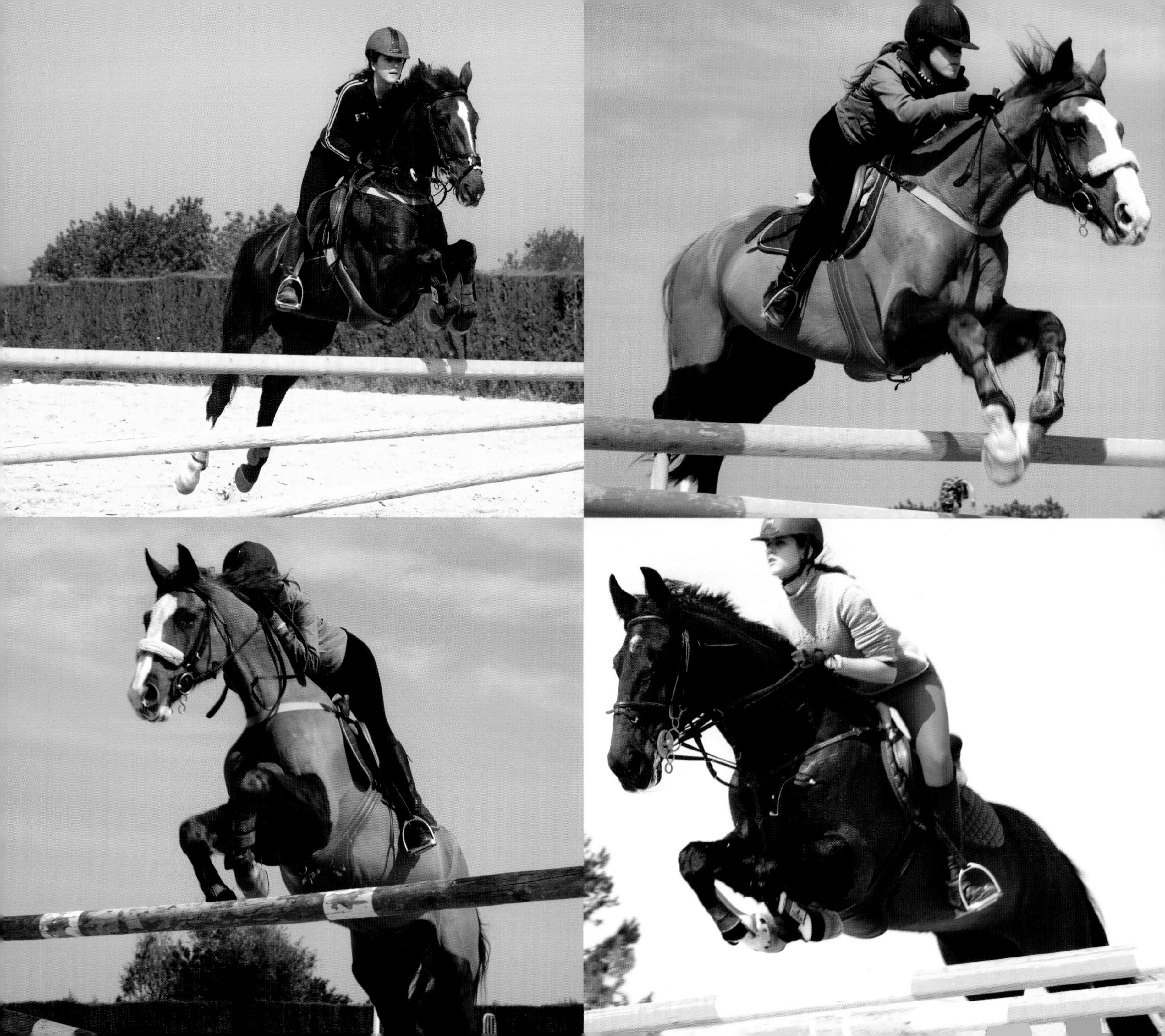

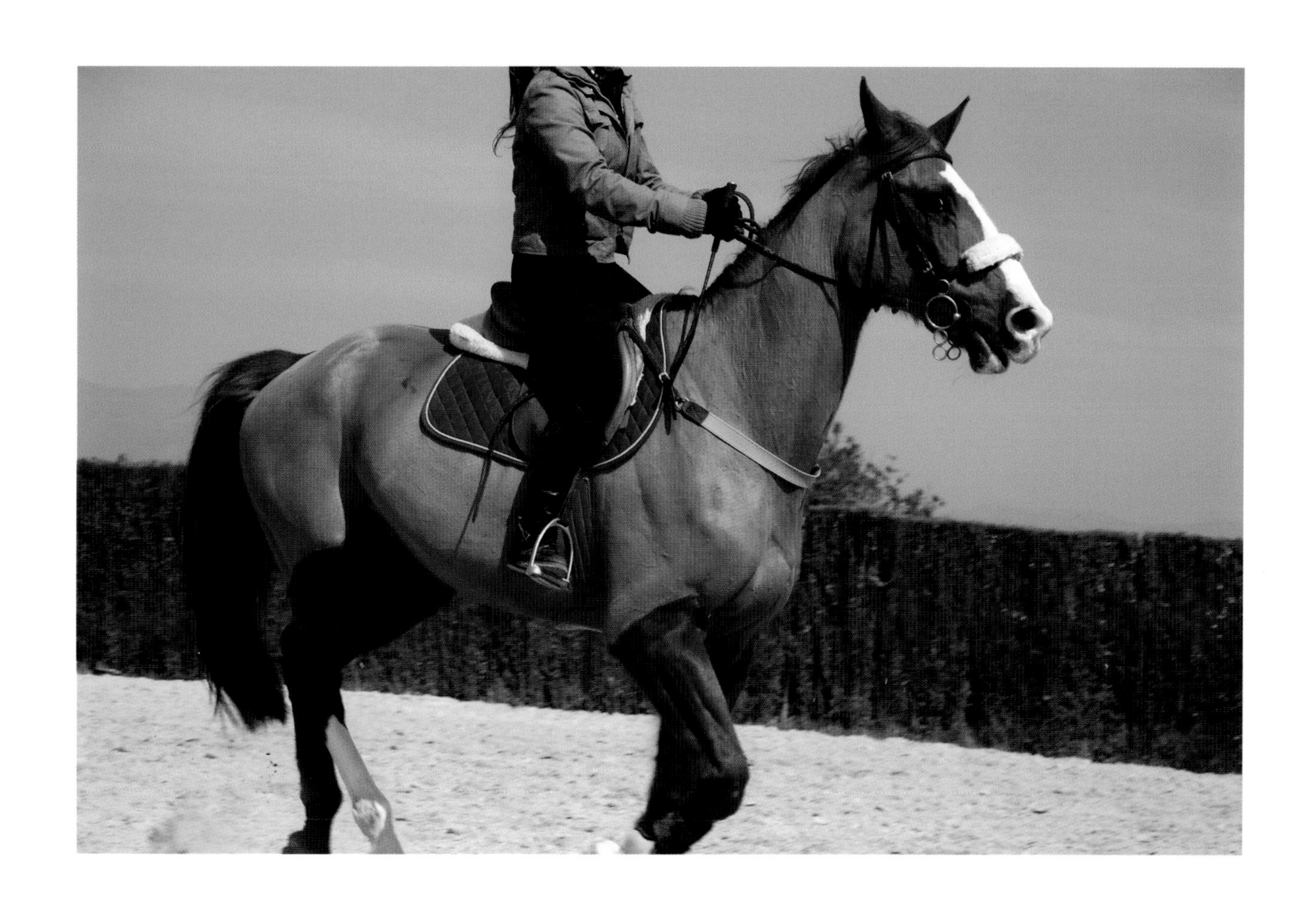

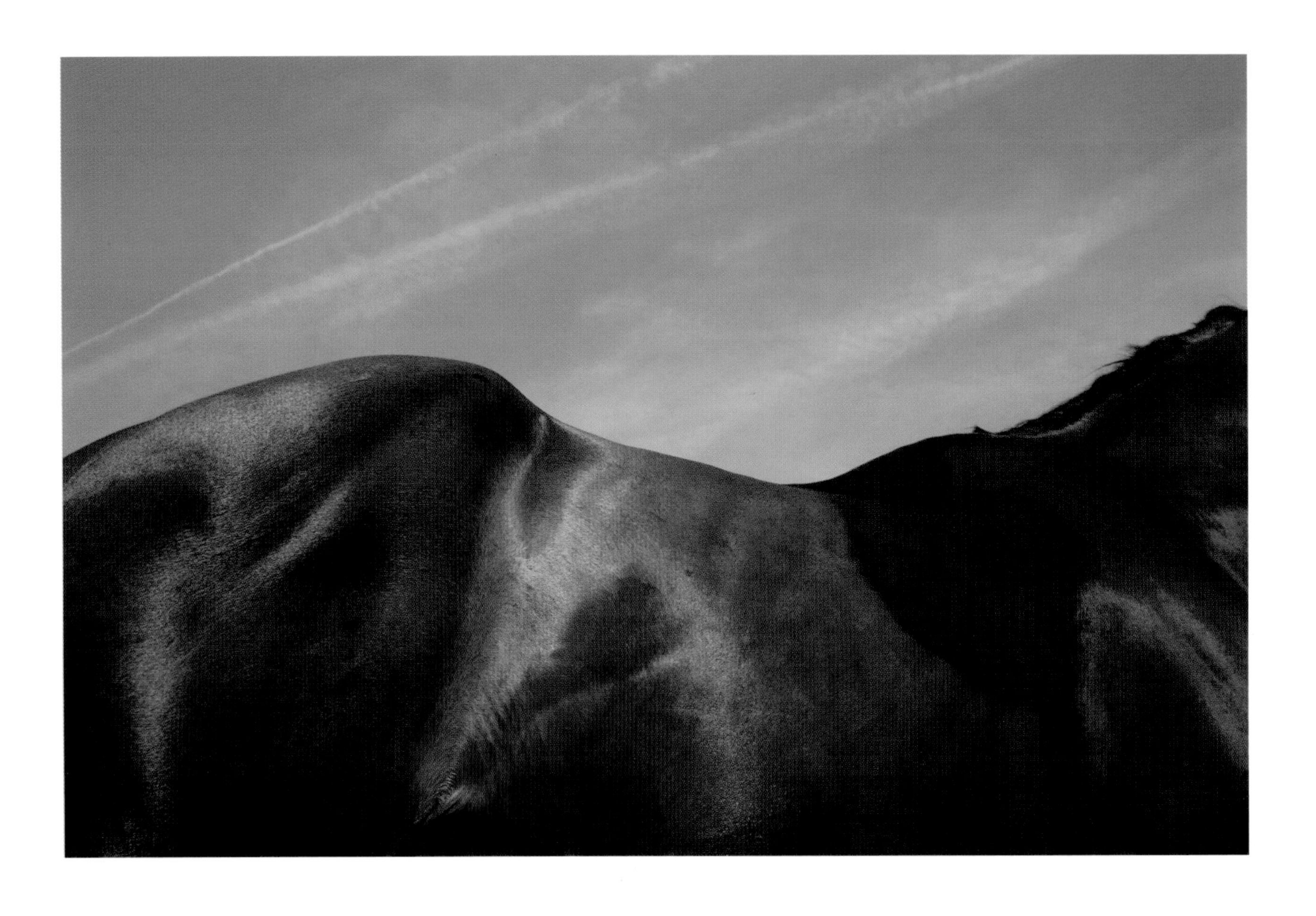

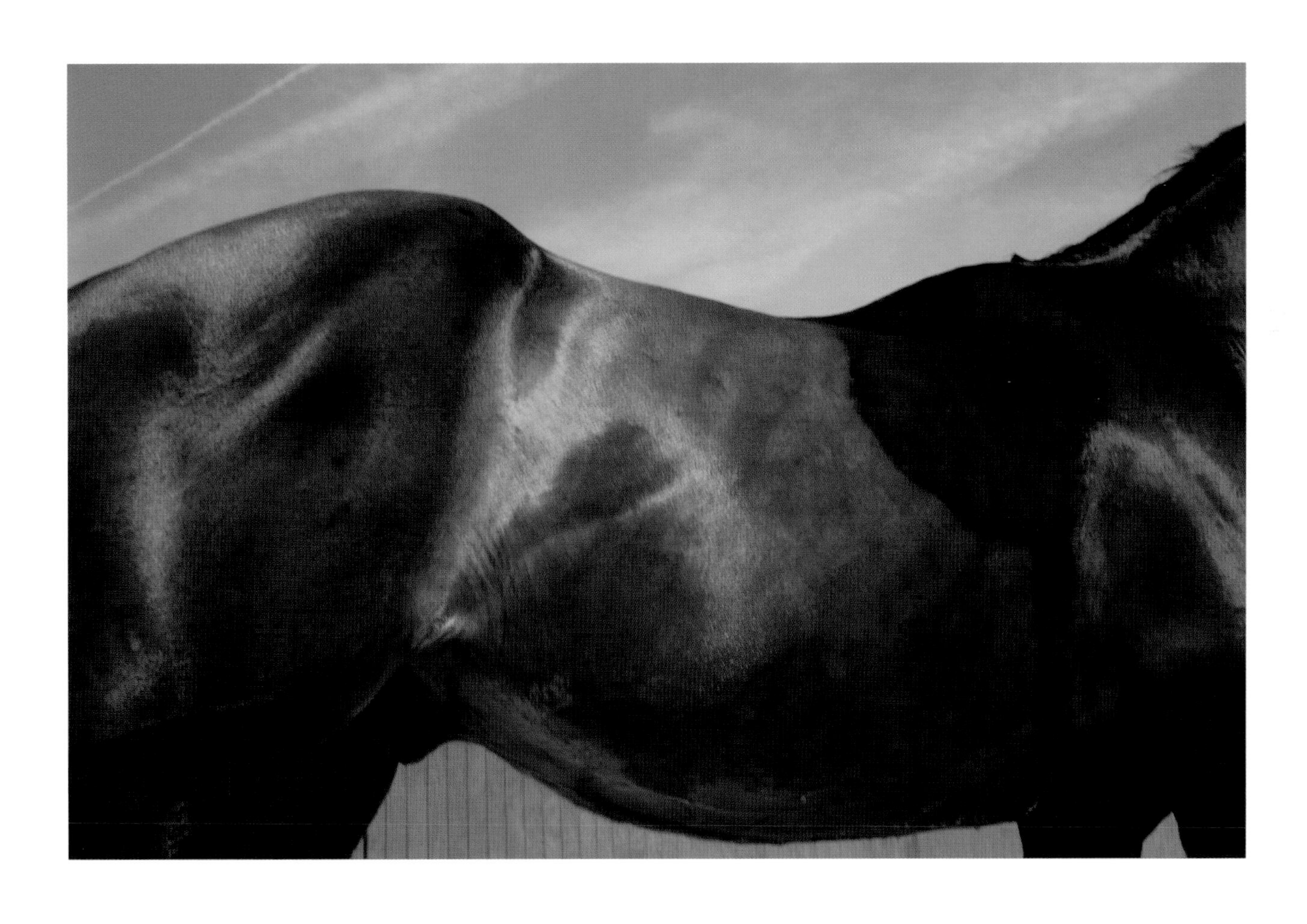

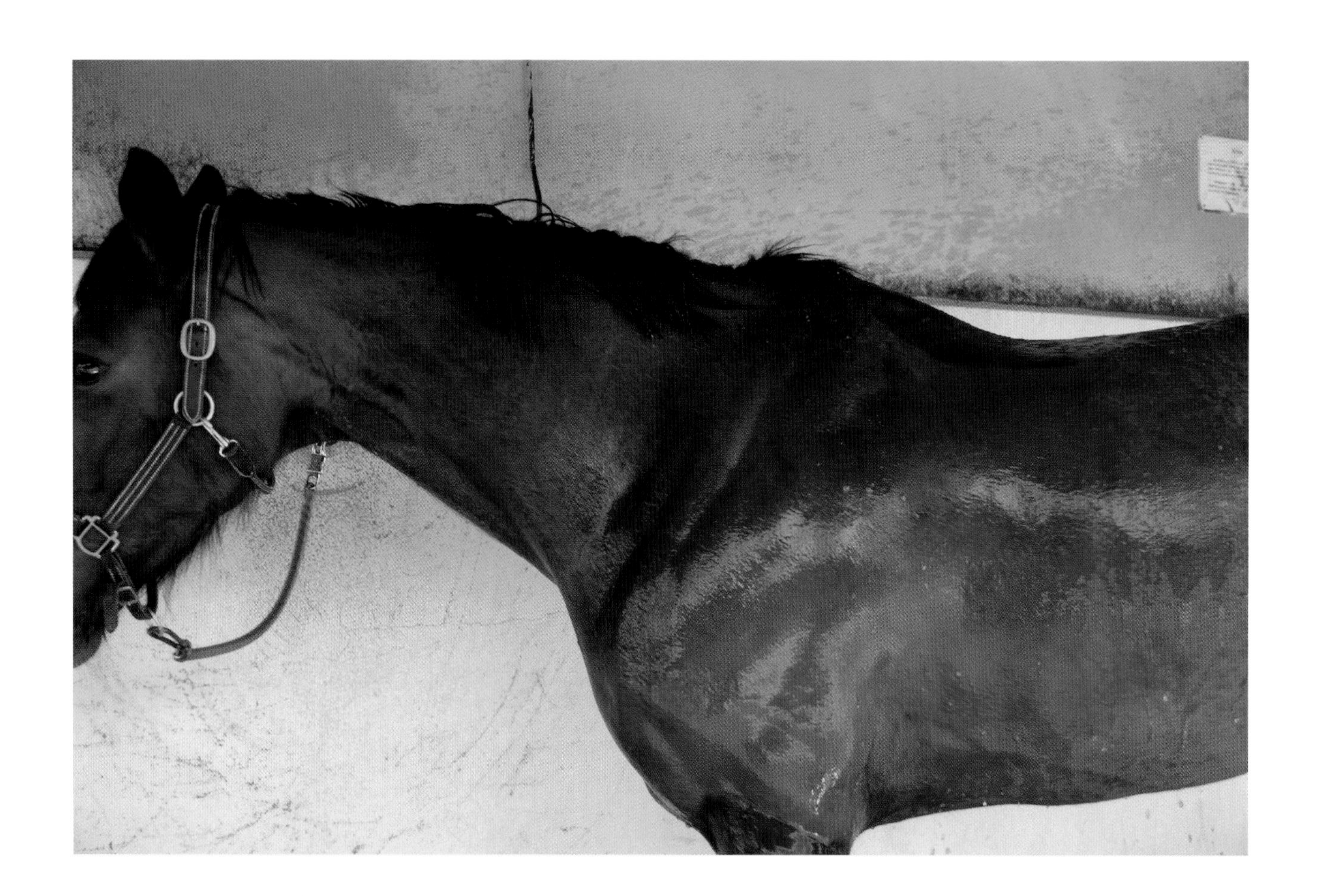

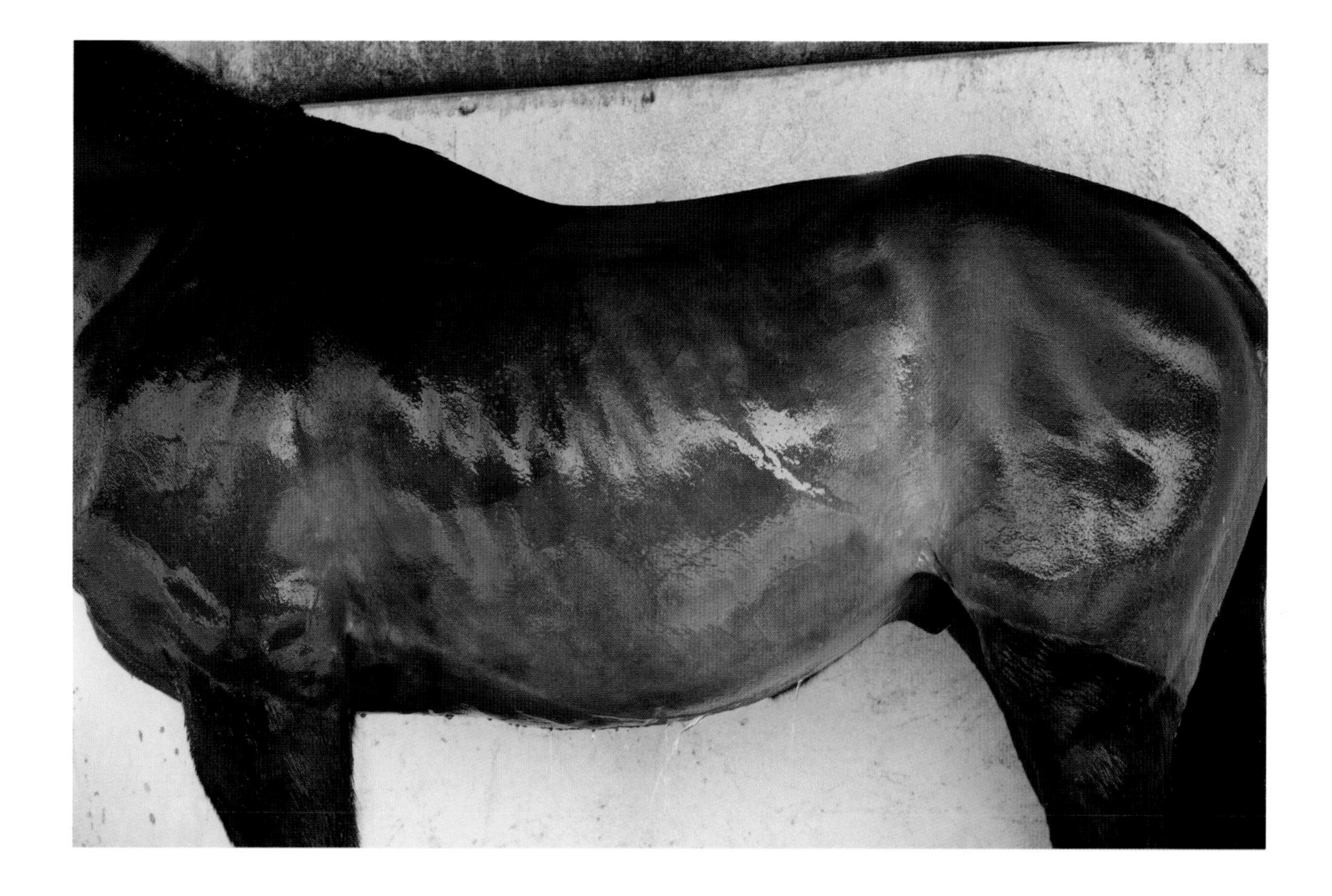

P105

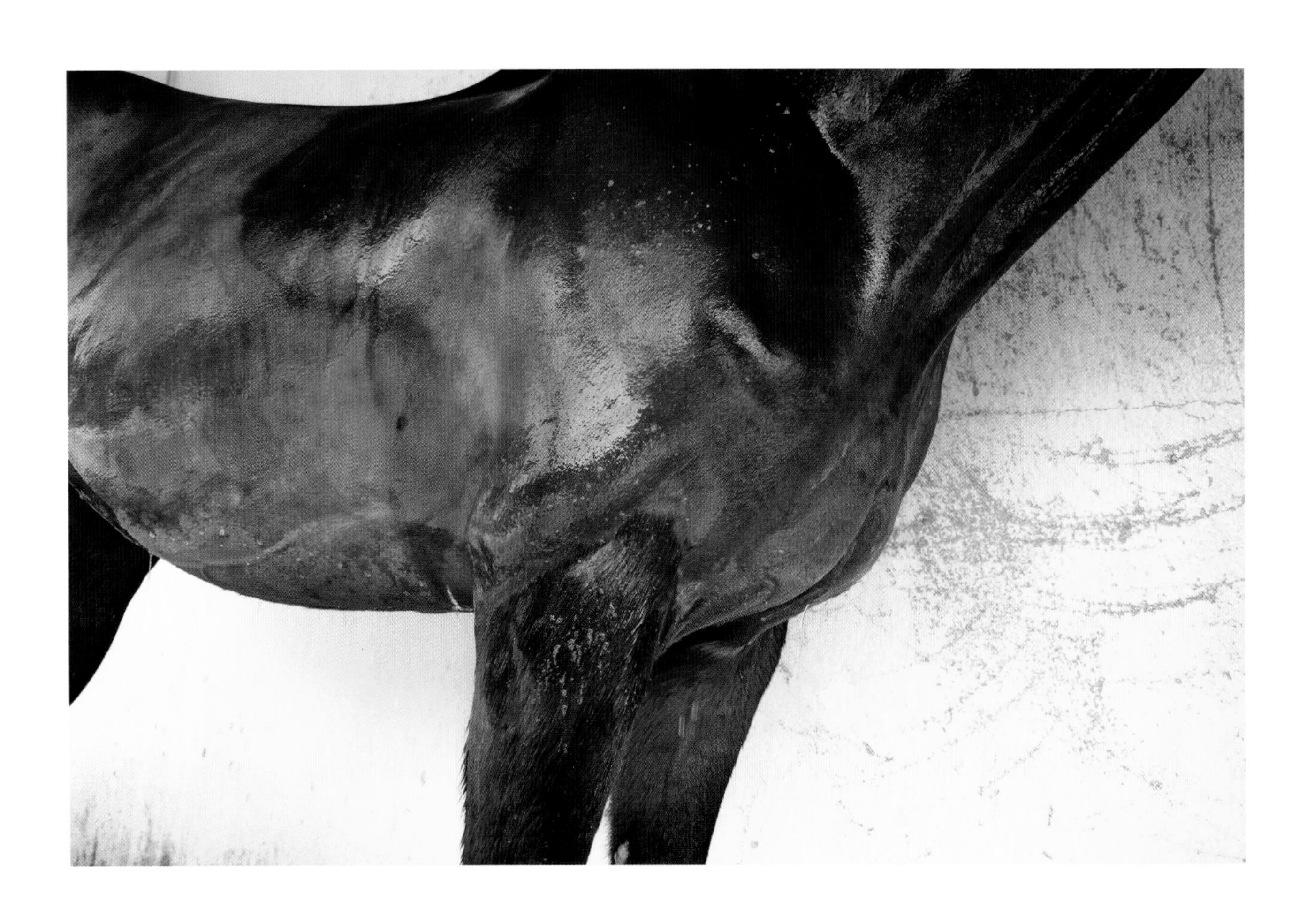

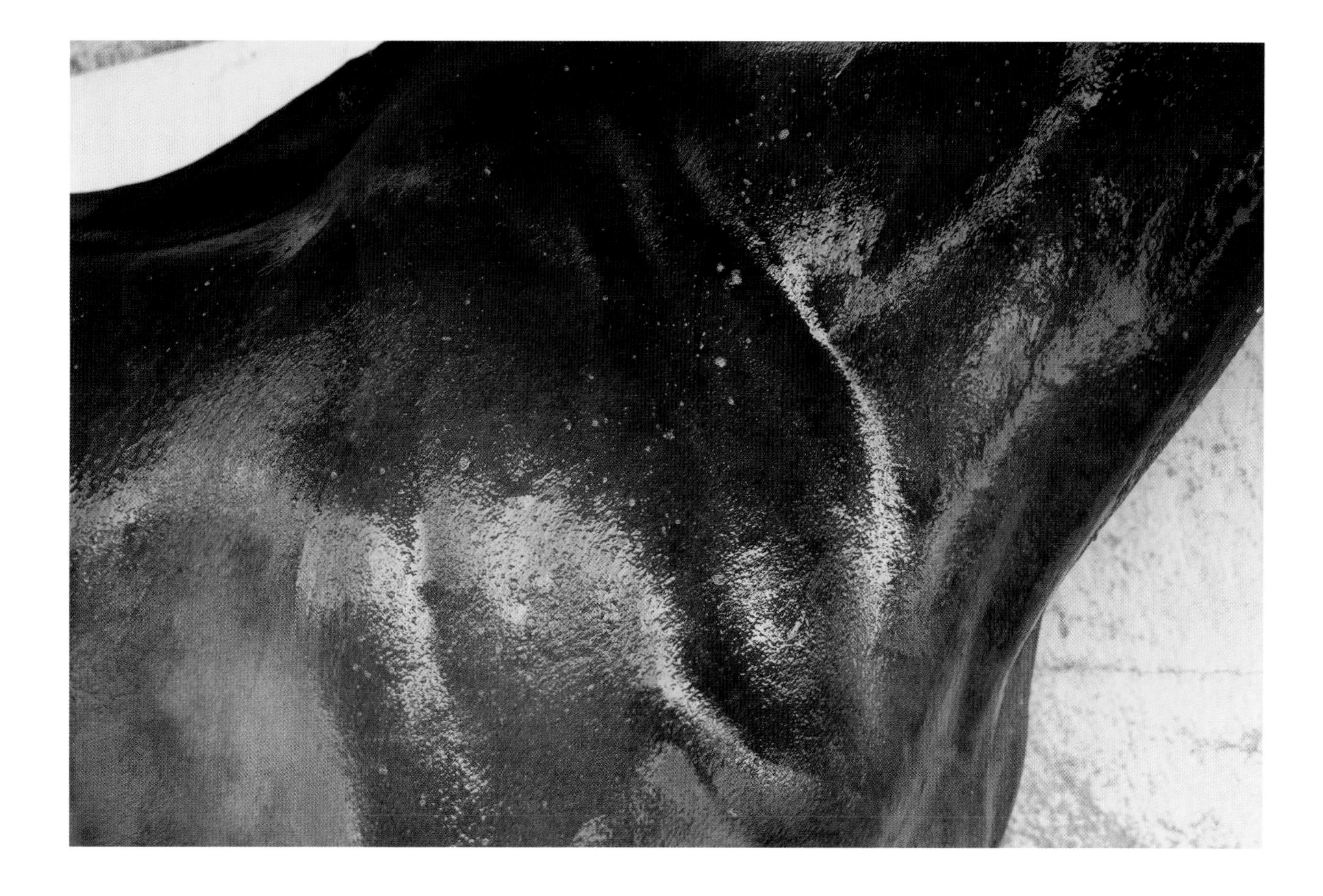

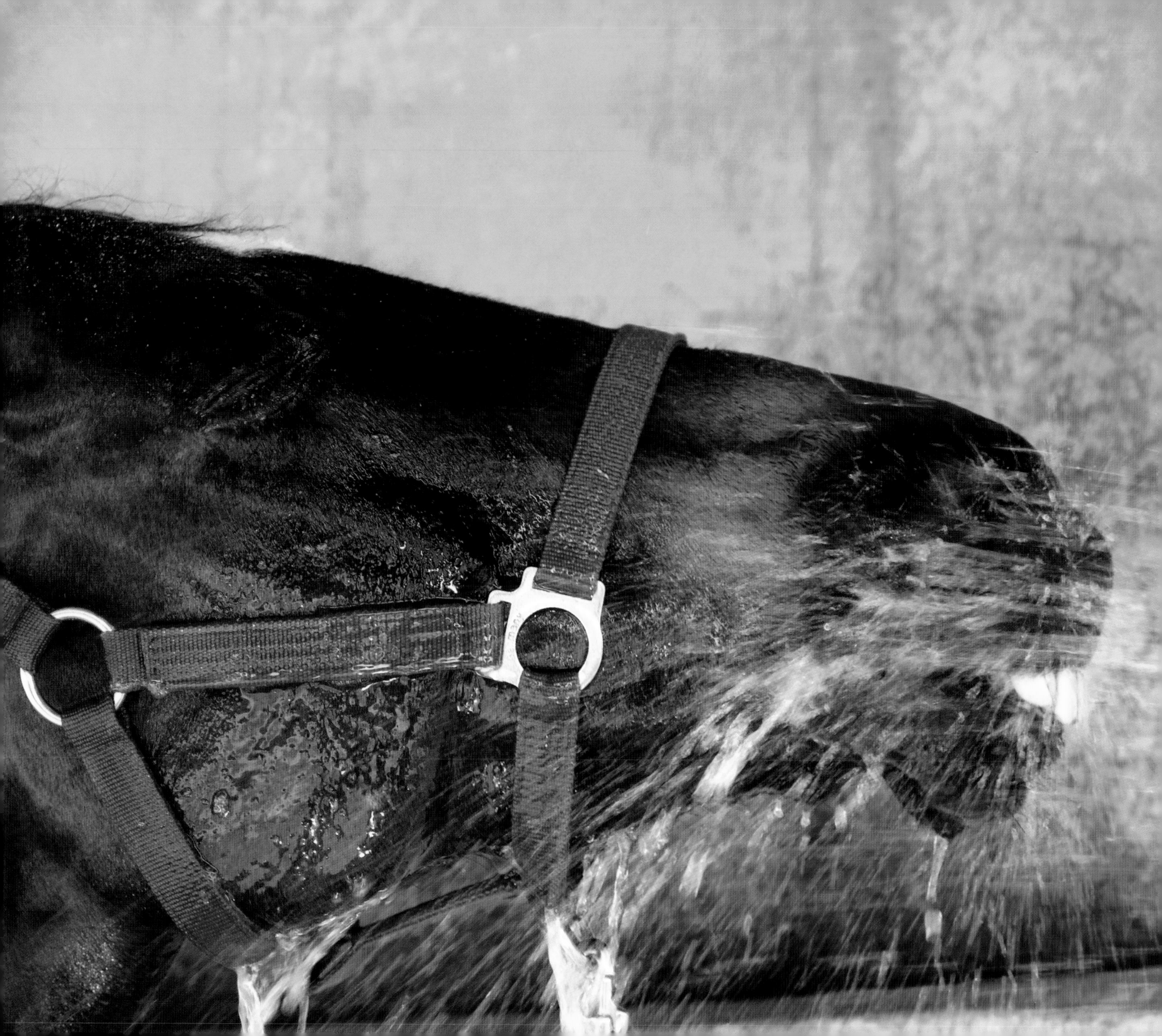

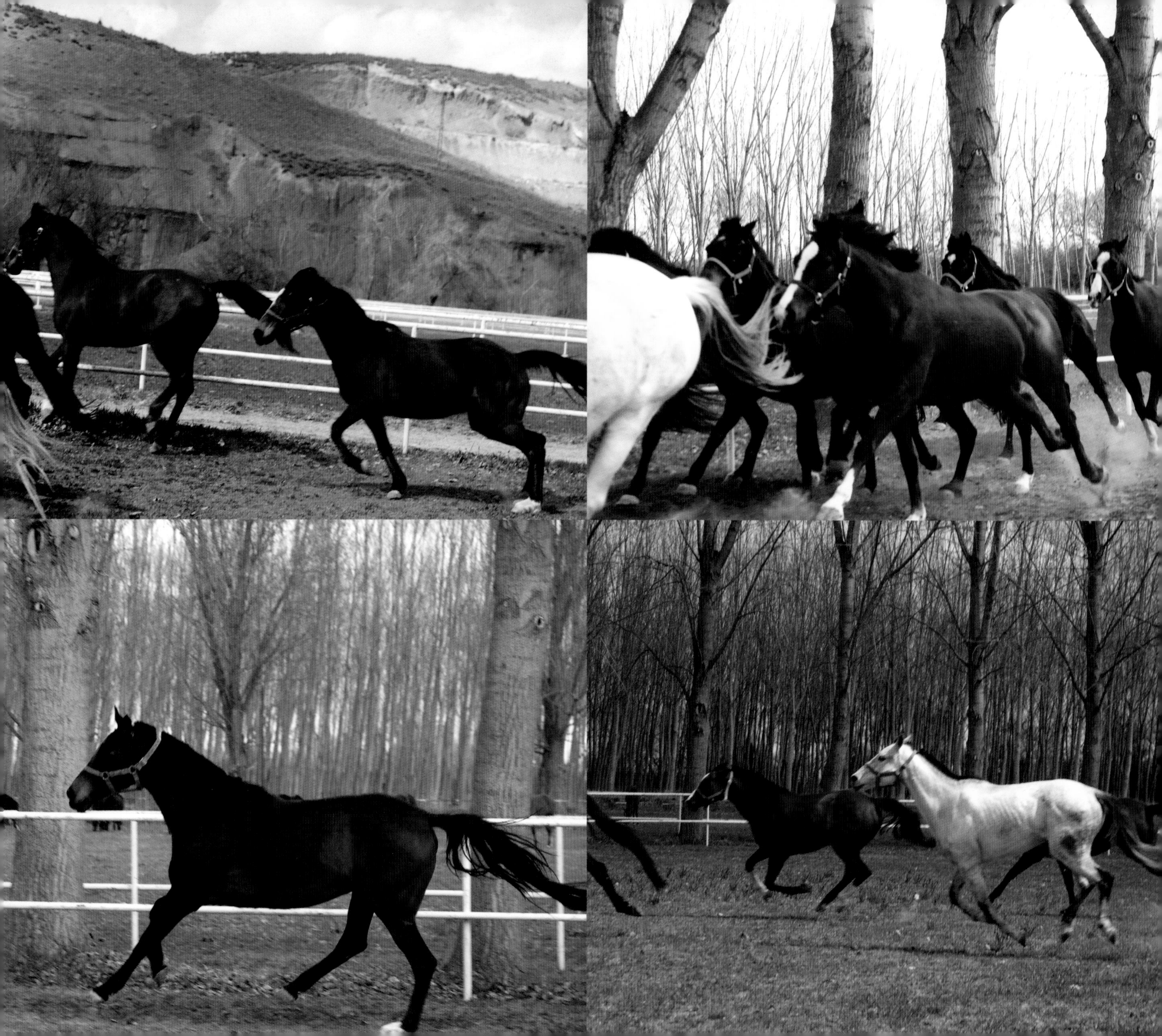

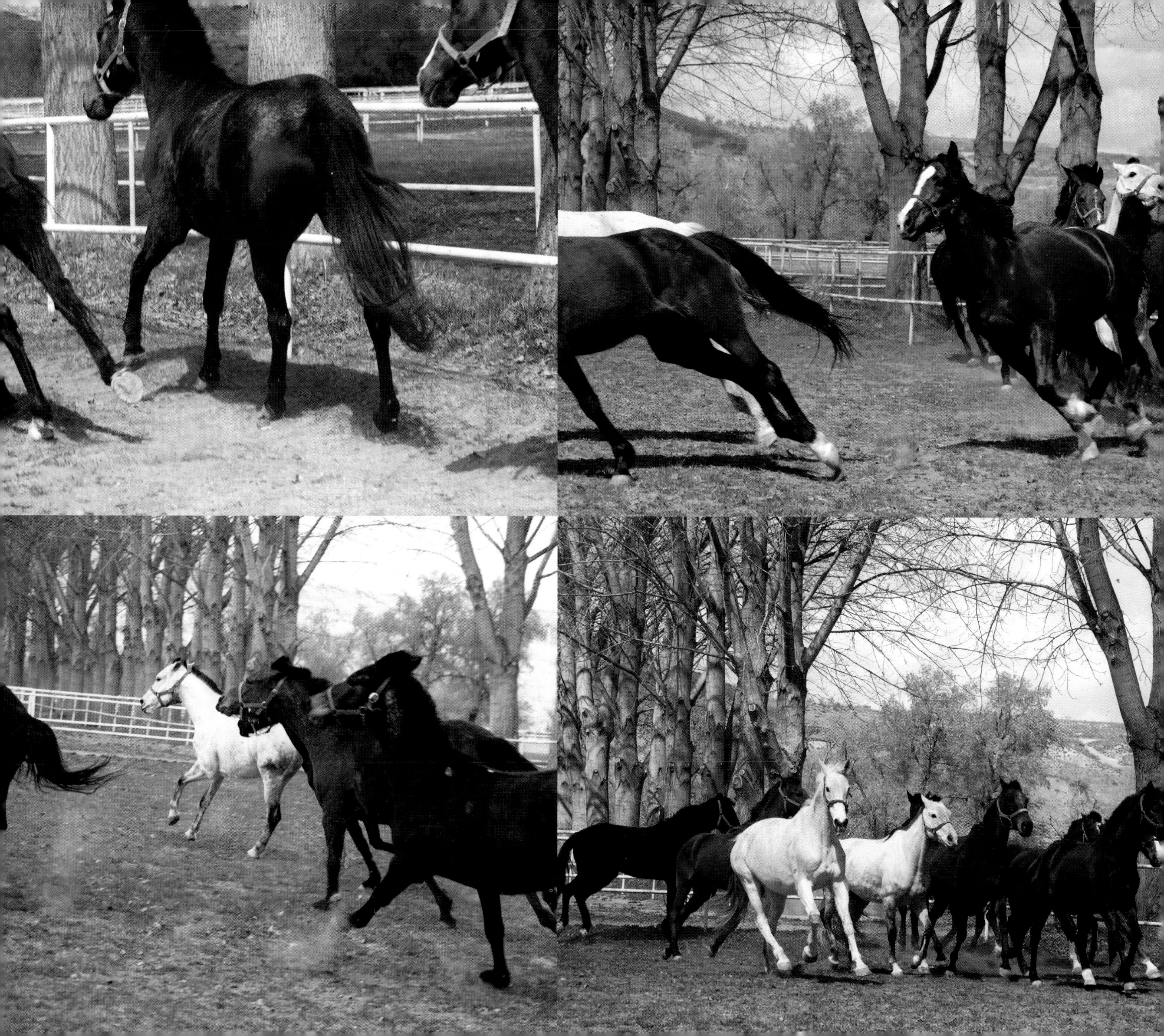

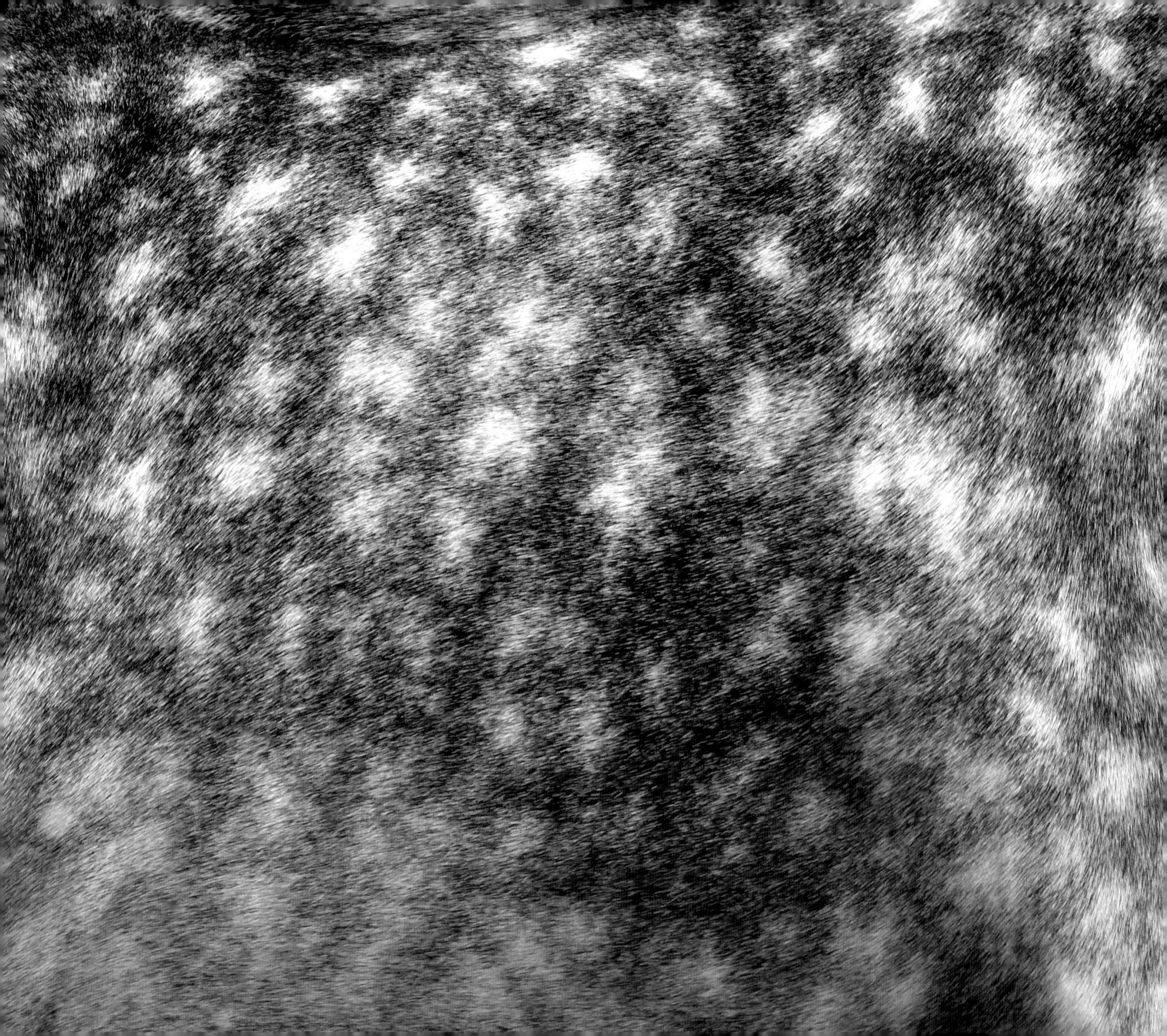

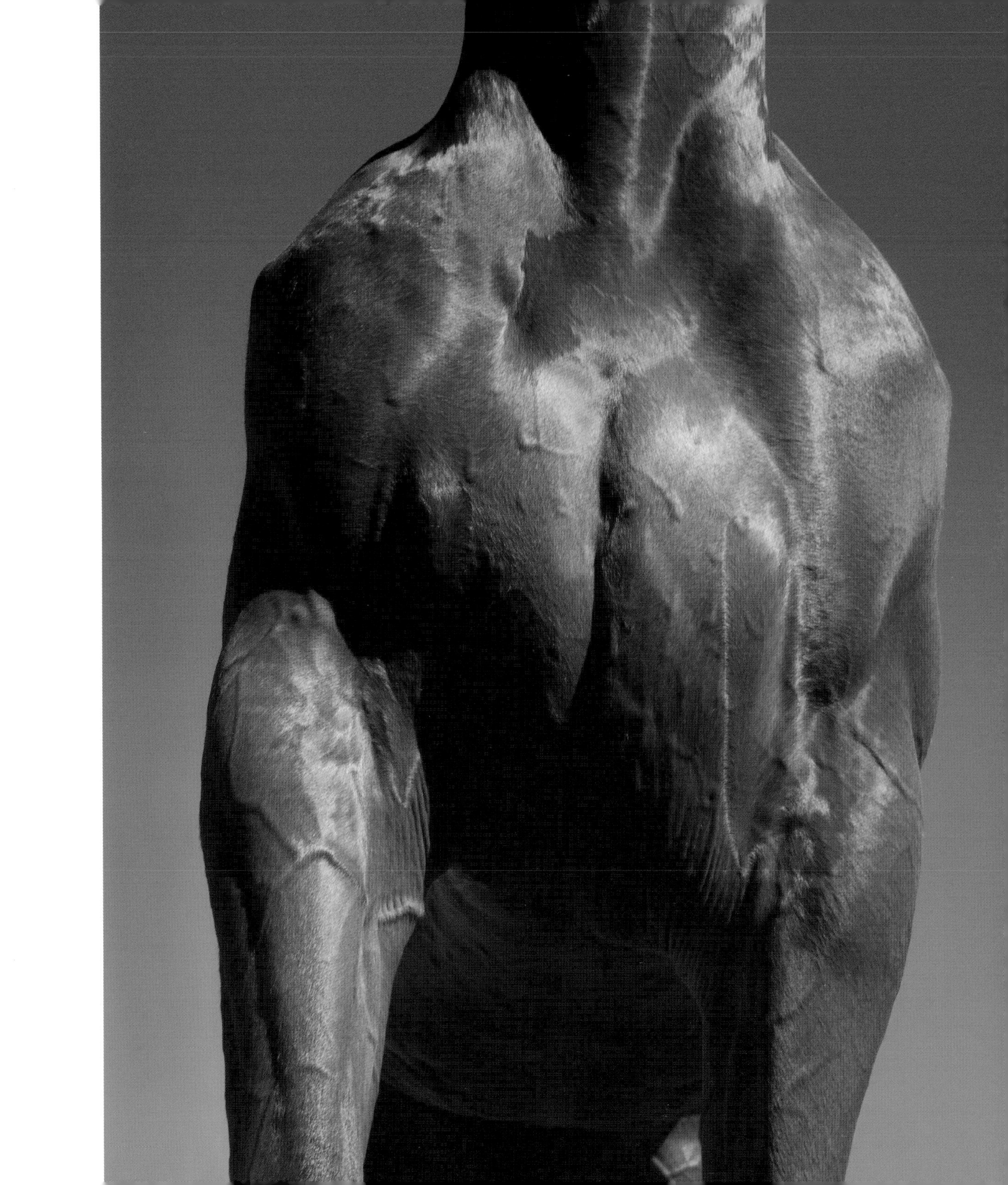

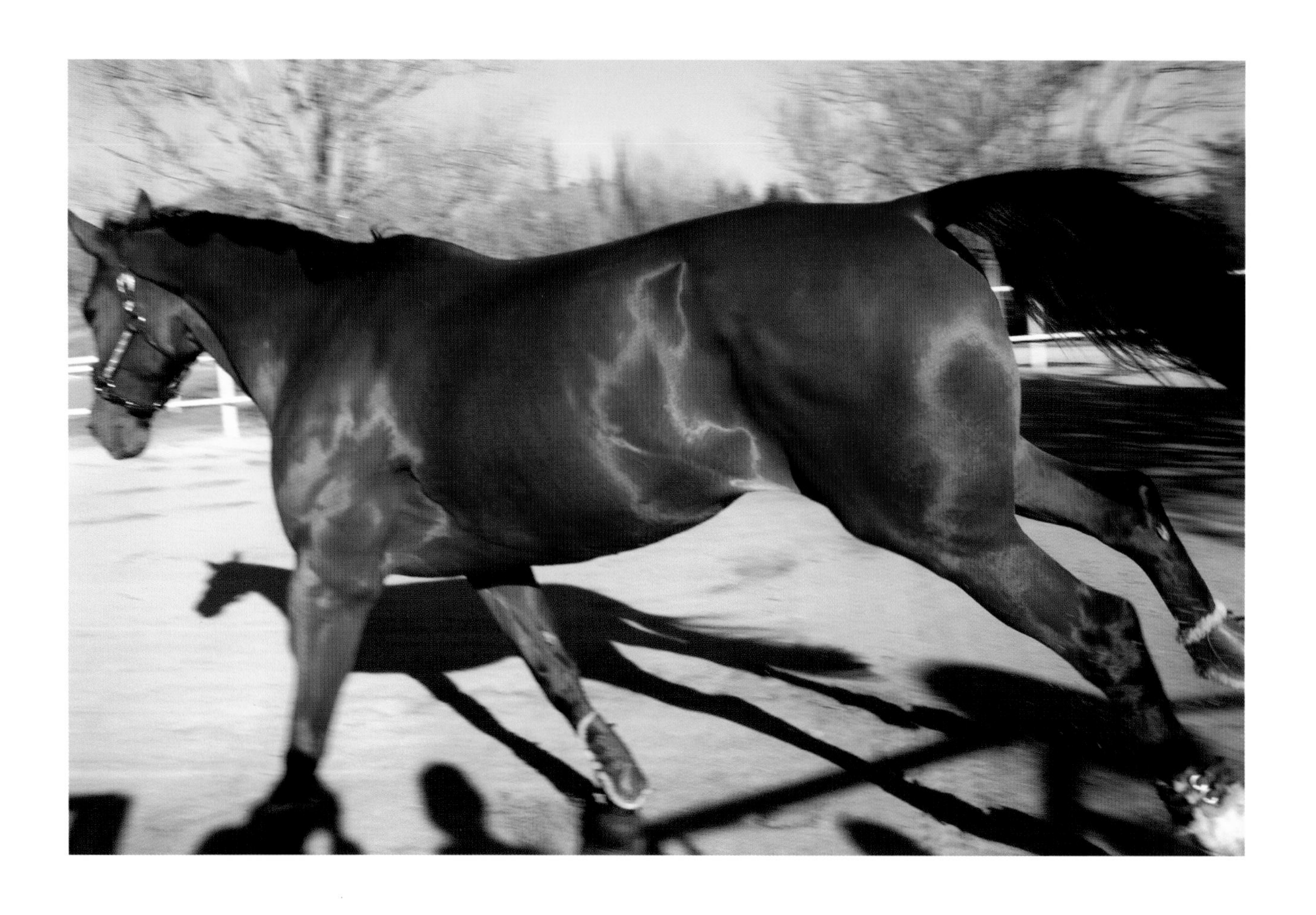

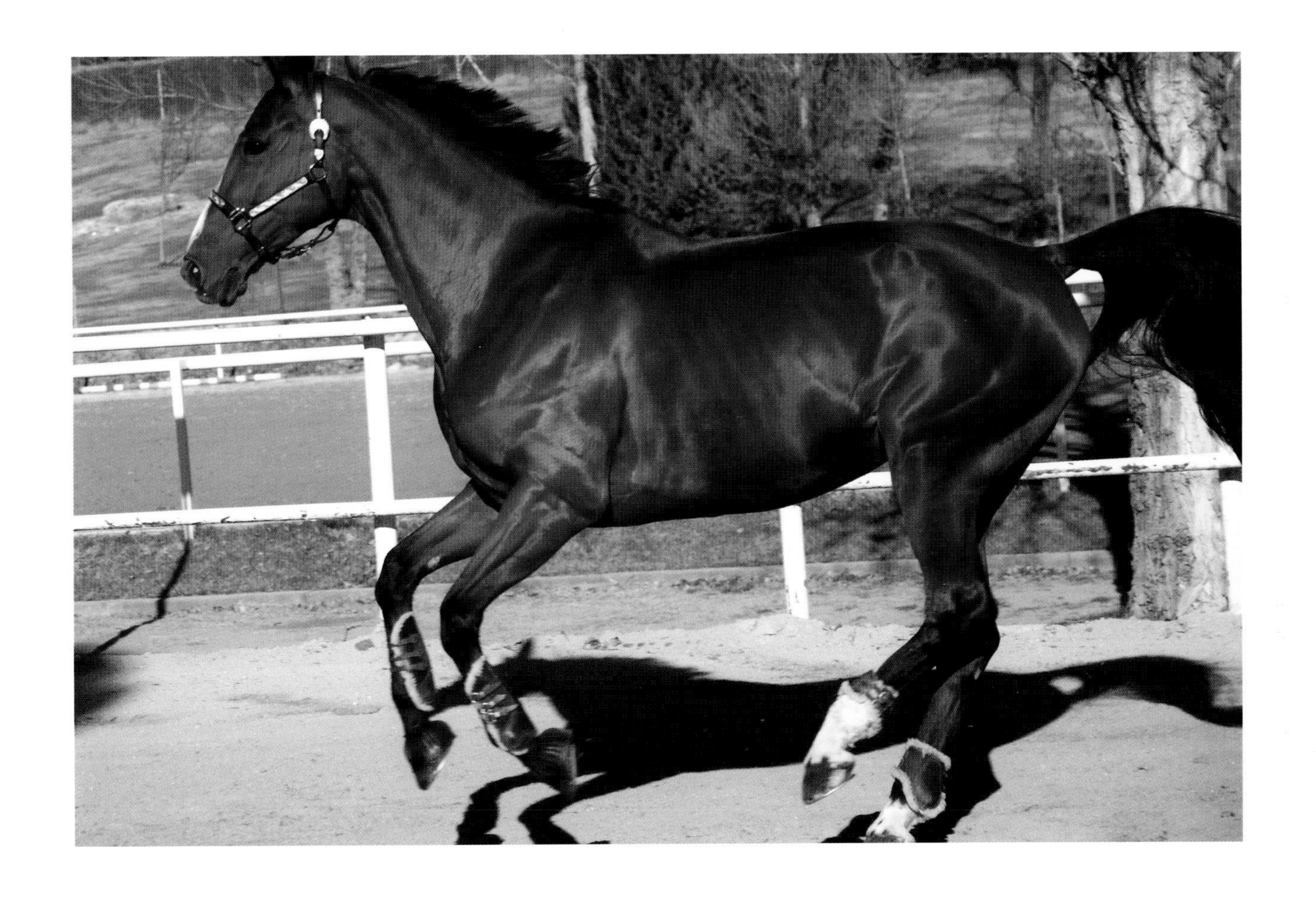

P115

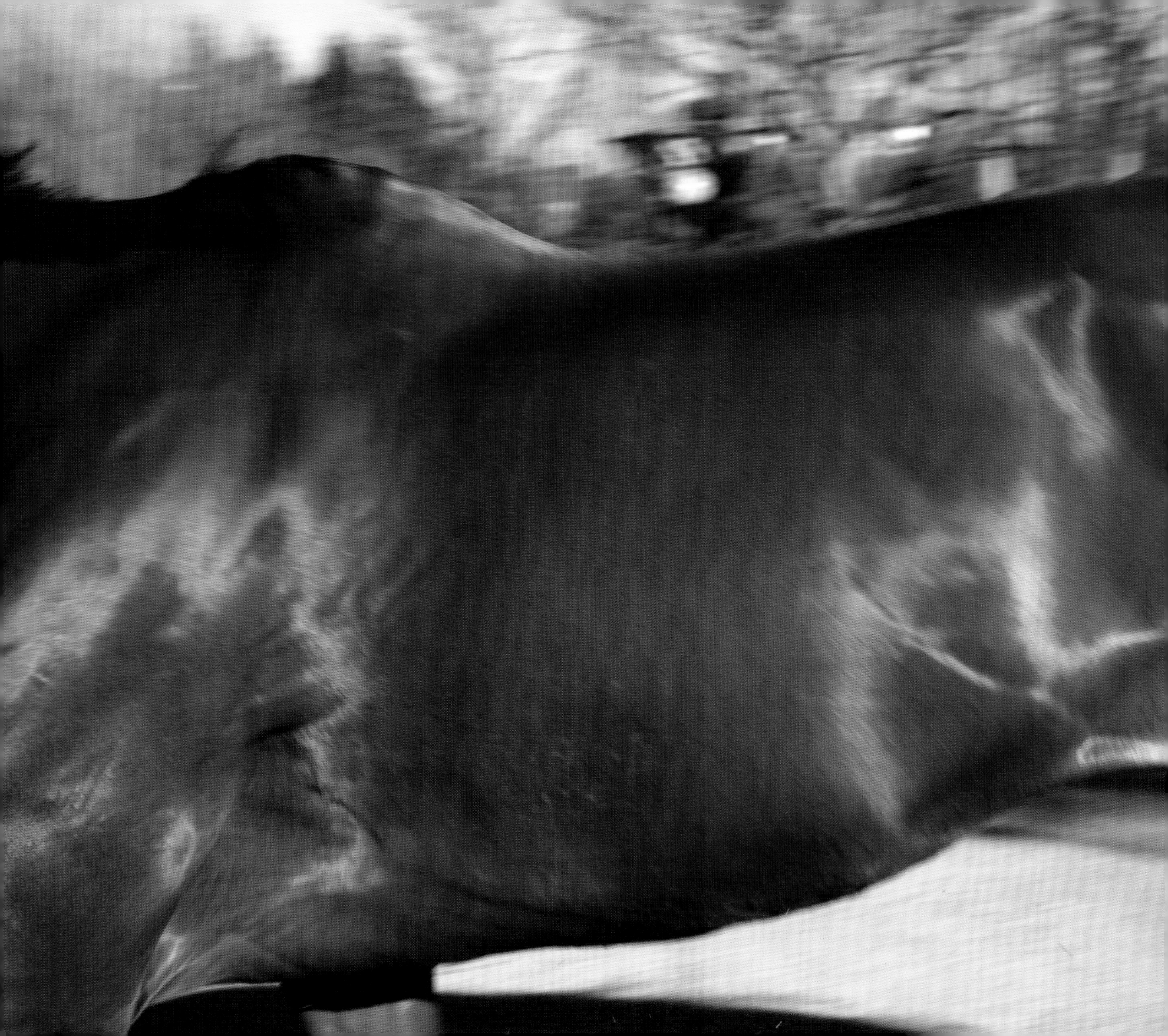

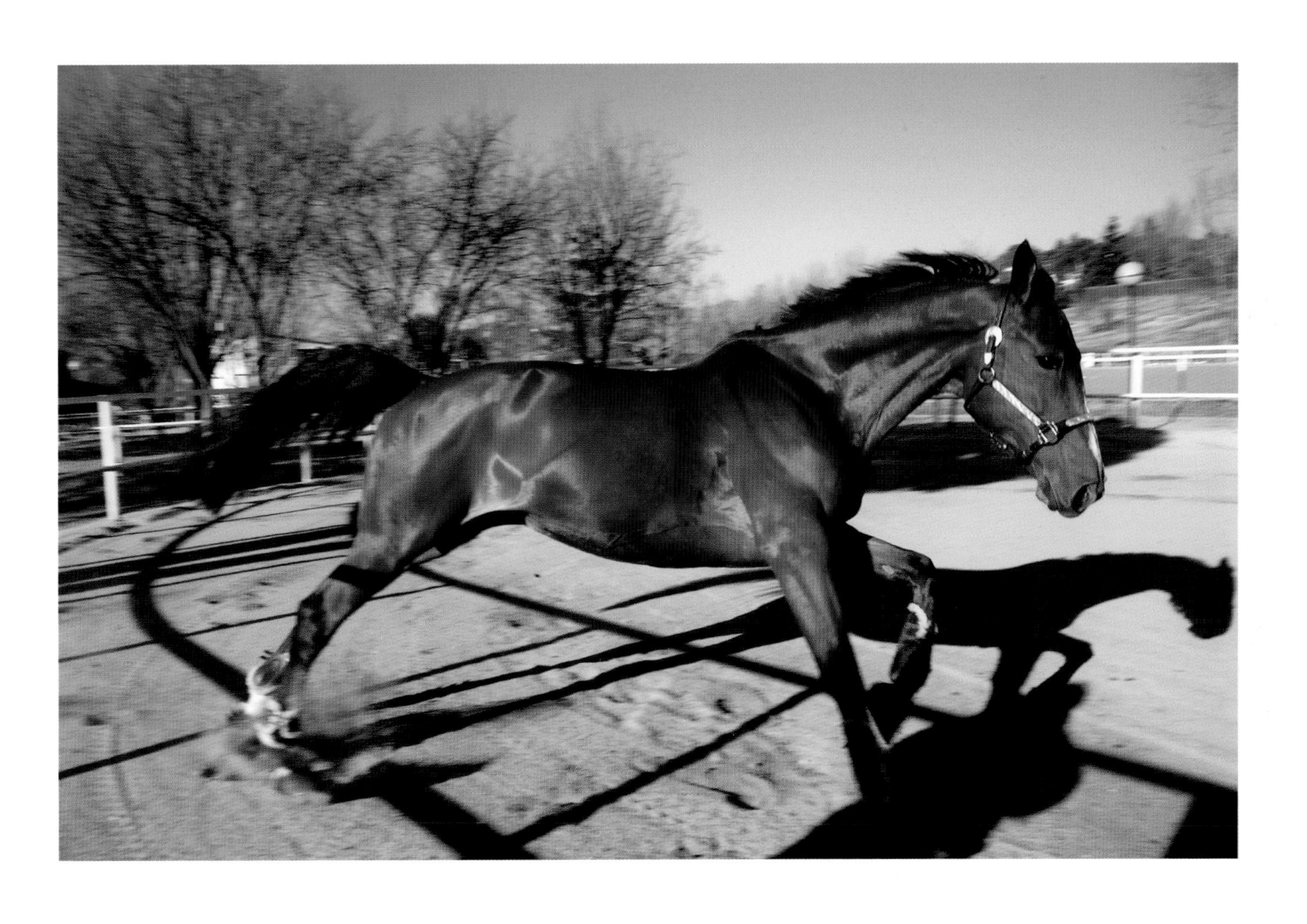

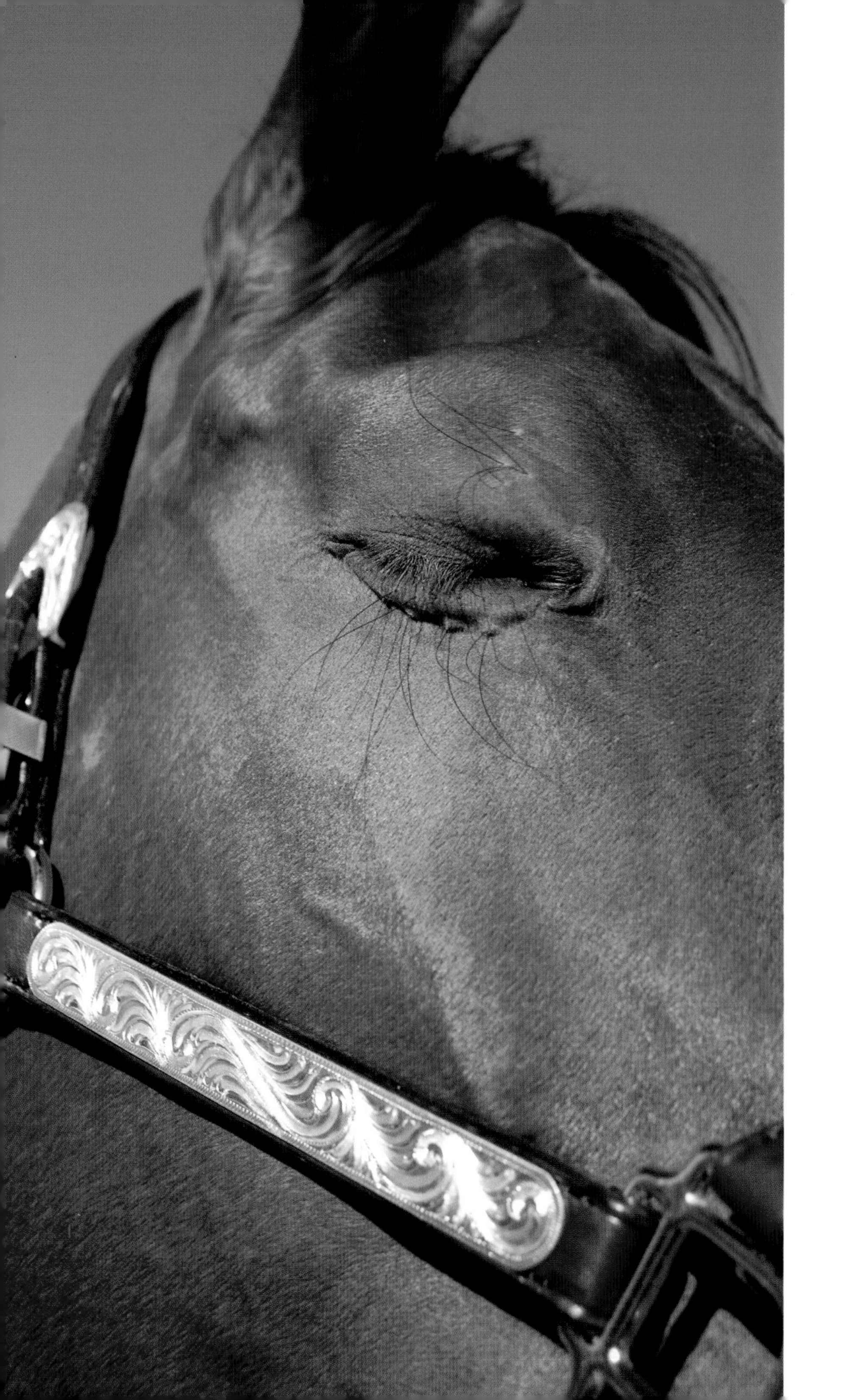

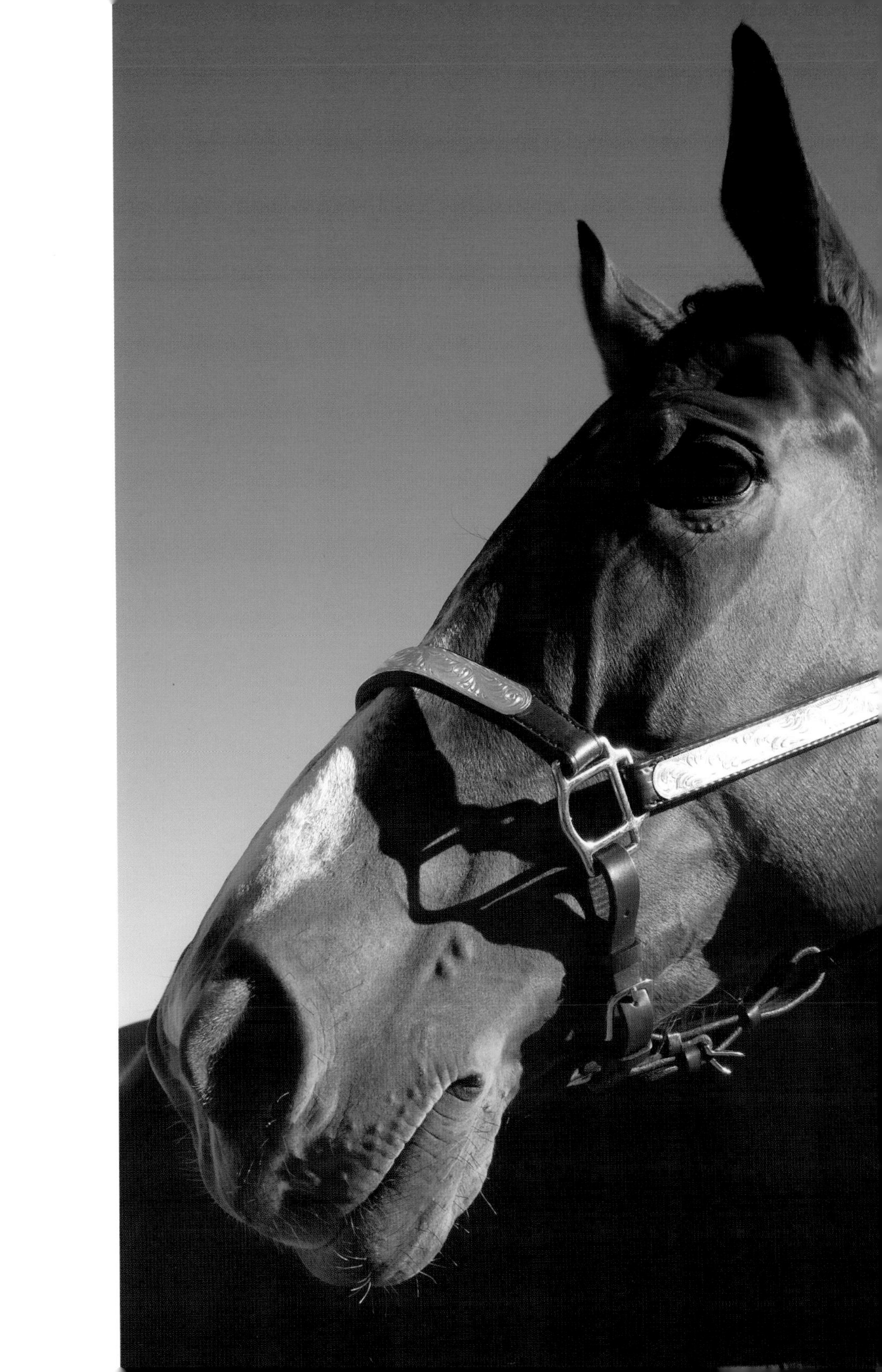

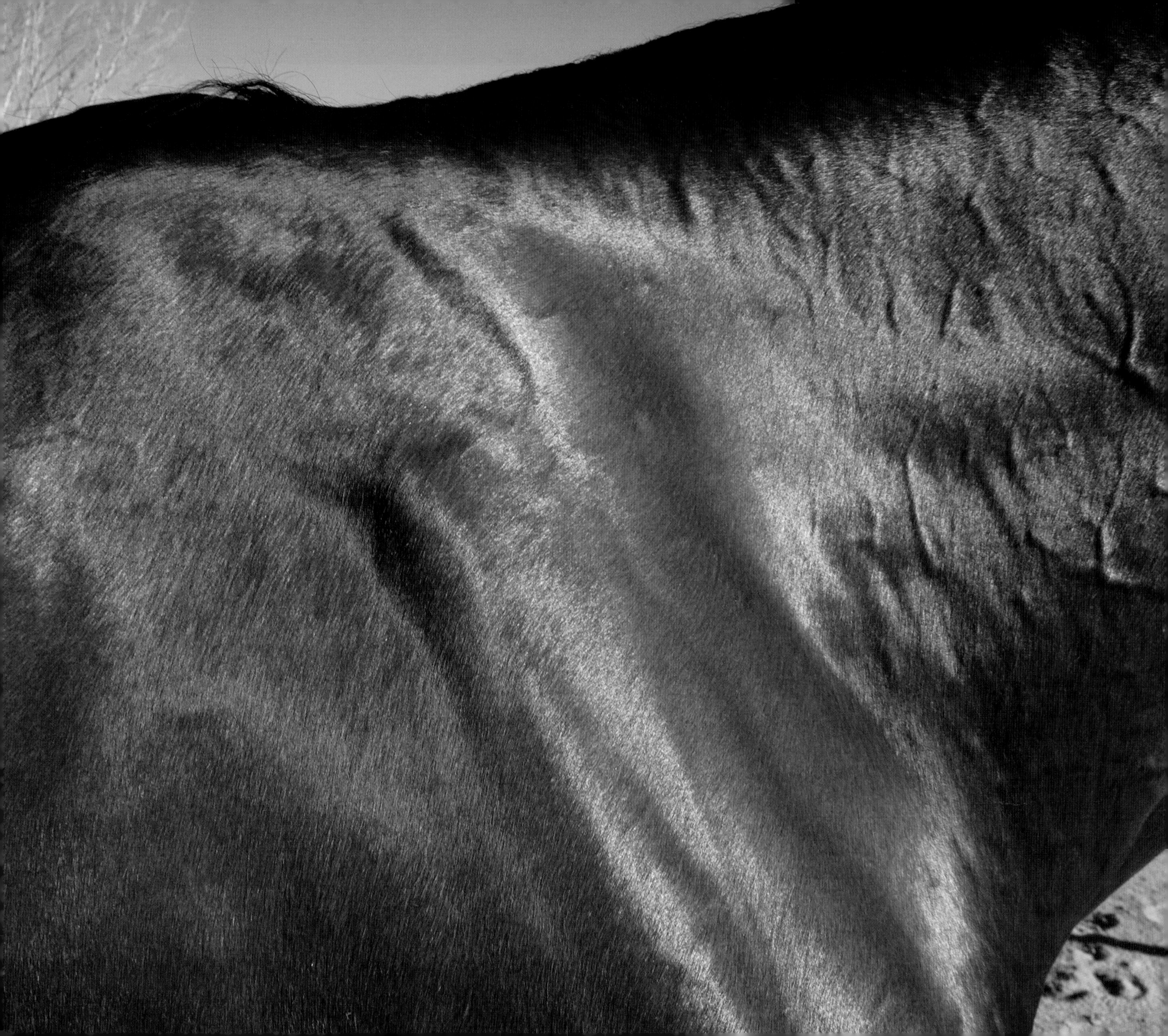

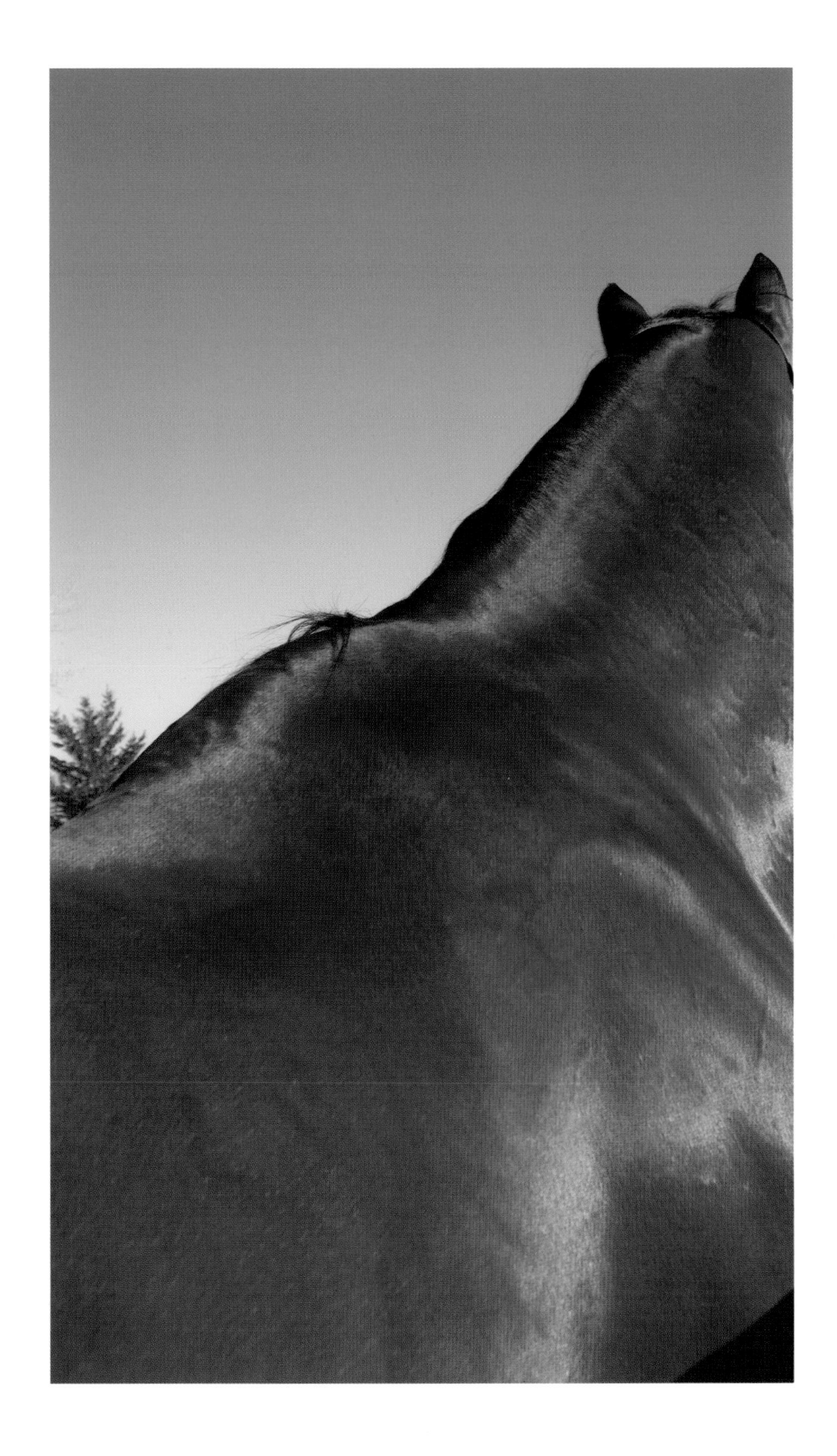

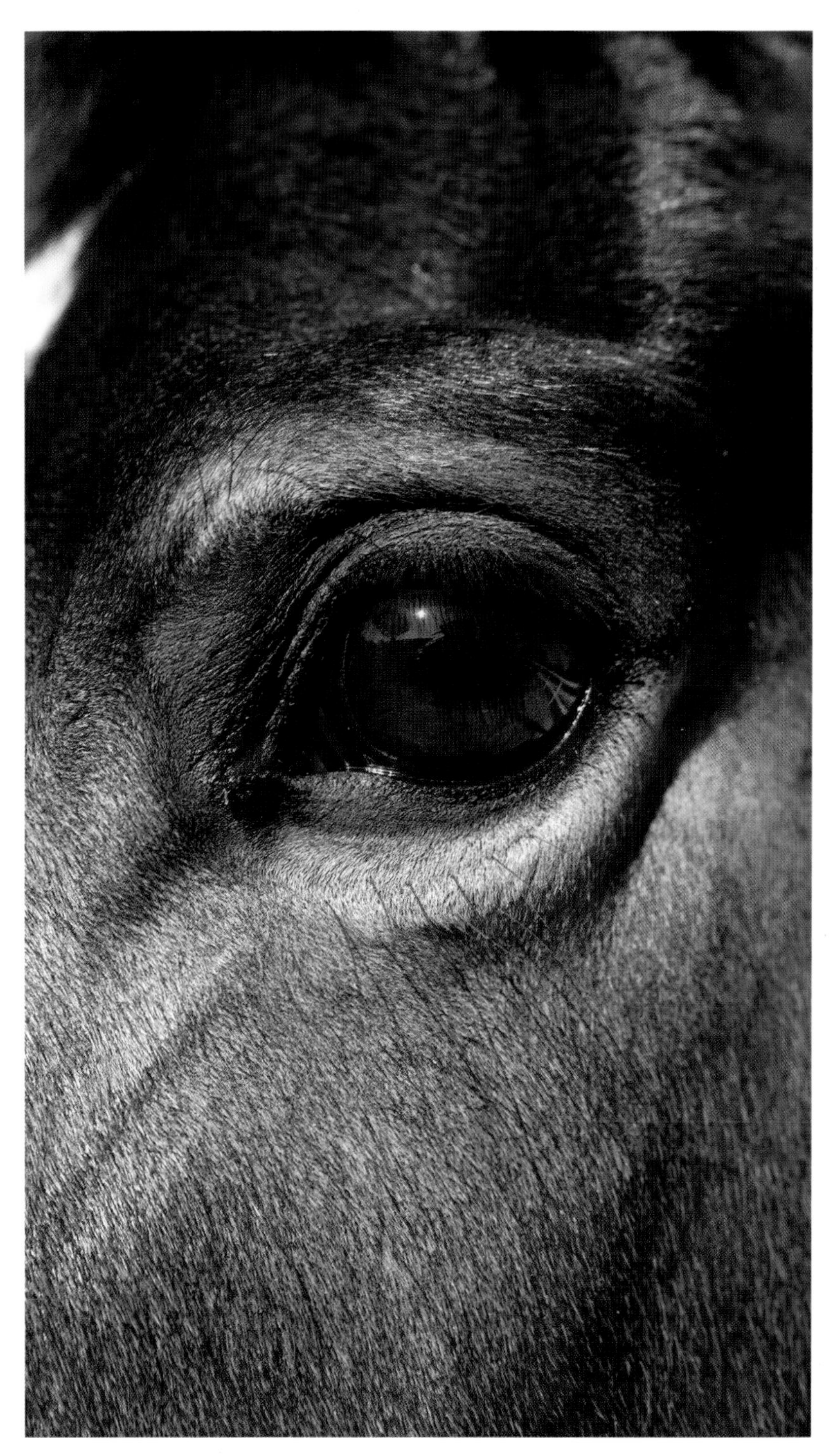

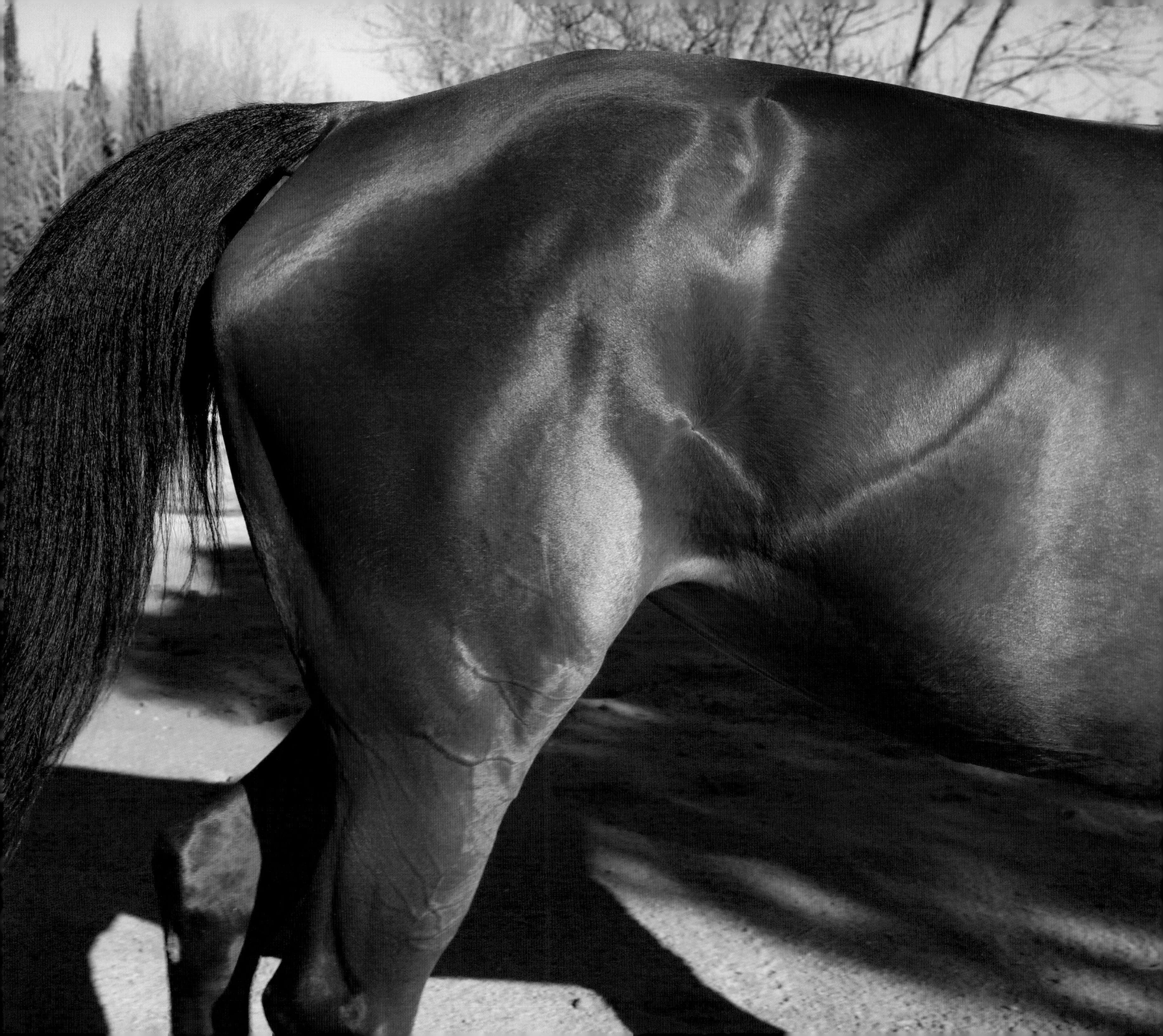

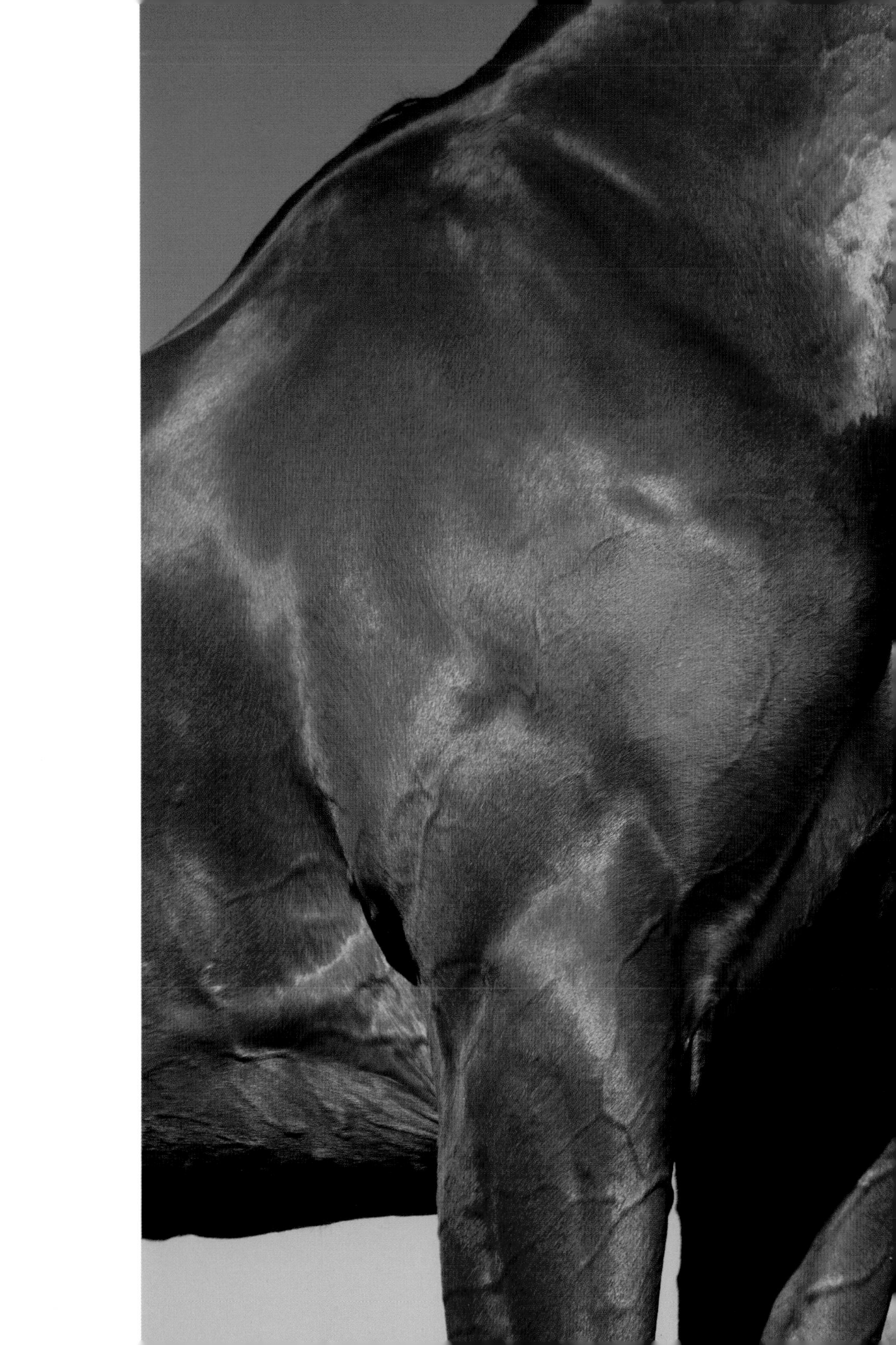

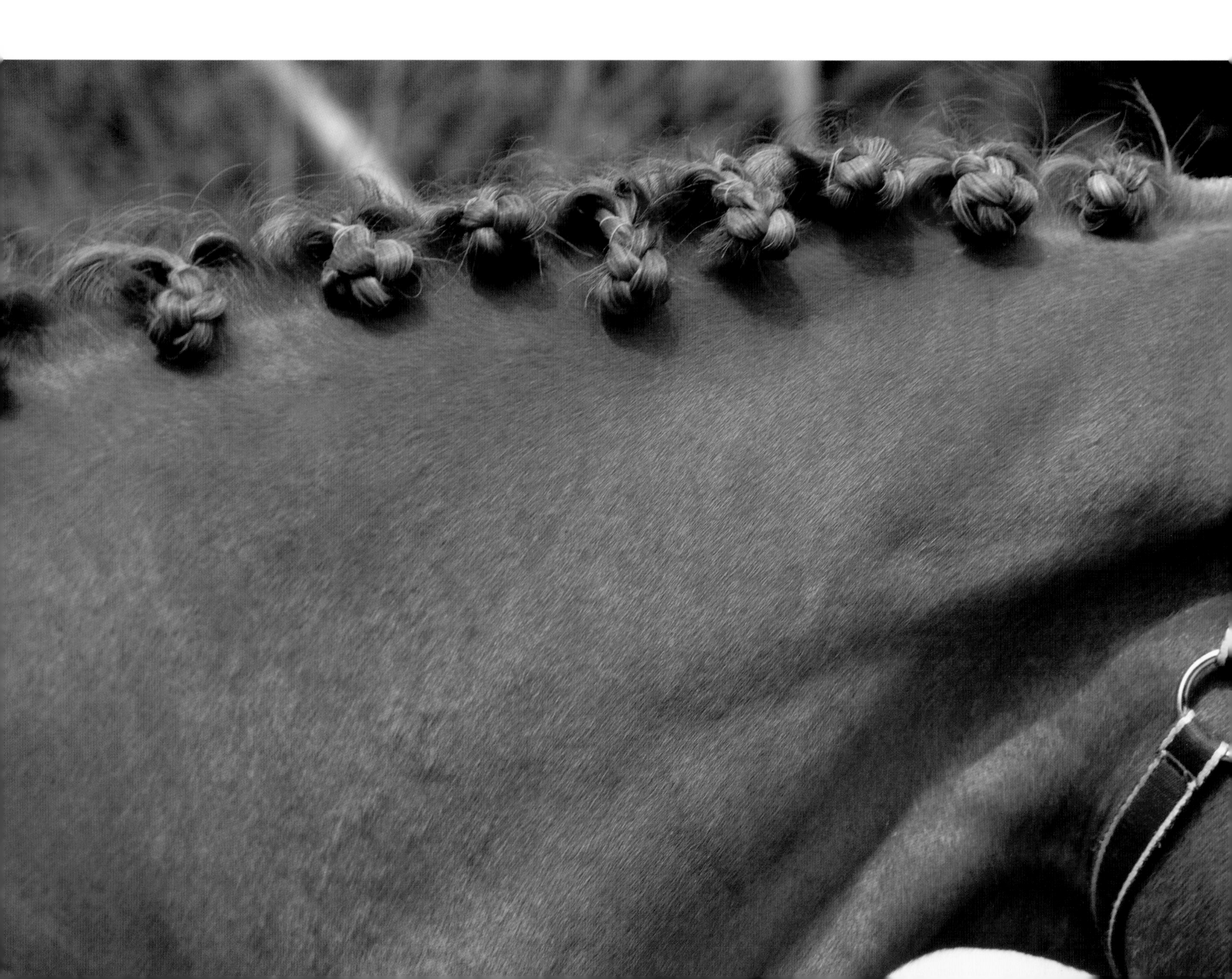

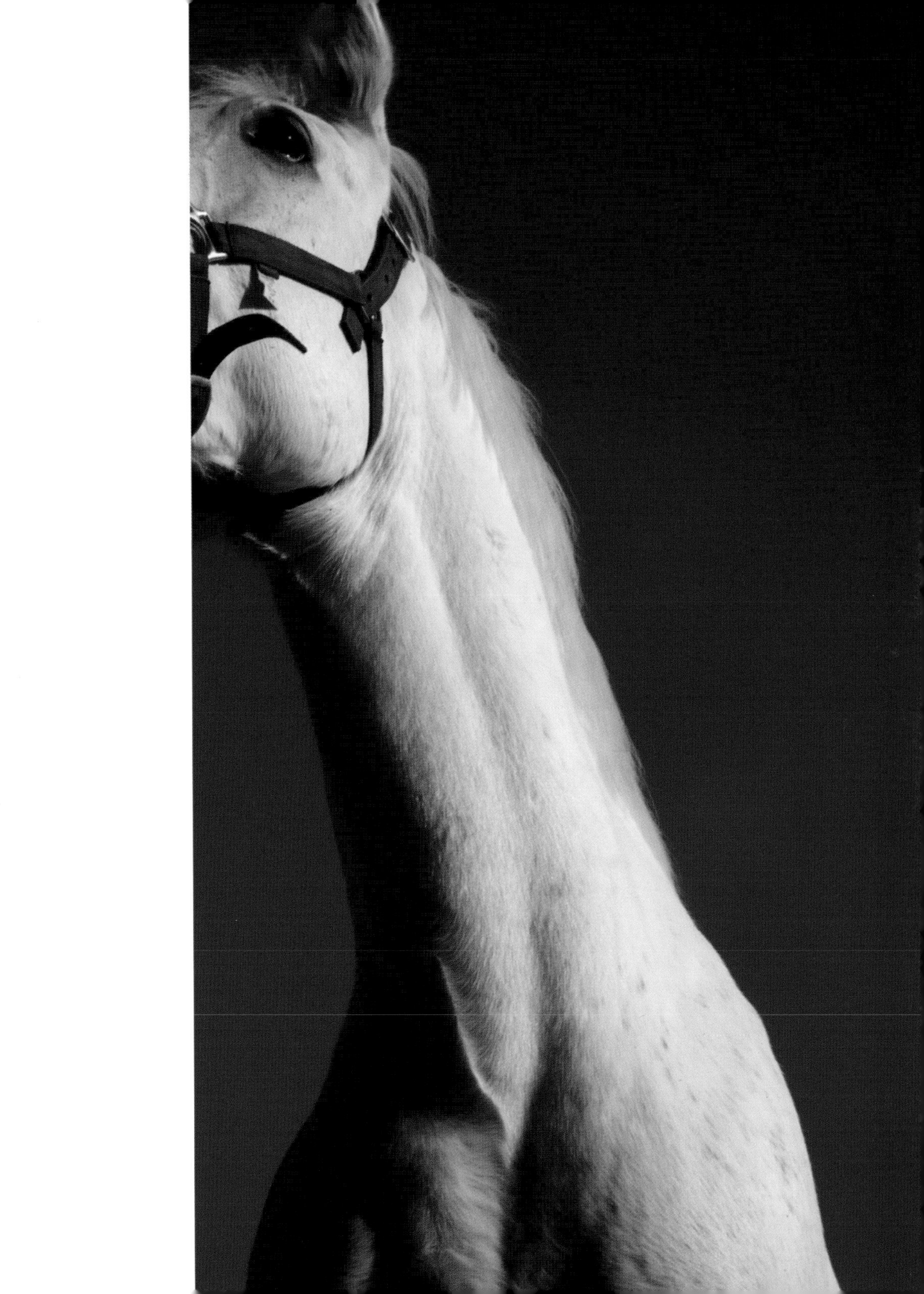

P126

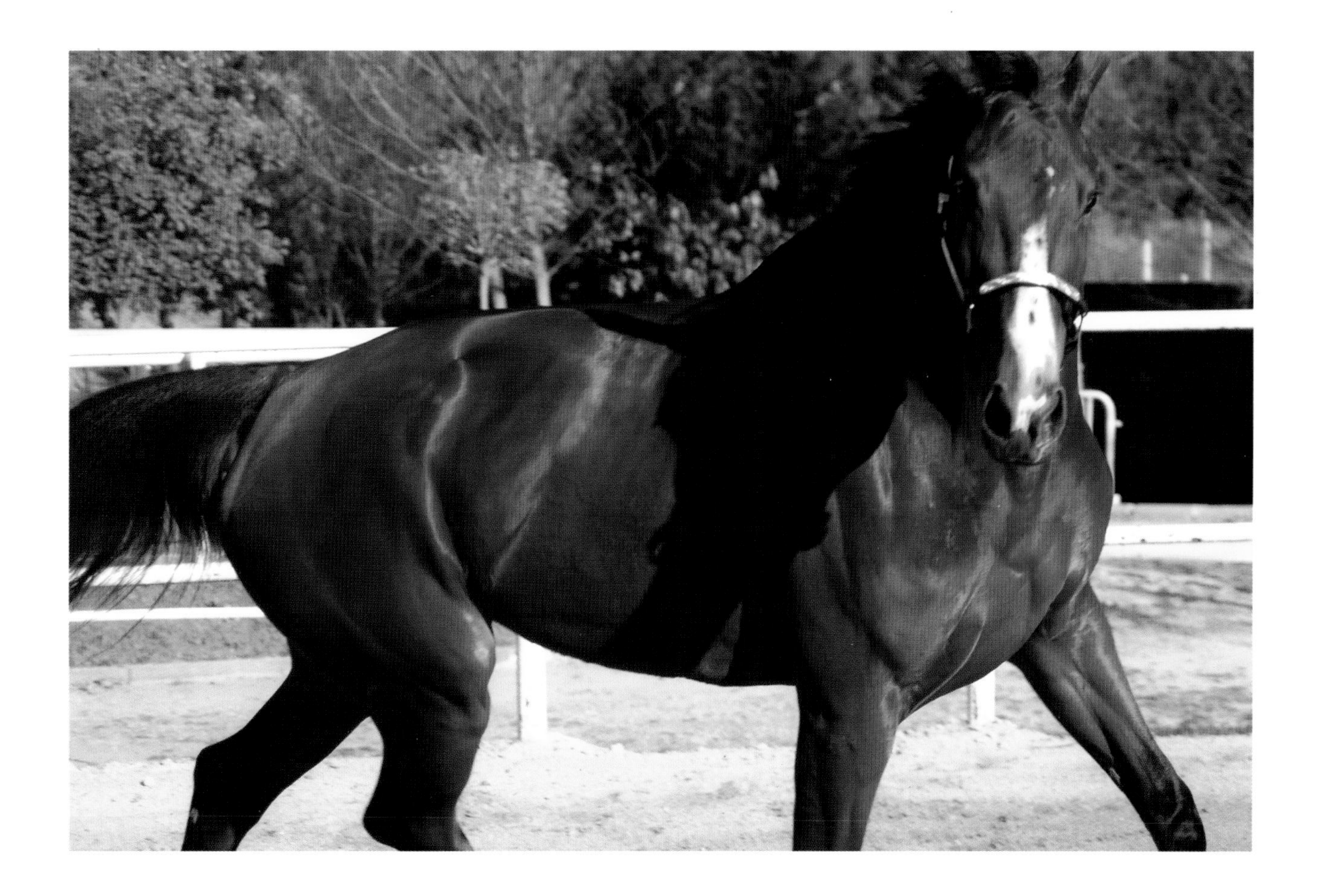

P127

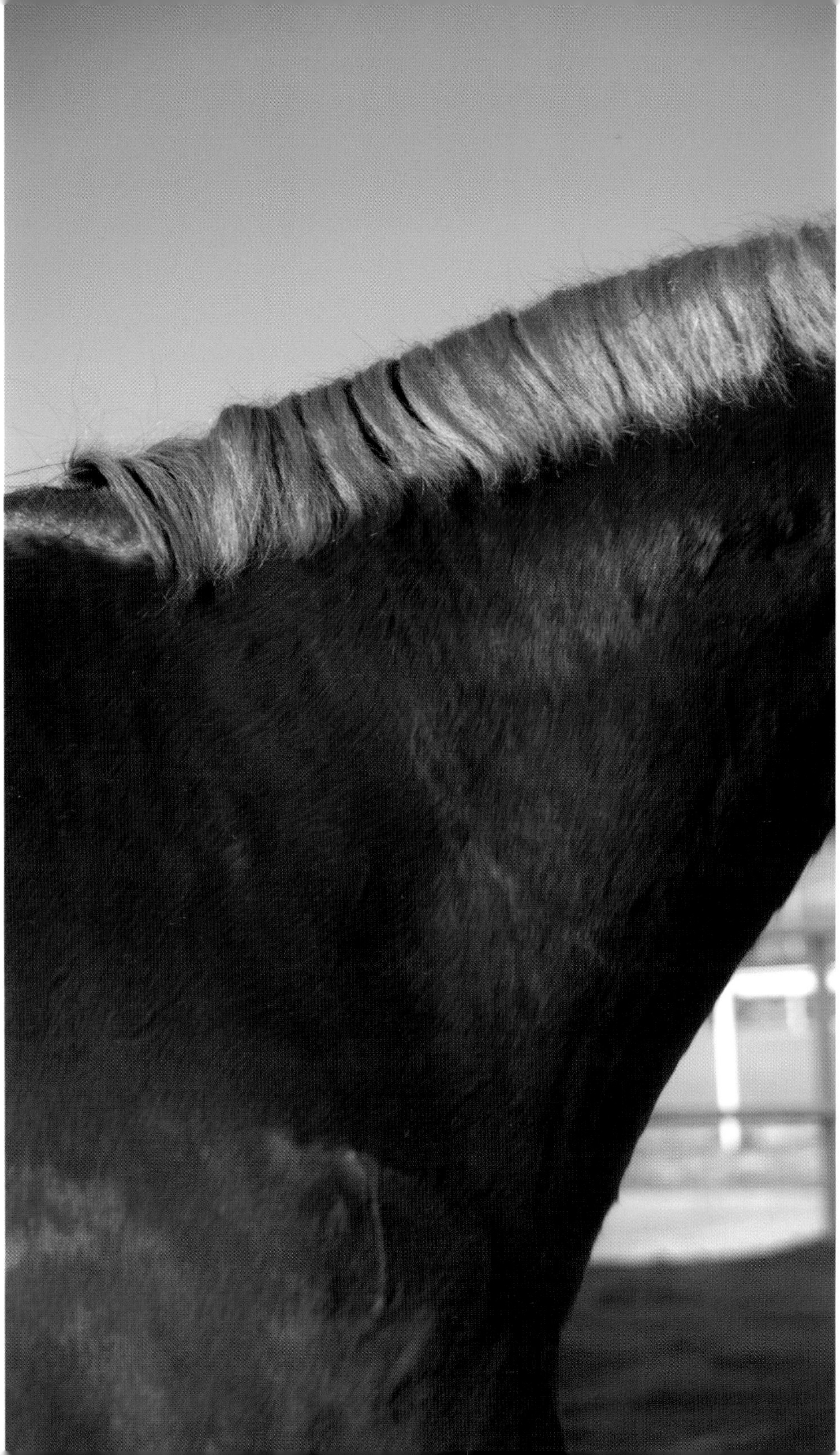

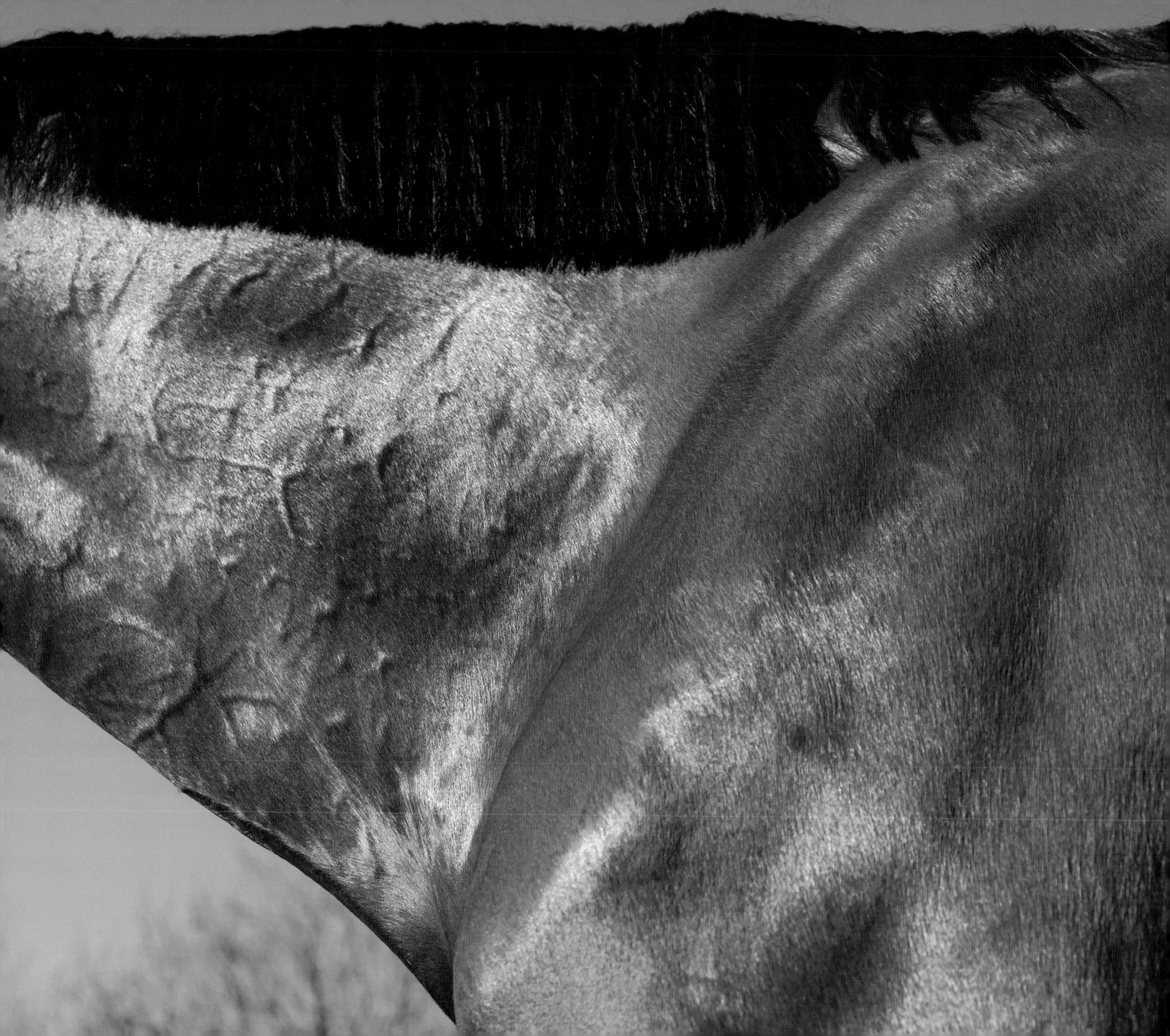

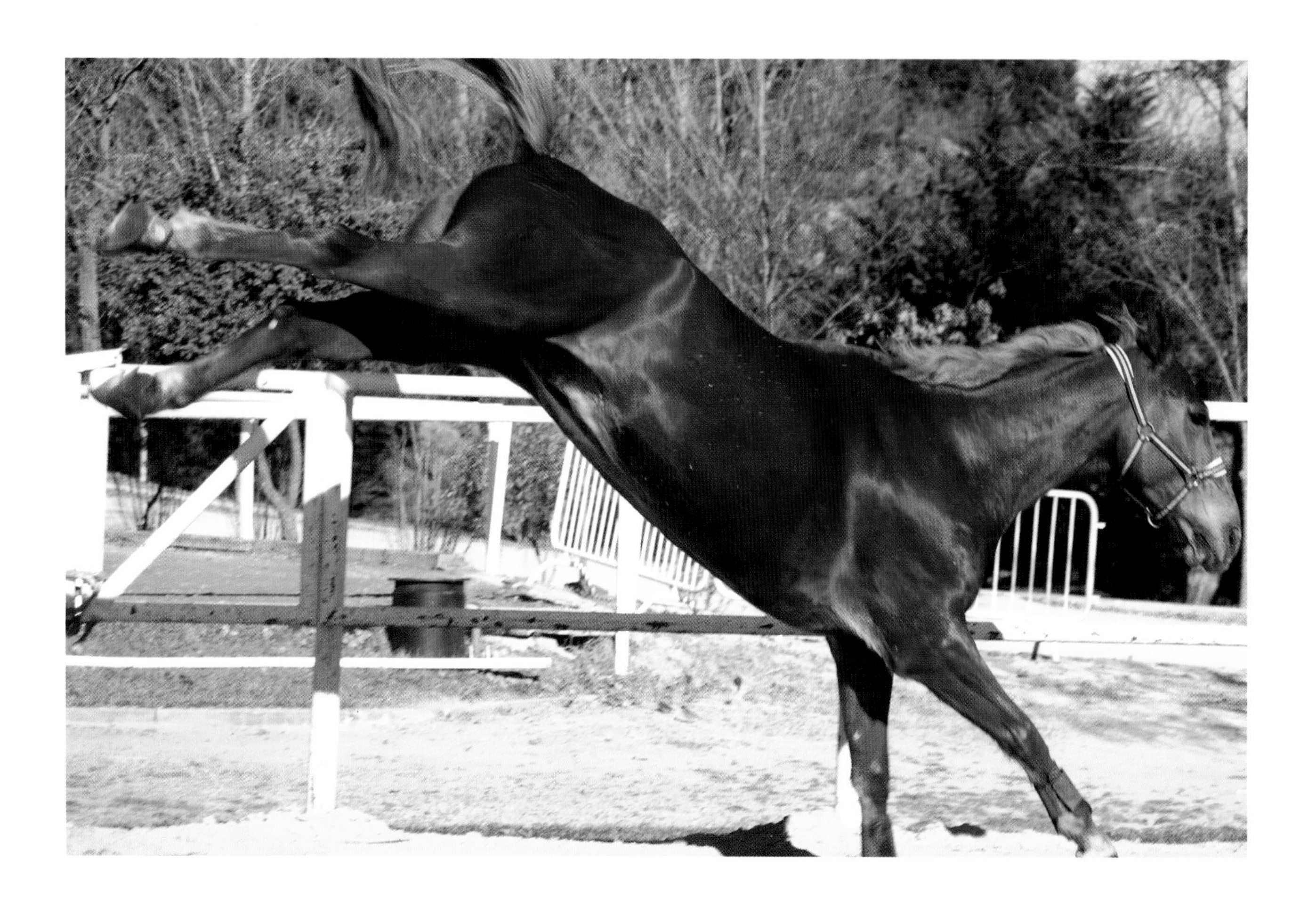

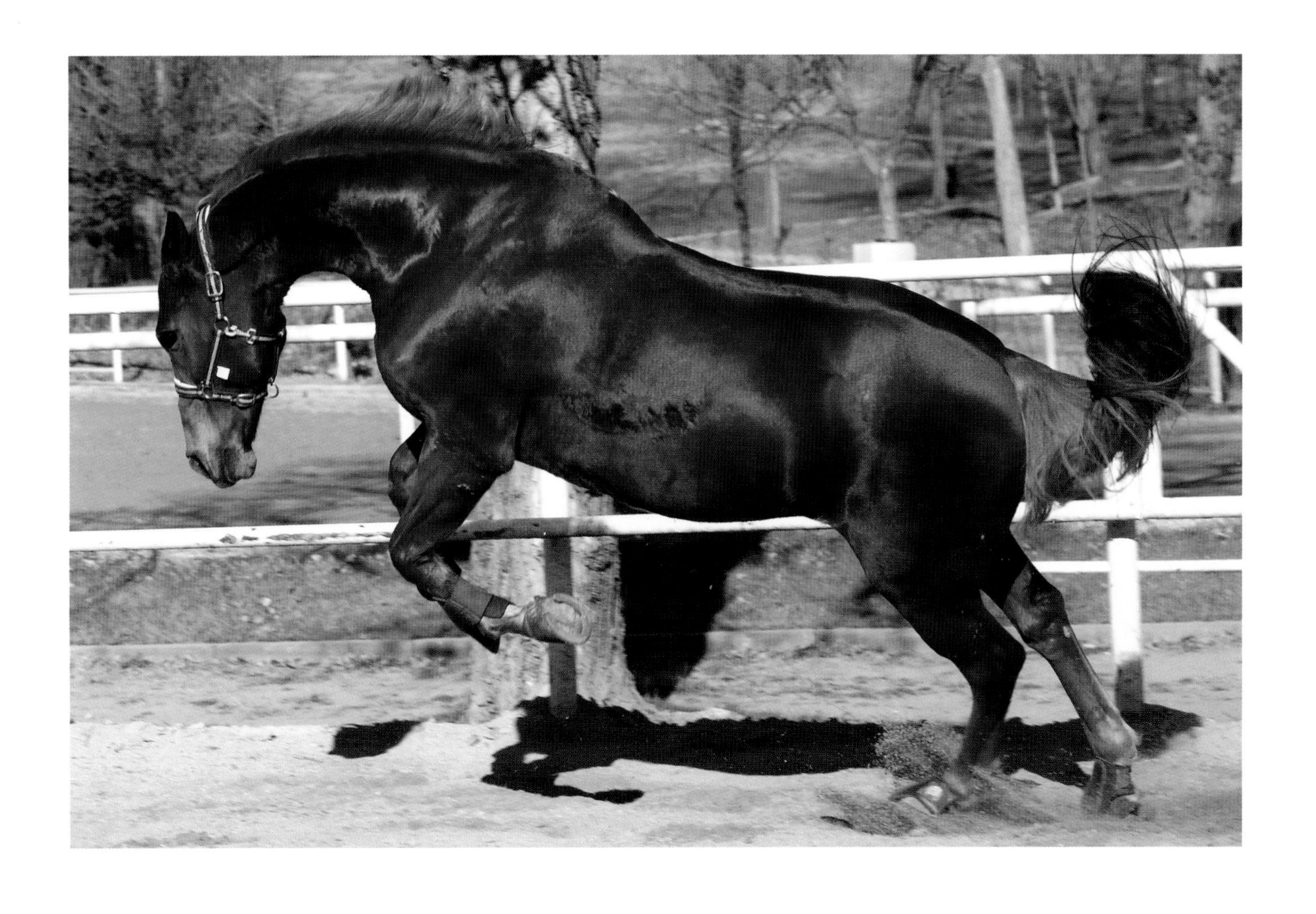

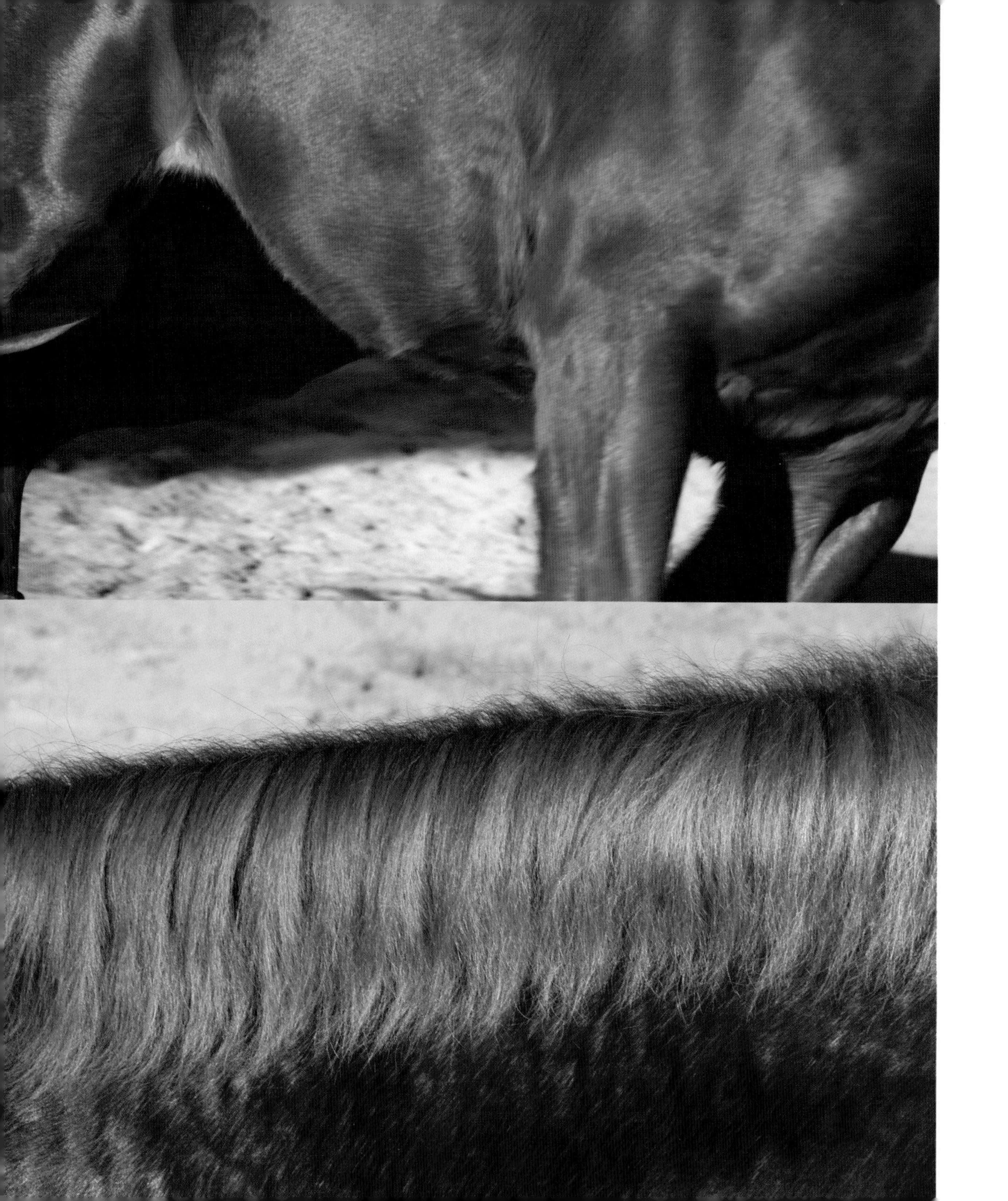

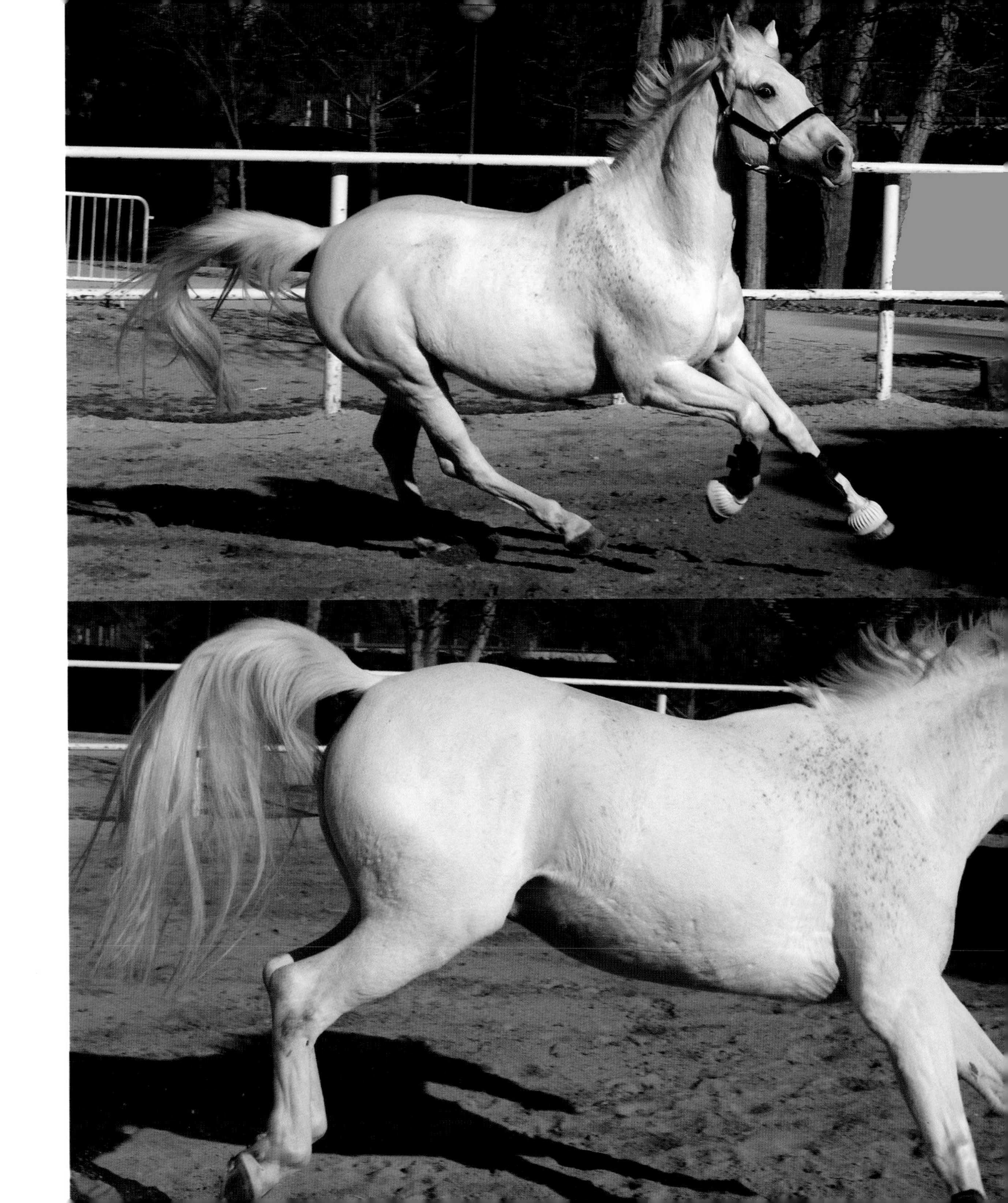

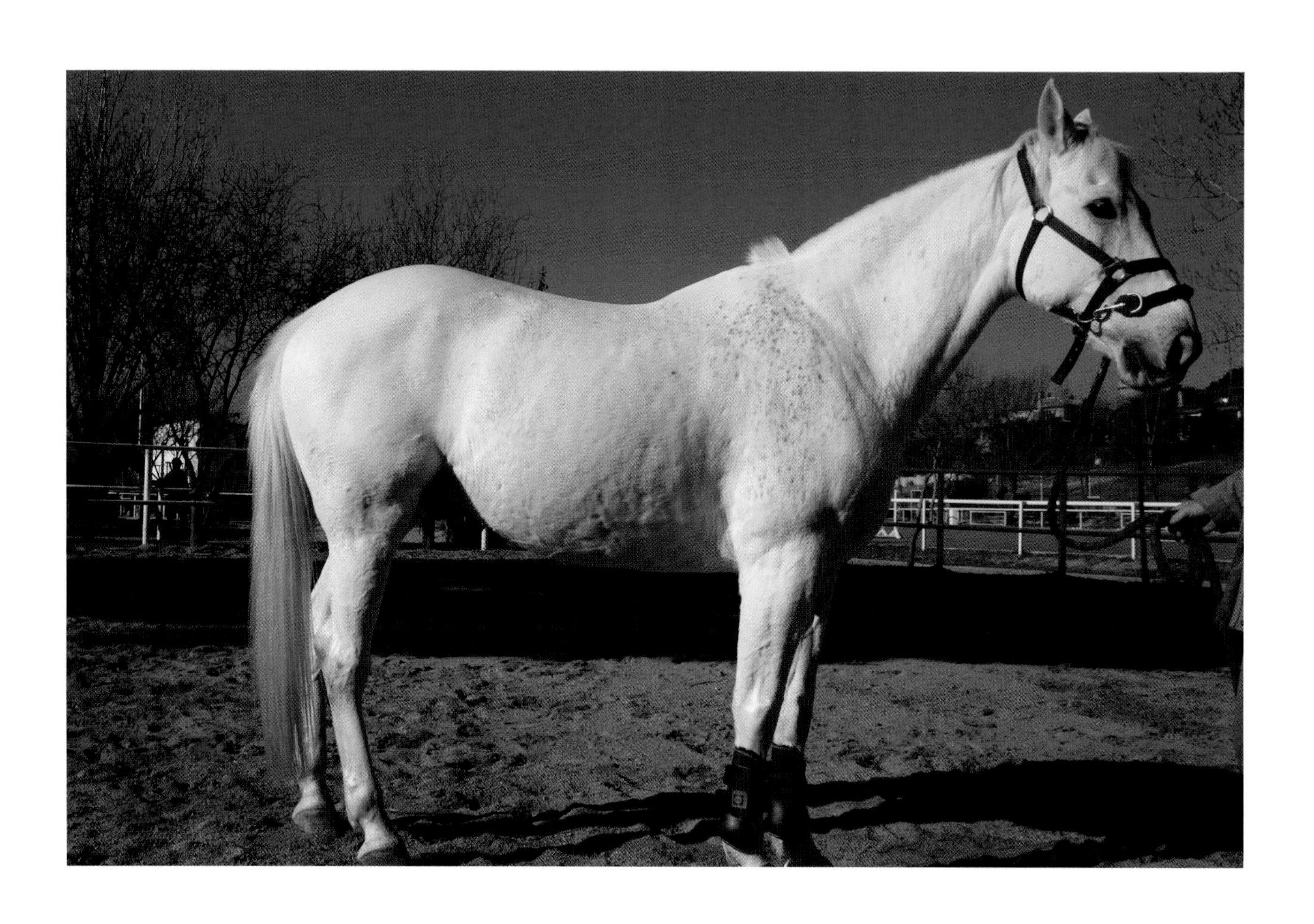

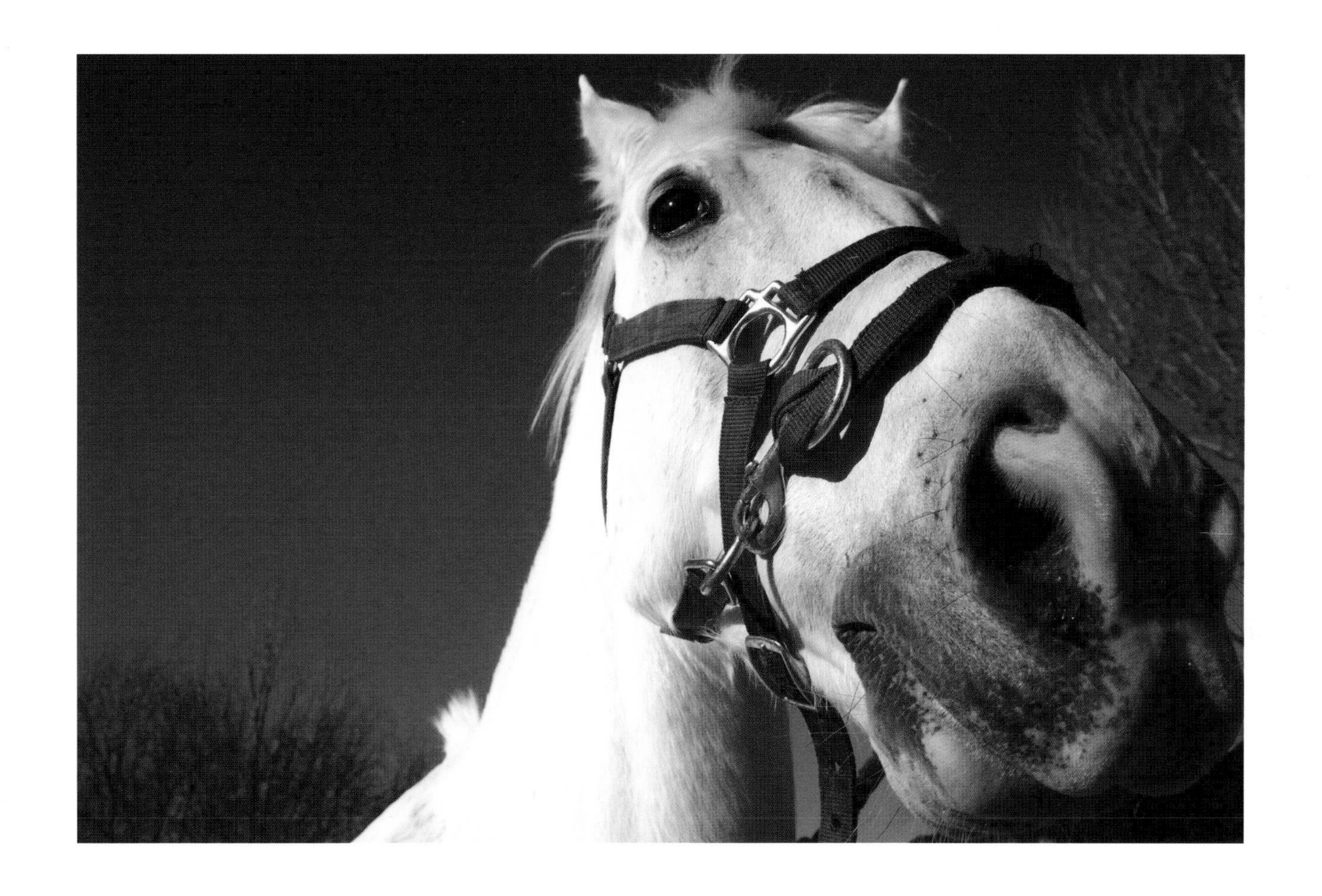

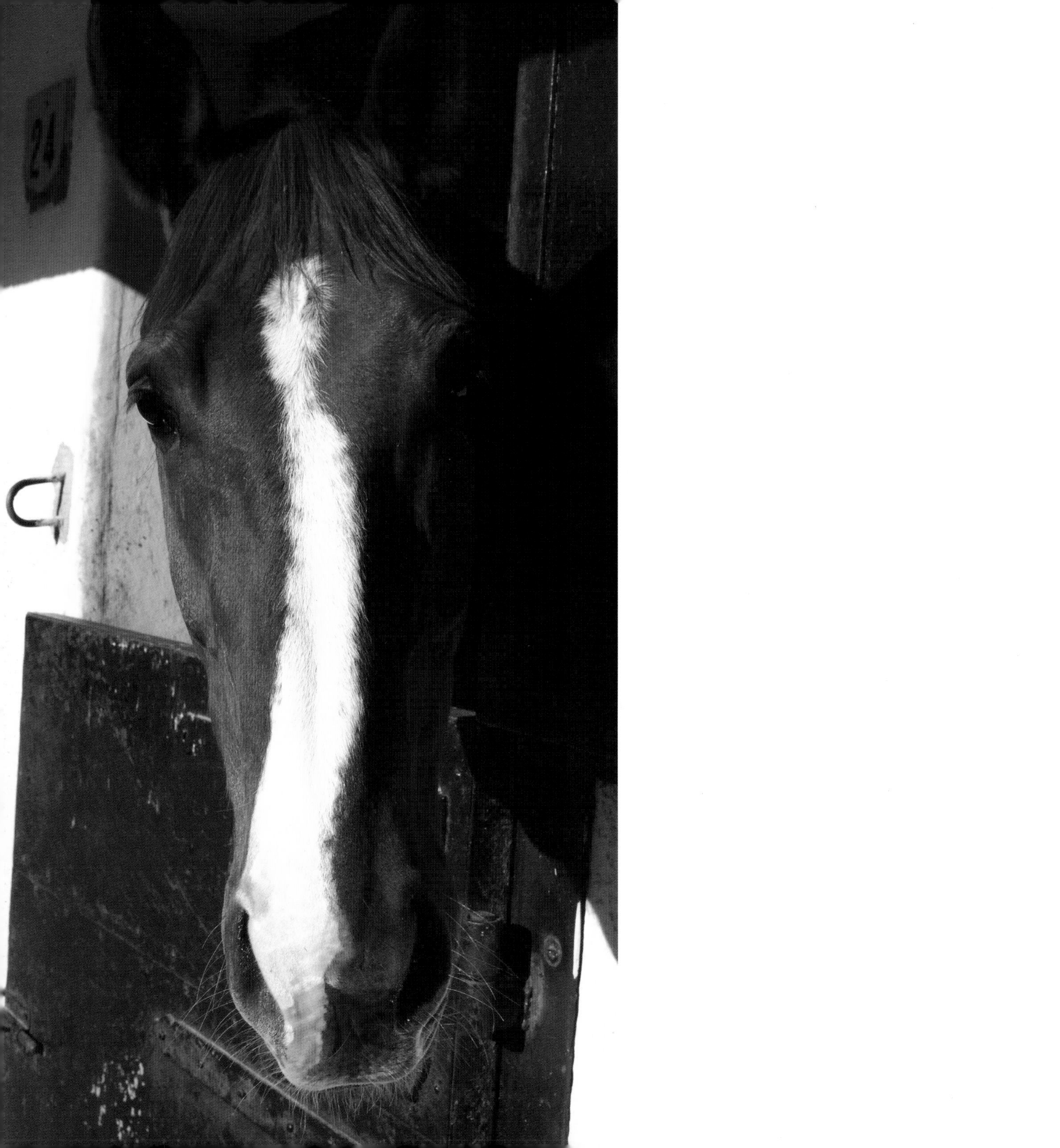
24

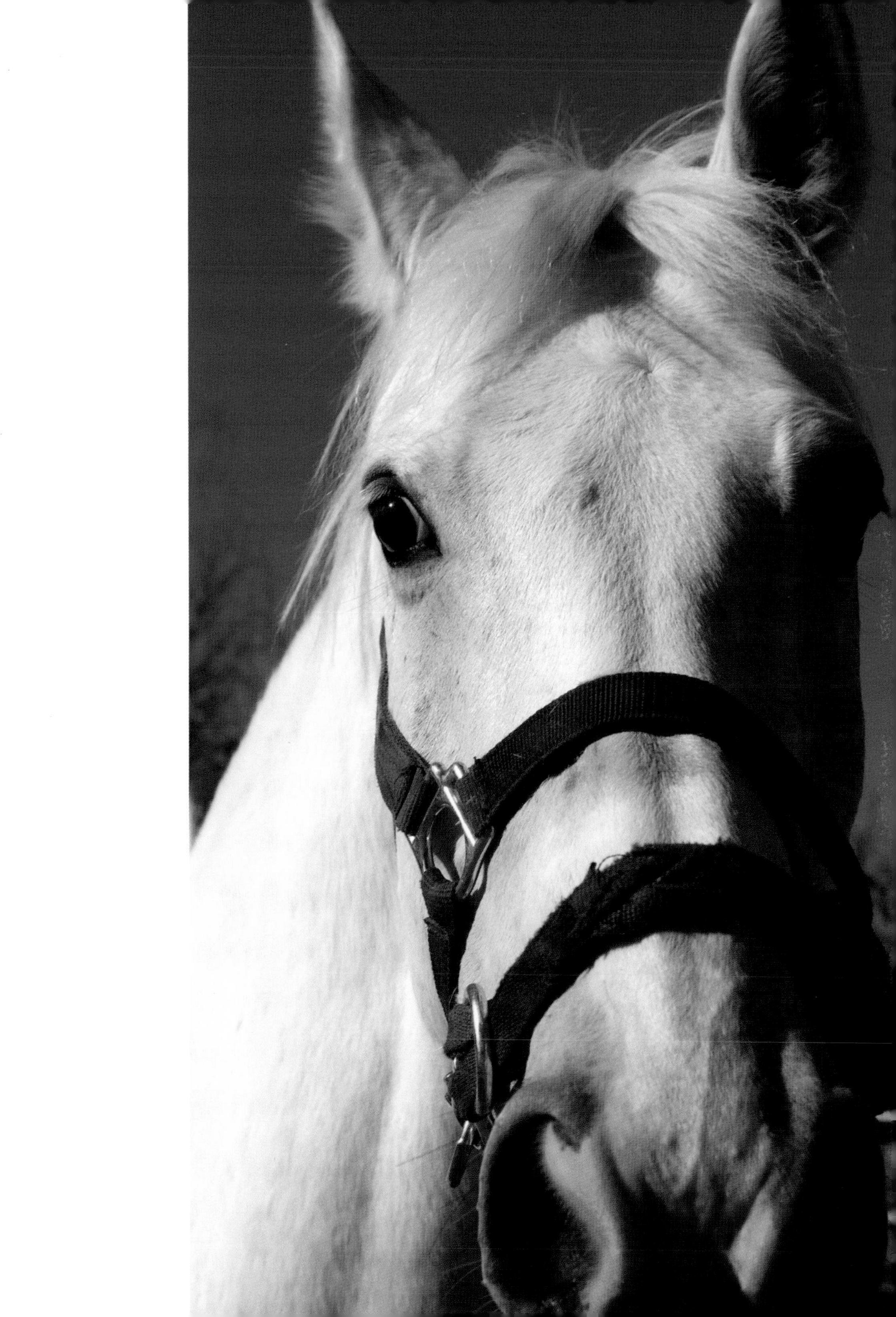

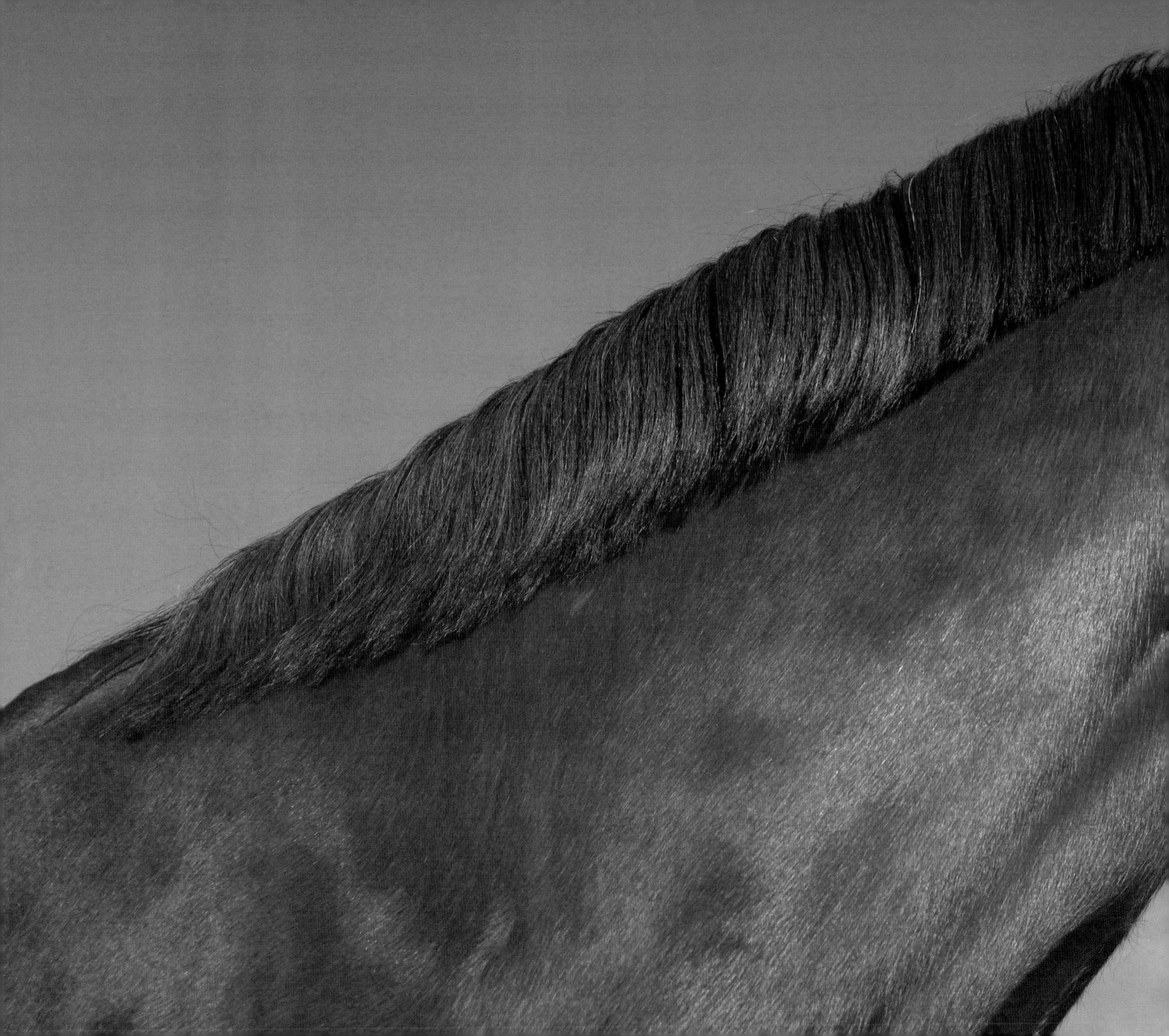

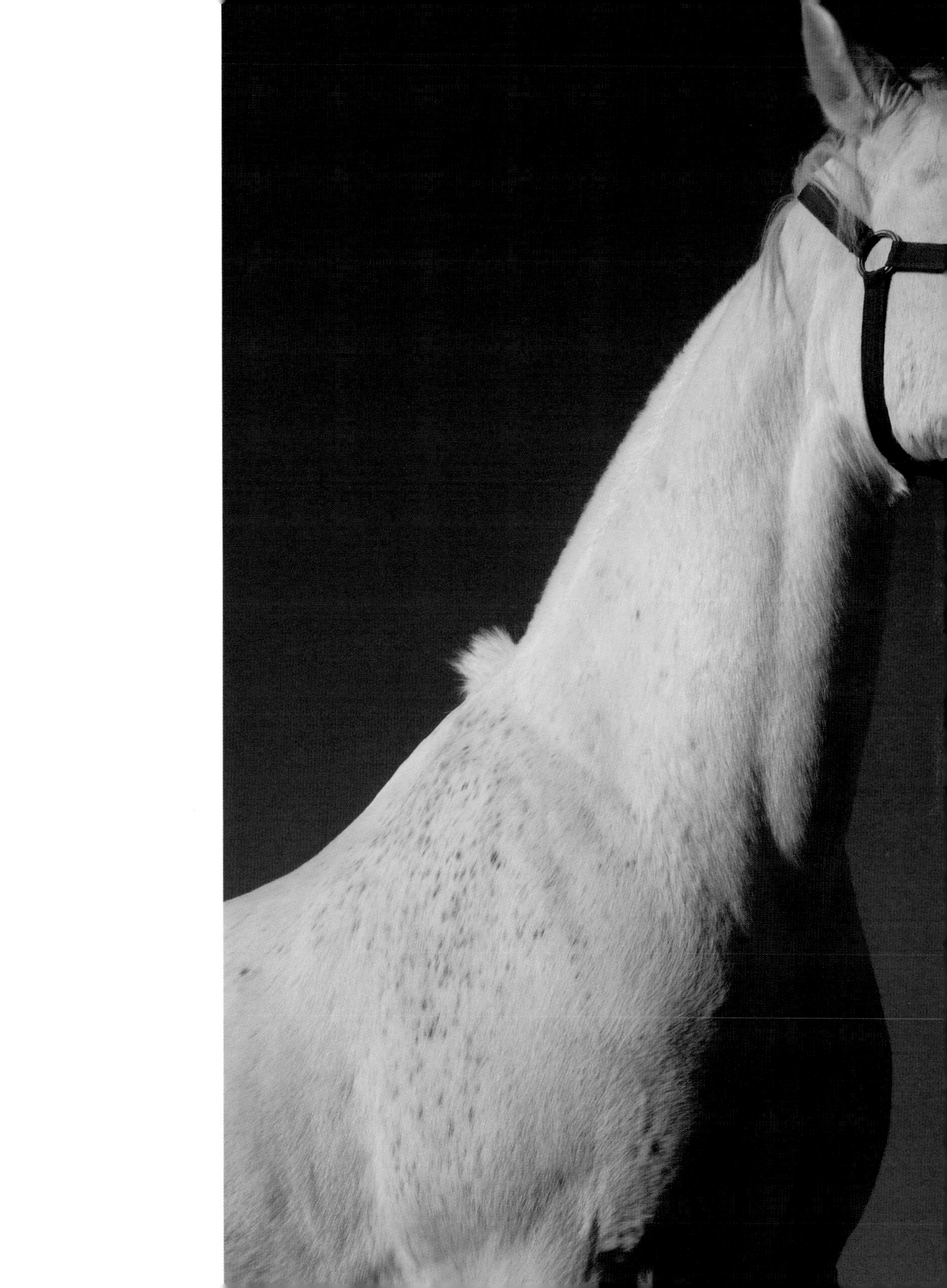

P140

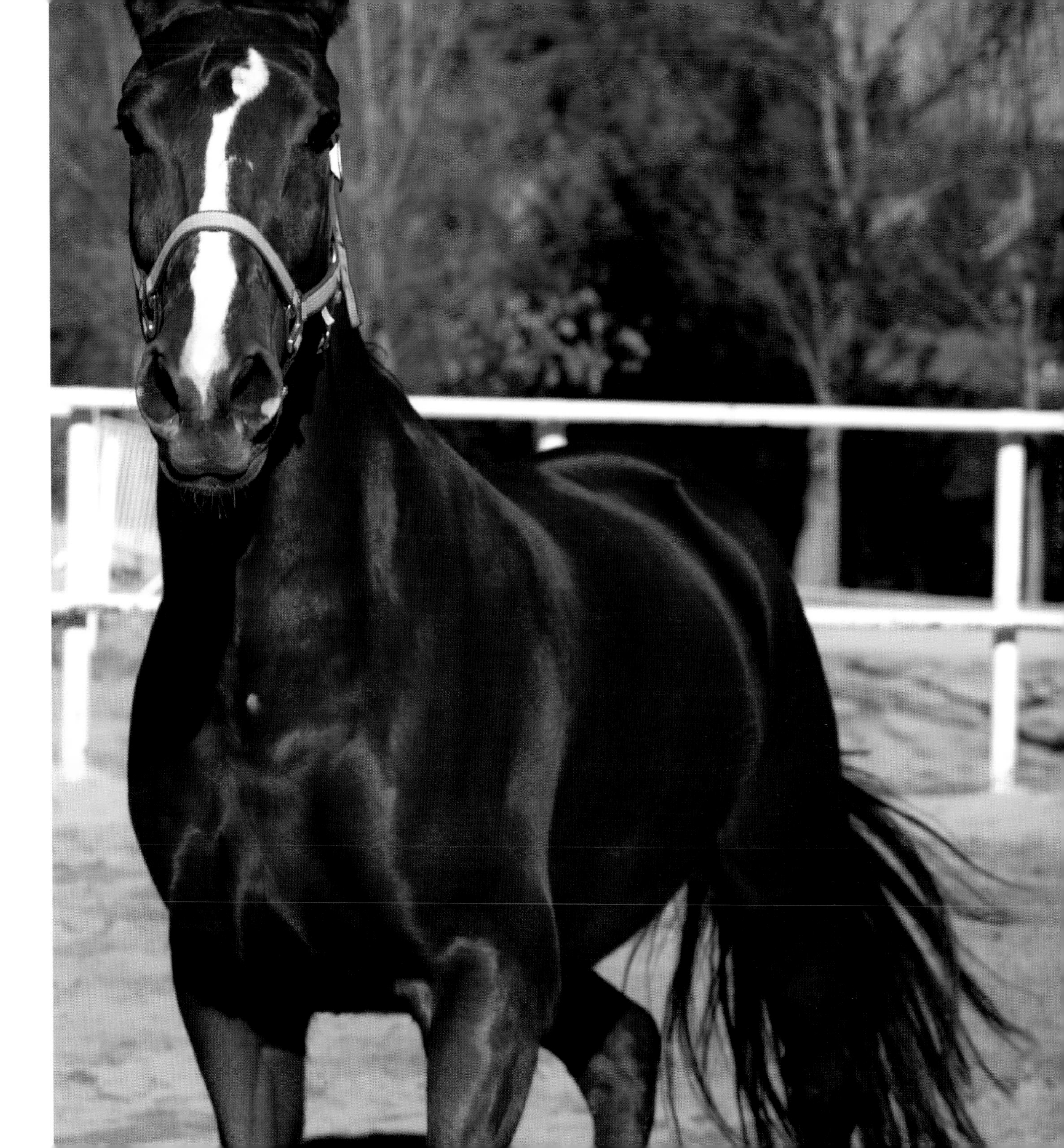

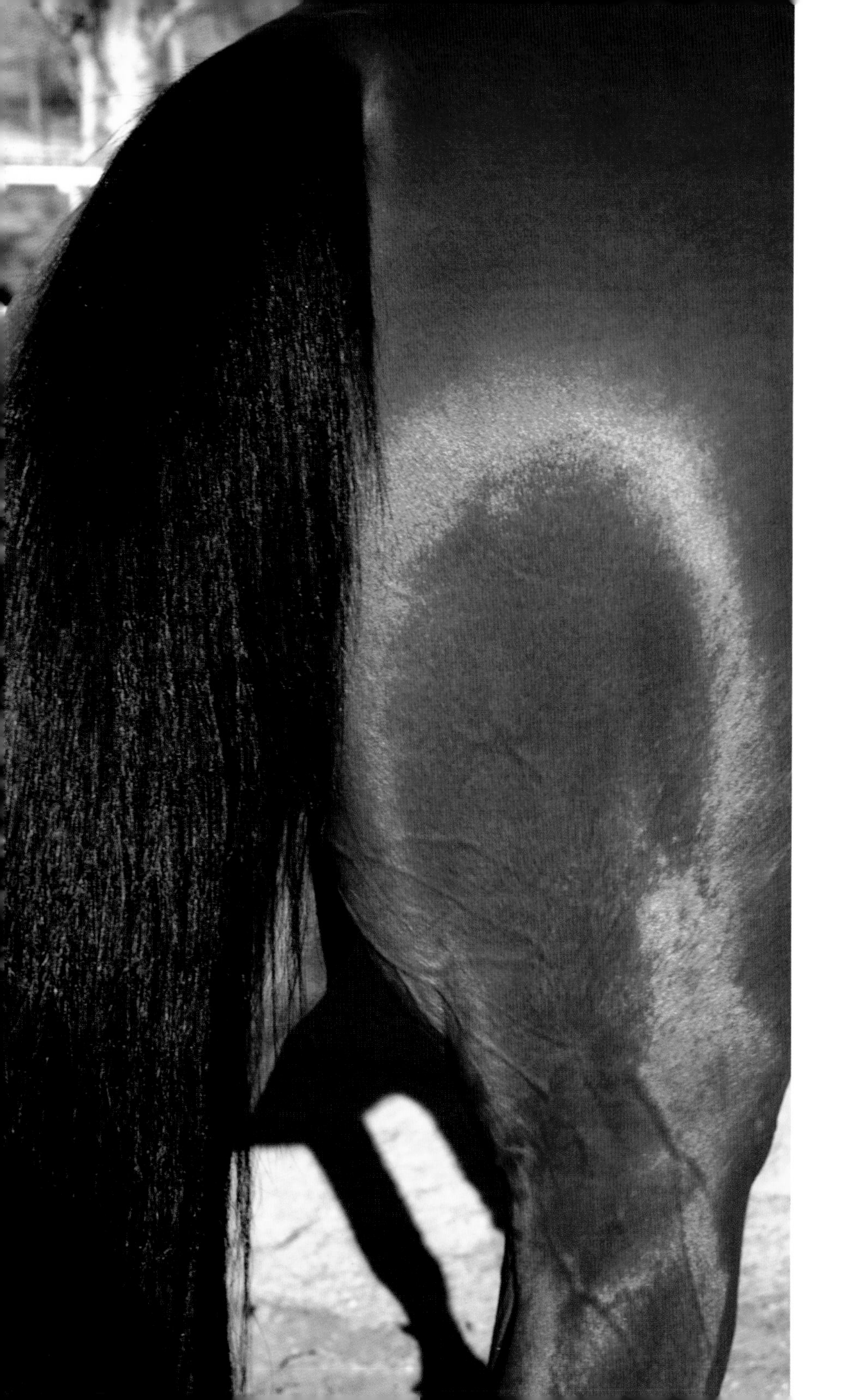

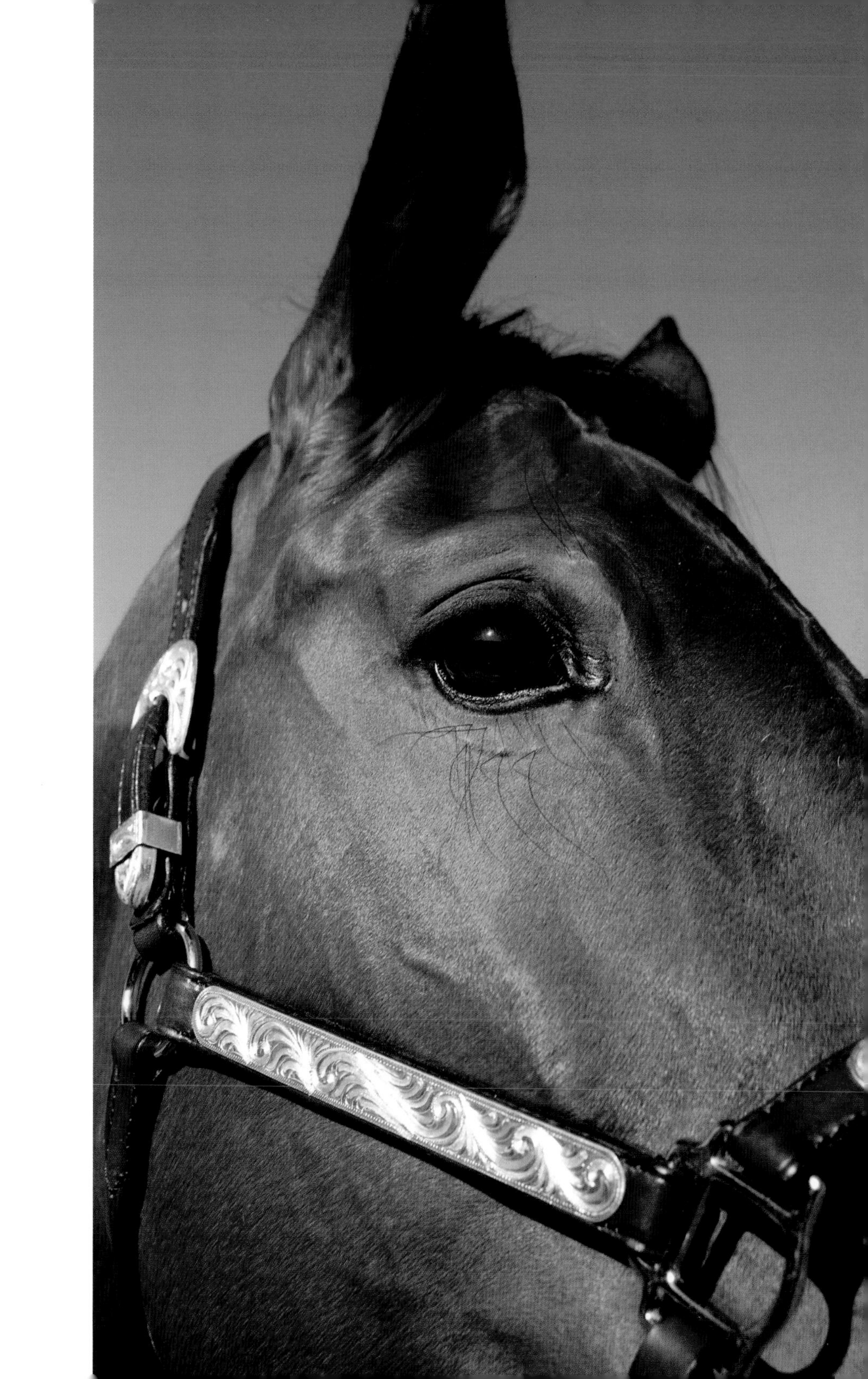

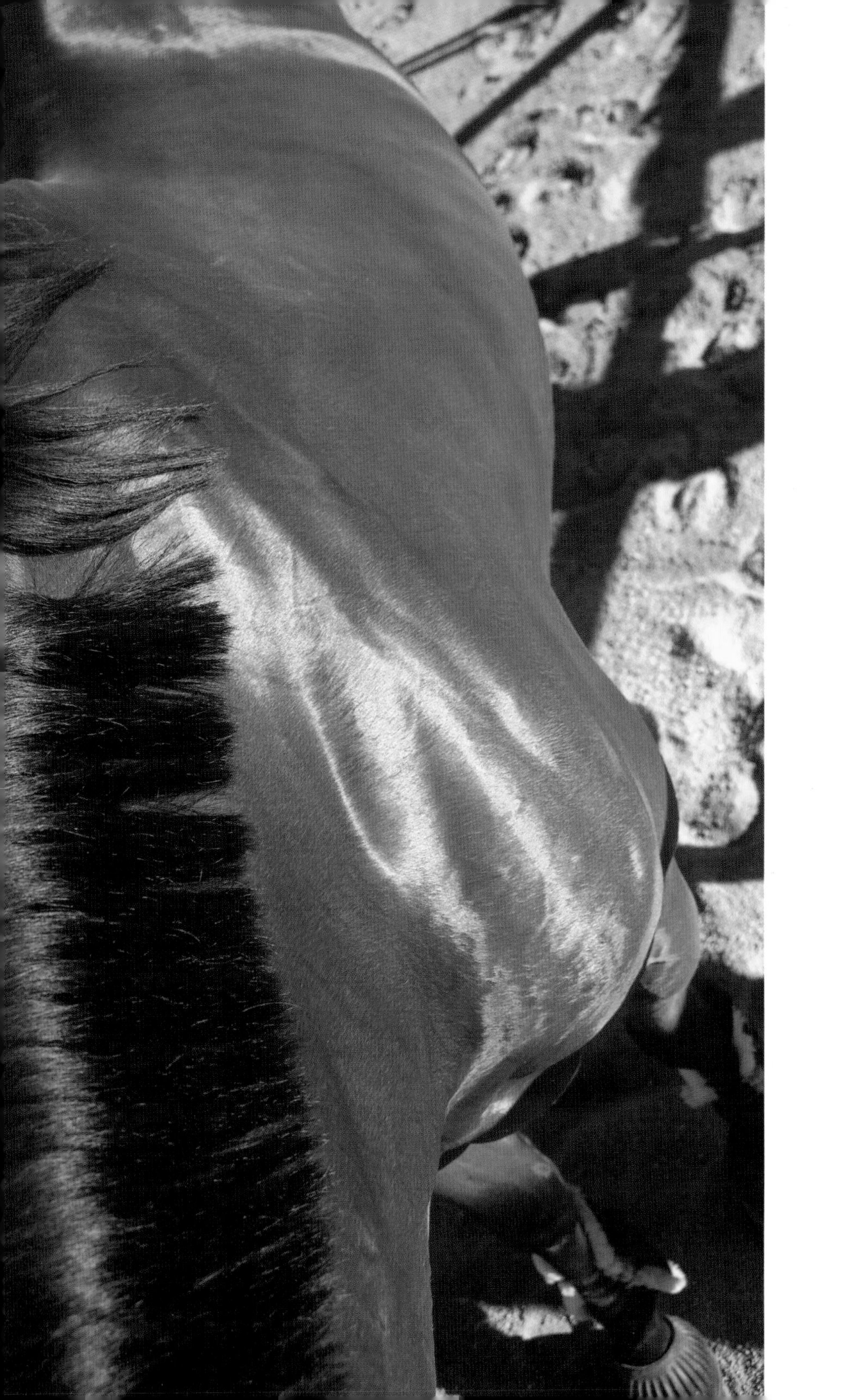

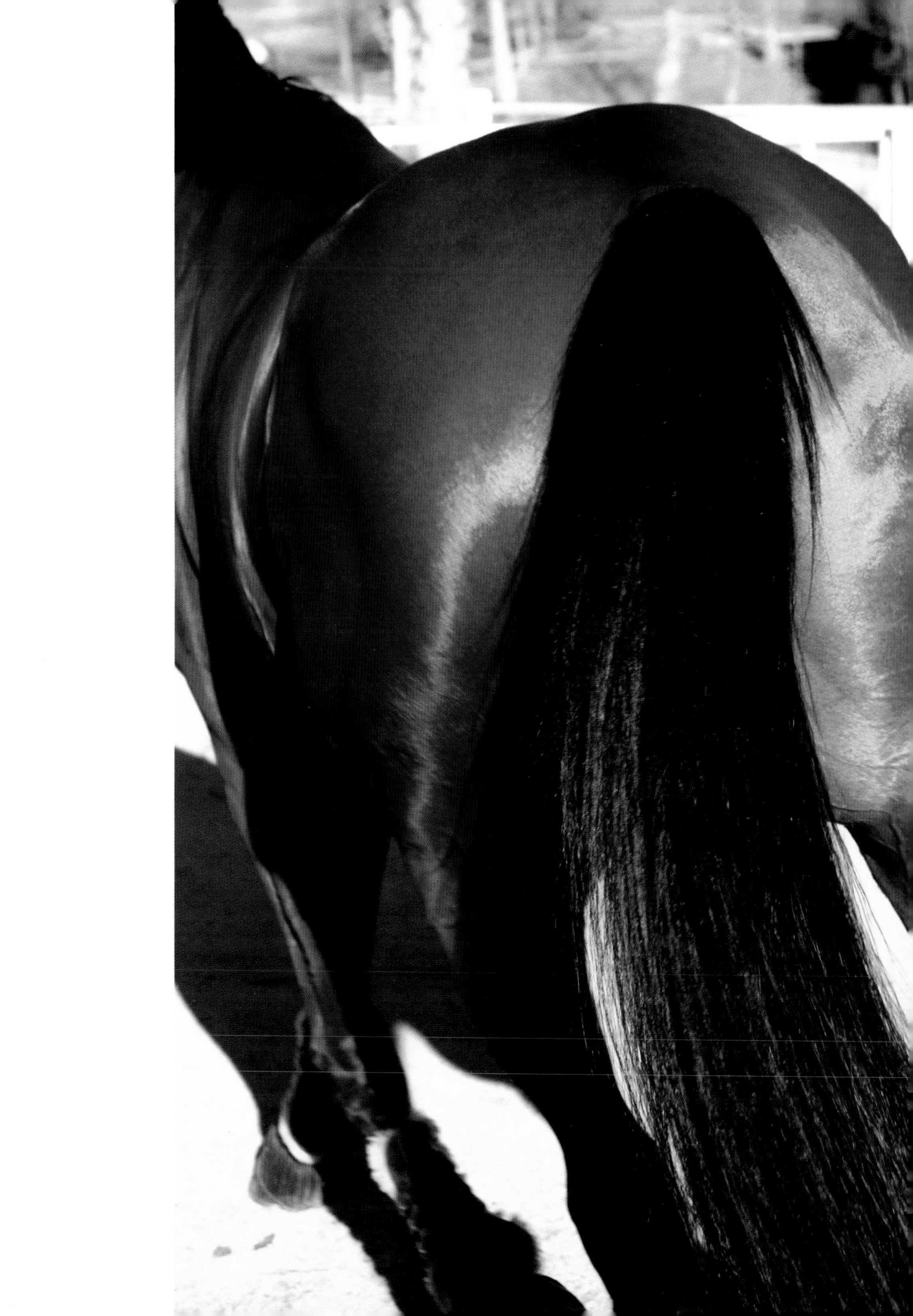

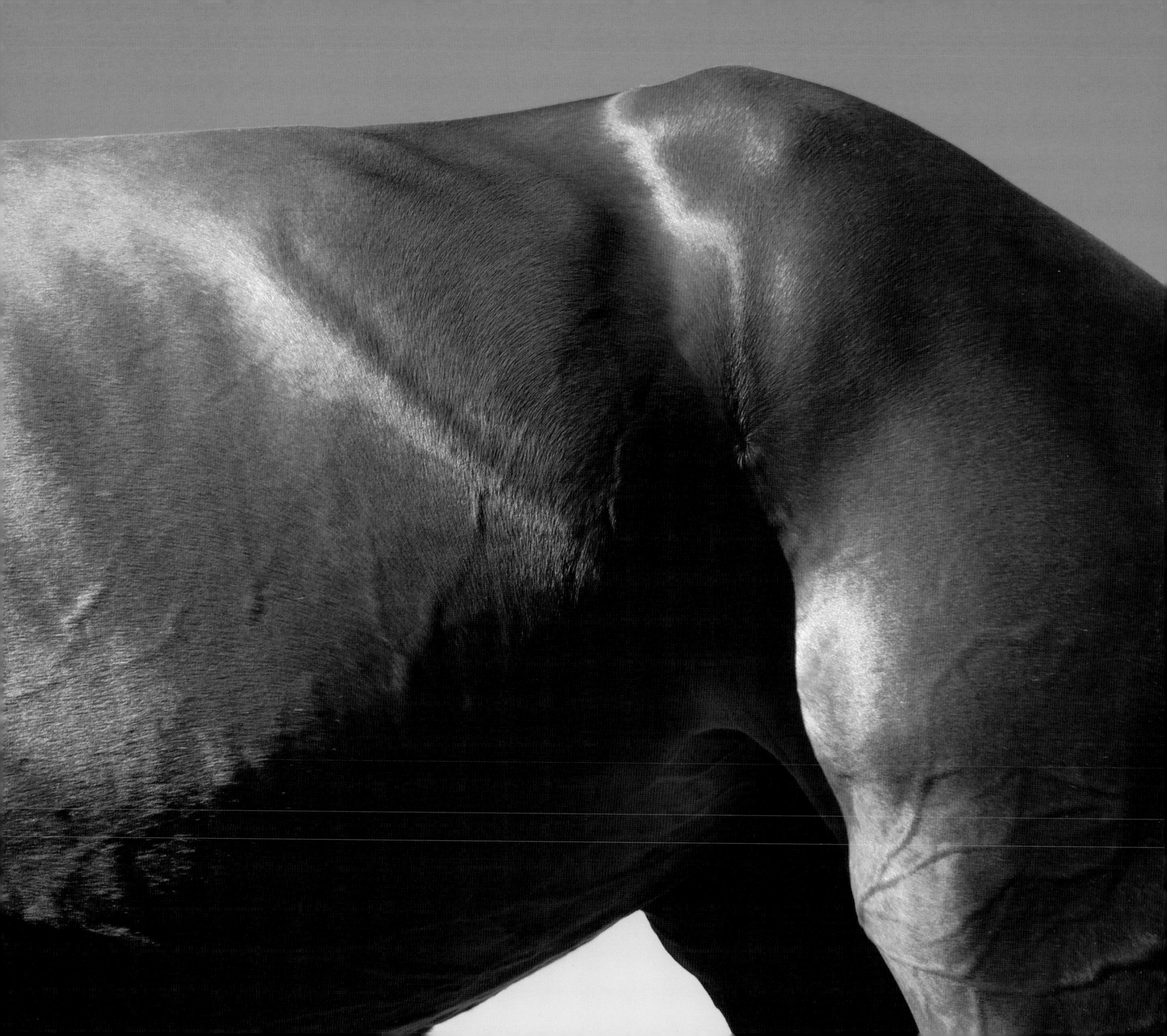

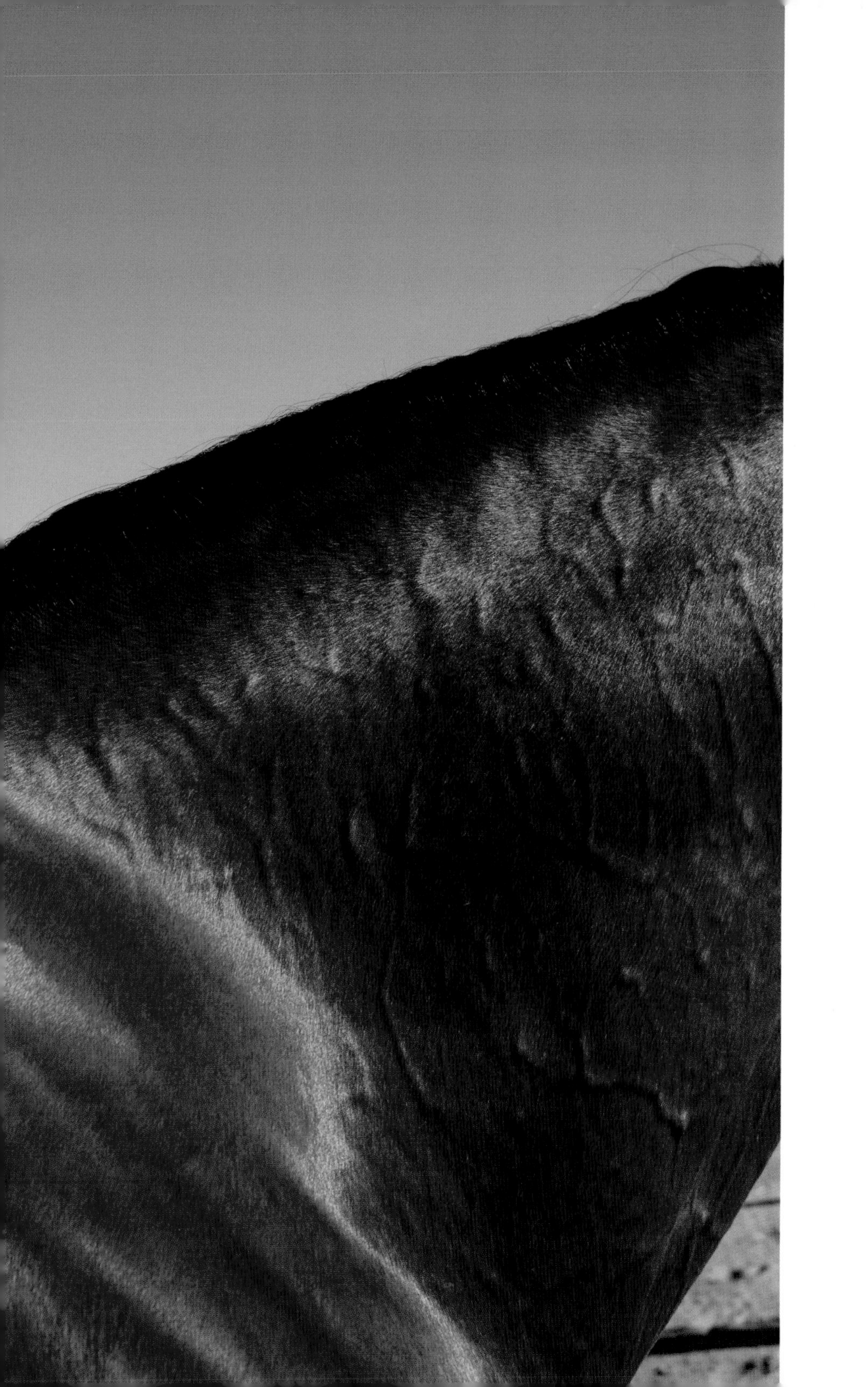

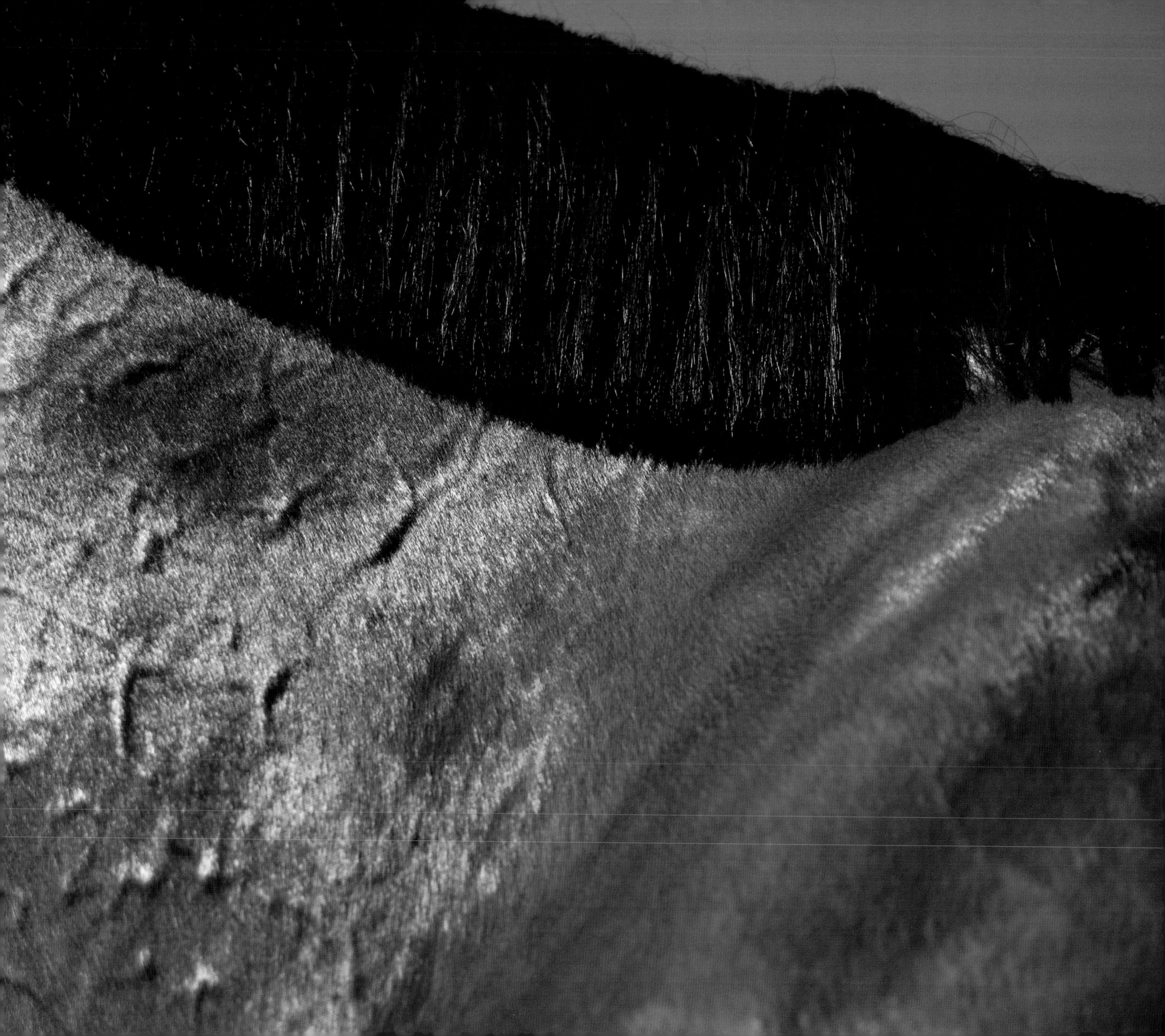

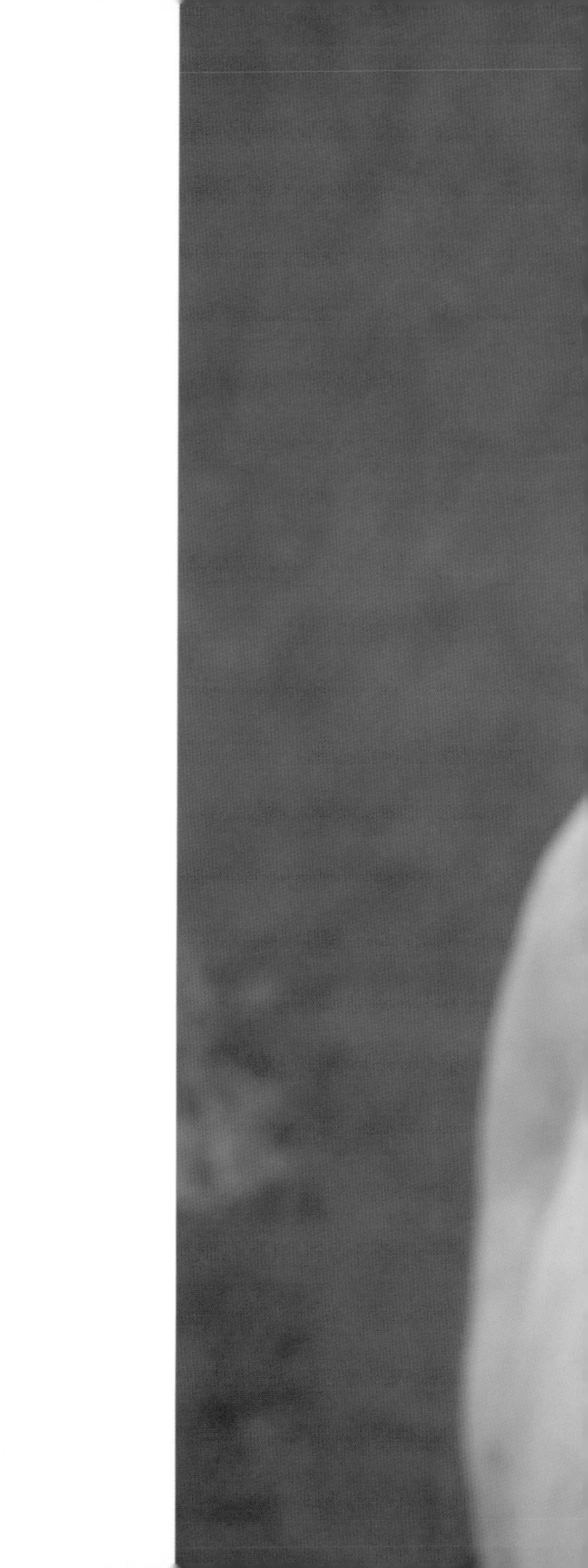

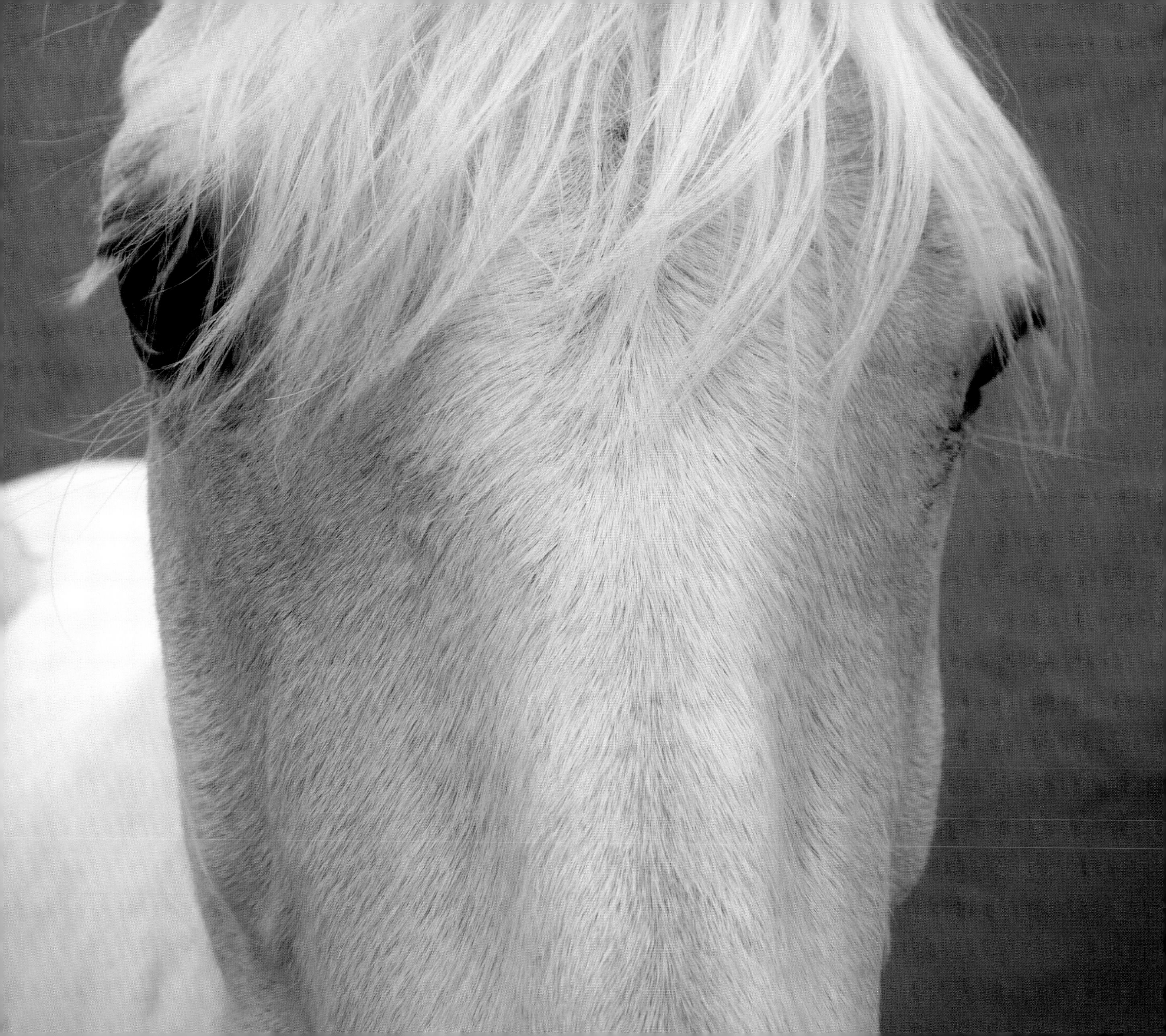

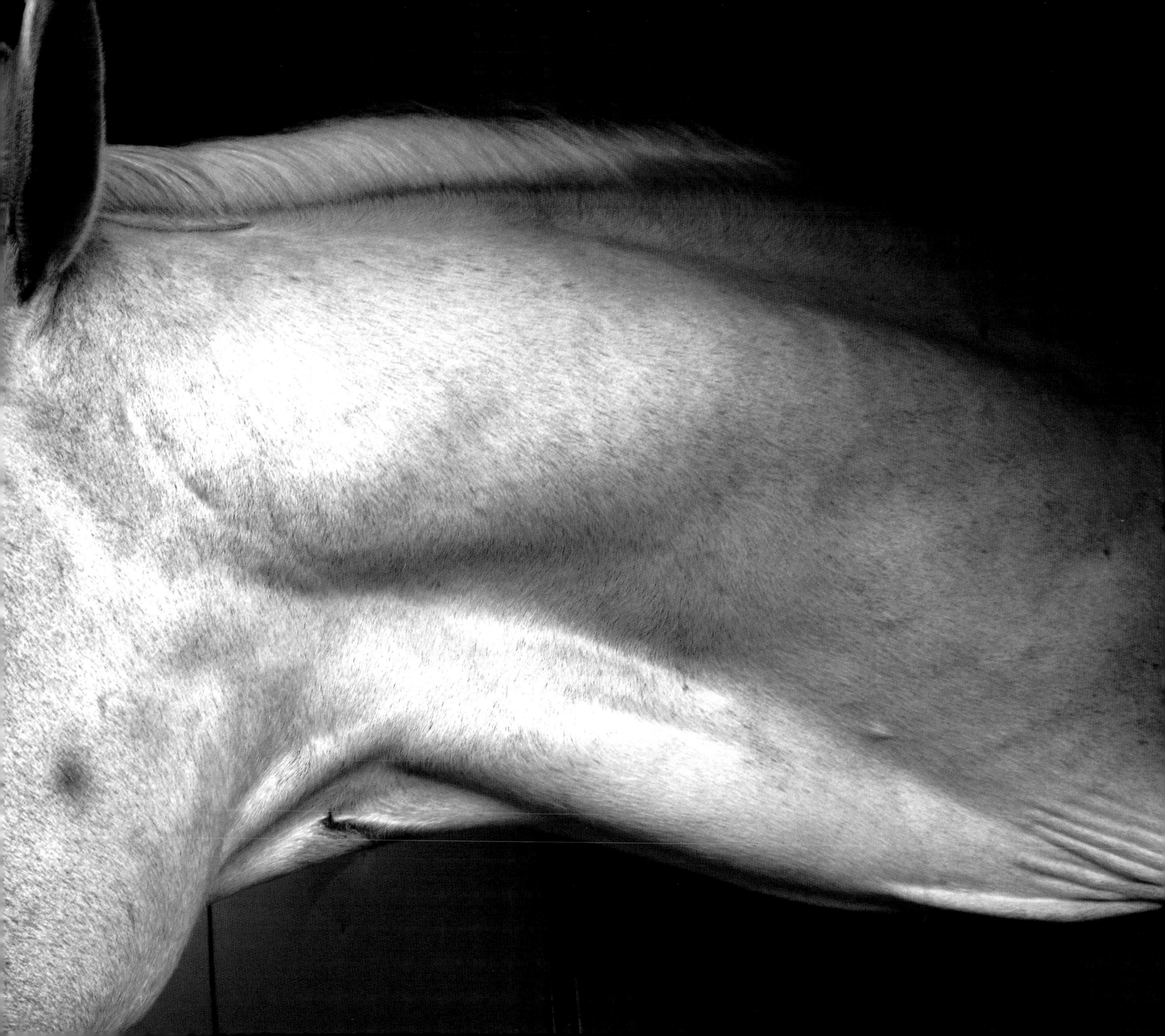

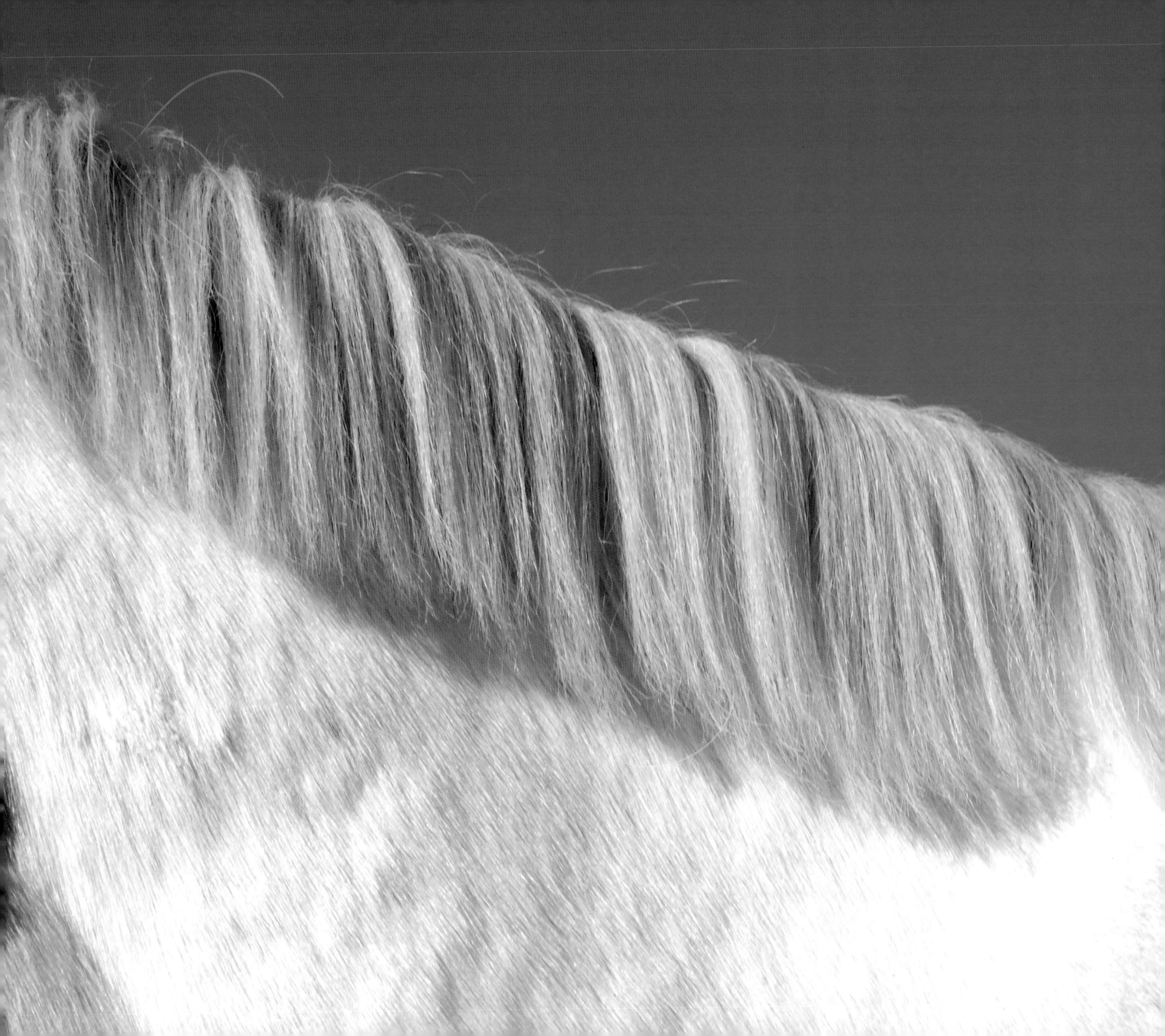

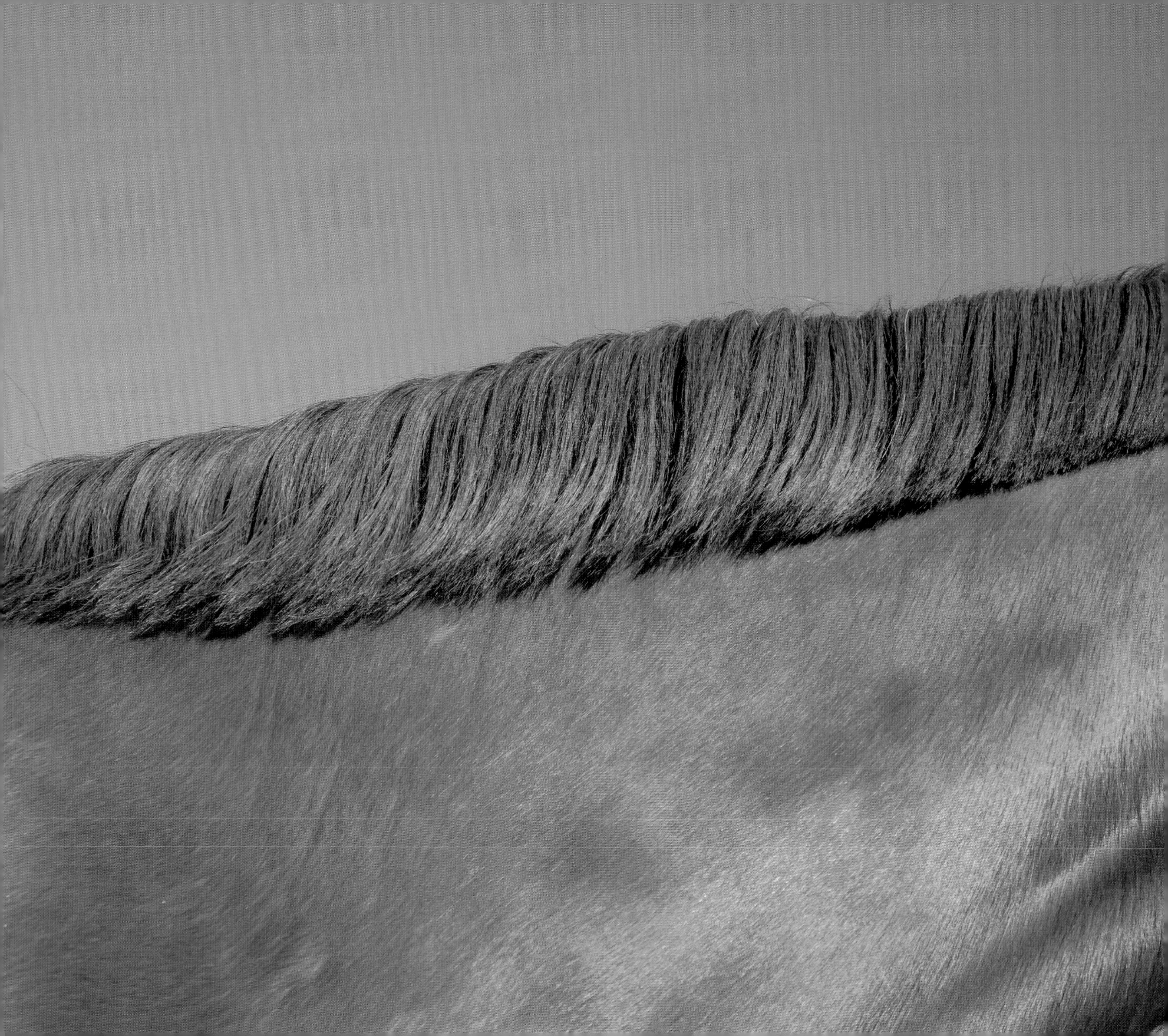

INDEX

P157